Safeguarding 6G: Security and Privacy for the Next Generation

RIVER PUBLISHERS SERIES IN DIGITAL SECURITY AND FORENSICS

The "River Publishers Series in Security and Digital Forensics" is a series of comprehensive academic and professional books which focus on the theory and applications of Cyber Security, including Data Security, Mobile and Network Security, Cryptography and Digital Forensics. Topics in Prevention and Threat Management are also included in the scope of the book series, as are general business Standards in this domain.

Books published in the series include research monographs, edited volumes, handbooks and textbooks. The books provide professionals, researchers, educators, and advanced students in the field with an invaluable insight into the latest research and developments.

Topics covered in the series include-

- Blockchain for secure transactions
- Cryptography
- Cyber Security
- Data and App Security
- Digital Forensics
- Hardware Security
- IoT Security
- Mobile Security
- Network Security
- Privacy
- Software Security
- Standardization
- Threat Management

For a list of other books in this series, visit www.riverpublishers.com

Safeguarding 6G: Security and Privacy for the Next Generation

Ramjee Prasad

CTIF Global Capsule (CGC), Denmark

Ana Koren

Croatia

River Publishers

Routledge
Taylor & Francis Group
NEW YORK AND LONDON

Published 2025 by River Publishers
River Publishers
Broagervej 10, 9260 Gistrup, Denmark
www.riverpublishers.com

Distributed exclusively by Routledge
605 Third Avenue, New York, NY 10017, USA
4 Park Square, Milton Park, Abingdon, Oxon OX14 4RN

Safeguarding 6G: Security and Privacy for the Next Generation / by Ramjee Prasad, Ana Koren.

Routledge is an imprint of the Taylor & Francis Group, an informa business

ISBN 978-87-7004-794-4 (hardback)
ISBN 978-87-7004-822-4 (paperback)
ISBN 978-87-7004-796-8 (online)
ISBN 978-87-7004-795-1 (master ebook)

The authors dedicate this book to the family and friends.

Contents

Preface

महाभूतान्यहङ्कारो बुद्धिरव्यक्त मेव च |
इन्द्रियाणि दशैकं च पञ्च चेन्द्रियगोचराः || 6||

mahā-bhūtāny ahankāro buddhir avyaktam eva cha
indriyāṇi daśhaikaṁ cha pañcha chendriya-gocharāḥ

Translation

The field of activities is composed of the five great elements, the ego, the intellect, the unmanifest primordial matter, the eleven senses (five knowledge senses, five working senses, and mind), and the five objects of the senses.

इच्छा द्वेष: सुखं दु:खं सङ्घातश्चेतना धृति: |
एतत्क्षेत्रं समासेन सविकारमुदाहृतम् || 7||

ichchha dveṣhaḥ sukhaṁ duḥkhaṁ saṅghātaśh chetanā dhṛitiḥ
etat kṣhetraṁ samāsena sa-vikāram udāhṛitam

Translation

Desire and aversion, happiness and misery, the body, consciousness, and the will—all these comprise the field and its modifications.

THE BHAGAVAD GITA (13.6-7)

In the rapidly evolving landscape of telecommunications, each generation of network technology has brought profound changes and advancements. From the analogue beginnings of 1G to the digital transformation of 2G, the high-speed capabilities of 3G, the multimedia potential of 4G and the connectivity revolution of 5G, the journey has been remarkable. Now, as we stand on the cusp of the 6G era, this book aims to explore and demystify the complex and multifaceted security and privacy challenges that lie ahead.

The idea for this book was born out of the recognition that 6G is not merely an incremental upgrade over its predecessors but a transformative leap that will redefine connectivity, intelligence and security. The promise of 6G extends far beyond faster speeds and lower latency; it envisions a future where networks are deeply integrated with artificial intelligence, where connectivity transcends terrestrial boundaries, and where new paradigms of communication and interaction emerge. This book seeks to provide a comprehensive examination of the security and privacy implications of such a transformative technology.

Writing this book has been driven by the urgent need to address the critical security and privacy issues that will accompany the deployment of 6G networks. As researchers, practitioners and policymakers, we must anticipate and mitigate the risks associated with these advanced technologies to ensure a safe and secure digital future. Our goal is to equip readers with the knowledge and insights necessary to navigate the complex security landscape of 6G, from emerging threats posed by quantum computing to the ethical and regulatory considerations that will shape the deployment of these networks.

This book is intended for a diverse audience, including researchers, engineers, policymakers and anyone interested in the future of telecommunications. We have endeavoured to present a balanced perspective, combining technical depth with practical insights to make the content accessible and relevant. By exploring real-world applications, advanced security mechanisms and the latest research developments, we hope to stimulate interest and foster a deeper understanding of 6G security and privacy.

The journey to 6G is still in its early stages, and much remains to be discovered and developed. This book is a contribution to the ongoing dialogue and research in this field. It is our hope that it will inspire further exploration, innovation and collaboration among the global community of stakeholders involved in shaping the future of telecommunications.

As we embark on this journey together, we invite you to delve into the pages that follow, to explore the challenges and opportunities of 6G and to join us in envisioning a secure and connected future. The insights and knowledge contained within this book are the result of collective efforts and contributions from experts across the globe. We extend our gratitude to all those who have shared their expertise and insights, making this work possible.

Welcome to the exploration of 6G security and privacy. We hope you find this book both informative and inspiring, and we look forward to the innovations and advancements that will undoubtedly emerge as we move towards the realisation of 6G networks.

Acknowledgement

We would like to thank the numerous contributors, reviewers and experts who have provided invaluable insights and feedback throughout the development of this book. Special thanks go to our colleagues and research partners whose dedication and collaboration have been instrumental in bringing this work to fruition. Additionally, we extend our gratitude to our families and friends for their unwavering support and encouragement.

List of Figures

List of Tables

List of Abbreviations

3GPP	3rd generation partnership project
6G-AITS	6G autonomous intelligent transportation systems
Adam	Adaptive moment estimation
AE	Adversarial examples
AES	Advanced encryption standard
AI	Artificial intelligence
AKA	Authentication and key agreement
AN	Anchor node
APD	Avalanche photodiode
APT	Advanced persistent threats
AQI	Air quality index
AR	Augmented reality
AV	Autonomous vehicle
B5G	Beyond 5G
BER	Bit error rate
BIM	Basic iterative method
BPQS	Blockchained post-quantum signatures
CALEA	Communications assistance for law enforcement act
CCPA	California consumer privacy act
CMA-ES	Covariance matrix adaptation evolution strategy
CNN	Convolutional neural network
CSA	Cloud security alliance
DDoS	Distributed denial-of-service
DE	Differential evolution
DLT	Distributed ledger technology
DoS	Denial of service
DPA	Data processing agreement
DPO	Data protection officer

DPoS	Delegated proof of stake
DSA	Dynamic spectrum access
DT	Digital twin
ECC	Elliptic curve cryptography
EPP	Endpoint protection platform
ESV	Entropy source validation
ETSI	European telecommunications standards institute
EU	European union
FG QIT	Focus group on quantum information technology
FGSM	Fast gradient sign method
FQSCS	Fully quantum-safe cryptographic state
FWA	Fixed wireless access
GAN	Generative adversarial networks
GDPR	General data protection regulation
GNFS	General number field sieve
GPU	Graphics processing unit
GSM	Global system for mobile communications
HDQKD	High-dimensional quantum key distribution
HHI	Heinrich hertz institute
HIDS	Host-based intrusion detection system
HIPAA	Health insurance portability and accountability act
HSP	Hidden subgroup problem
IAM	Identity and access management
IDR	Intrusion detection and response
IDS	Intrusion detection system
IEEE	The institute of electrical and electronics engineers
IET	Institution of engineering and technology
IETF	Internet engineering task force
IIoT	Industrial internet of things
IMT	International mobile telecommunications
IoBNT	Internet of Bio-Nano-Things
IoE	Internet of everything
IoMT	Internet of medical things
IoT	Internet of things

IPS	Intrusion prevention system
IPsec	Internet protocol security
ISO	International organization for standardization
ITER	Index transmission error rate
ITS	Intelligent transportation system
ITU	International telecommunication union
JTC	Joint technical committee
KEM	Key encapsulation mechanism
LMS	Leighton-Micali signature
LPWA	Low-power wide area
LSTM	Long short-term memory
LWE	Learning with errors
MCF	Multicore fibre
MFA	Multi-factor authentication
MIMO	Multiple input multiple output
MITM	Man-in-the-middle
ML	Machine learning
MRSS	Multi-RAT spectrum sharing
MSP	Managed service provider
MTC	Machine-type communication
NIDS	Network-based intrusion detection system
NIST	National institute of standards and technology
NLP	Natural language processing
NTN	Non-terrestrial network
OAM	Optical angular momentum
O-RAN	Open radio access network
OSS	Open-source software
OTA	Over-the-air
OWC	Optical wireless communication
PGD	Projected gradient descent
PII	Personally identifiable information
PMT	Photomultiplier tube
PoS	Proof of stake
PoW	Proof of work
PQC	Post-quantum cryptography
PRNG	Pseudo-random number generator
PSTN	Public switched telephone network

QBER	Quantum bit error rate
QFT	Quantum Fourier transform
QKD	Quantum key distribution
QoS	Quality of service
QRNG	Quantum random number generation
QSSWG	Quantum-safe security working group
QUESS	Quantum experiments at space scale
RAN	Radio access network
RAT	Remote access Trojans
RBAC	Role-based access control
ResNets	Residual networks
RF	Random forest
RMSprop	Root mean square propagation
RNN	Recurrent neural network
RSA	Rivest-Shamir-Adleman
RSSI	Received signal strength indicator
SC	Smart city
SEGM	Smart grid management
SGD	Stochastic gradient descent
SGX	Software guard extensions
SIDH	Supersingular Isogeny Diffie-Hellman
SIEM	Security information and event management
SIoMT	Smart IoMT
SME	Small- and medium-sized enterprise
SMPC	Secure multi-party computation
SNSPD	Single-photon detector
SPAD	Single-photon avalanche diode
SPDC	Spontaneous parametric down-conversion
SSO	Single sign-on
SVM	Support vector machine
SVP	Shortest vector problem
TEE	Trusted execution environment
TES	Transition-edge sensor
THz	Terahertz
TLS	Transport layer security
UAV	Unmanned aerial vehicle
UE	User equipment

VAE	Variational autoencoder
VLC	Visible light communication
VPN	Virtual private network
VR	Virtual reality
XAI	Explainable AI
XMSS	Extended Merkle signature scheme
XR	Extended reality
ZKP	Zero-knowledge proof

1

Introduction

As the deployment of 5G networks has expanded over the past few years, their limitations have become apparent, prompting the development into 6G networks as the next-generation of solution [1]. This chapter begins with a historical overview of earlier networking technologies and how they have shaped the current trends in 6G networking. The 6G system is anticipated to build upon the features and capabilities introduced with 5G, while incorporating new functionalities to provide enhanced services and value [2]. Key objectives include creating networks that promote digital inclusion, are both environmentally and economically sustainable, reduce complexity, manage increasing traffic demands and enable new services through features that complement mobile networks.

Despite the fact that the era of the 5G network has only recently fully unfolded, the limitations of 5G technology pushed the research of 6G networks. In March 2019, the world's first 6G summit was held in Finland, where leading communication experts collaborated to draft the inaugural 6G white paper, marking the unofficial birth of 6G as a research field. Since then, numerous governments and organisations have launched their own 6G research initiatives. For instance, the UK government has announced investments in technologies potentially useful for 6G networks, while the Academy of Finland has initiated the '6 Genesis' project focused on foundational research. But before continuing, let us go back to the very beginning.

1.1 From 1G to 6G: A 50-Year Evolution

If the initial 6G networks launch by 2030, it will mark approximately half a century since the advent of the first cellular network technology. This journey began with 1G, introduced in Japan in 1979. The analogue 1G network provided basic mobile communication capabilities but was plagued by issues such as inconsistent coverage, poor sound quality, limited vendor compatibility and significant security and privacy flaws. As phone services were not encrypted, both data transmissions and conversations were vulnerable to cloning, eavesdropping and unauthorised access. The absence of a standardised wireless protocol led to numerous drawbacks. Despite these drawbacks, it represented a revolutionary leap into the era of mobile communications, prompting other countries to launch their own networks in the early 1980s.

The digital transformation began with the commercial rollout of 2G technology [3] on the GSM (Global System for Mobile Communications) standard in Finland in 1991. 2G networks, leveraging digital modulation techniques like TDMA and CDMA, supported both voice and short message services. GSM emerged as the most widely used standard. GSM aimed to ensure security on par with the public switched telephone network (PSTN), offering features such as anonymity, authentication, signalling protection and user data protection. However, it faced significant security issues, such as one-way authentication, leaving users unable to verify network legitimacy, and limited encryption coverage. Shortly thereafter, 2.5G technologies like GPRS and EDGE introduced packet-switched domains, enabling the transfer of small data quantities over networks.

The demand for data spurred the development of 3G in 2001, offering peak data rates from 144 Kbps to 14 Mbps. By introducing high-speed data transmission, 3G enabled services like web browsing, TV streaming and video conferencing. Building on 2G/2.5G technologies, 3G incorporated more robust security measures, including two-way authentication and the authentication and key agreement (AKA) protocol. Despite these advancements, 3G networks remained vulnerable to IP traffic-related threats and attacks on the radio interface. UMTS became the predominant standard in Europe, Japan and China, while CDMA2000 was favoured in North America and South Korea.

With the advent of 4G, the landscape changed significantly. Launched first in South Korea with the WiMAX standard in 2006 and later with LTE deployments in Oslo and Stockholm in 2009, 4G provided download speeds up to 150 Mbps and upload speeds up to 50 Mbps. This advancement enabled true multimedia experiences on mobile networks, including video streaming and multiplayer gaming. However, it still fell short in terms of capacity, reach and latency necessary to fully support IoT ecosystems, smart cities and telehealth applications. Furthermore, the increased complexity and user interaction in 4G networks introduced new security and privacy vulnerabilities, including malicious software attacks and weaknesses in key management protocols.

This shortcoming led to the rollout of 5G, which started worldwide in 2019. Utilising shorter frequencies, or millimetre waves, between 30 and 300 GHz, 5G networks have significantly boosted performance. As of 2023, most 5G deployments are non-standalone, relying on underlying 4G infrastructure. Eventually, these will be replaced by standalone 5G networks featuring cloud-based virtualised cores. The deployment of 5G networks promises faster speeds, comprehensive systems and more secure architectures. Aiming to connect a vast number of devices, including IoT equipment, 5G networks address diverse security and privacy challenges across their architecture, from access networks to backhaul and core networks. While innovative technologies like NFV, SDN and cloud computing enhance network performance, they also introduce new vulnerabilities that must be managed to prevent attacks and ensure data privacy, which brings us, finally, to 6G (Figure 1.1).

But what exactly is a 6G network, and how is it different from 5G? Some experts were of the opinion that 6G should transcend merely being a faster version of 5G and instead represent a holistic enhancement of all aspects of 5G technology. They believed that coverage should extend beyond the ground level to include full undersea and surface coverage. Additionally, they envisioned 6G networks to boast significantly enhanced artificial intelligence (AI) capabilities. Many researchers saw 6G as an 'AI-empowered' network, where AI would be deeply integrated into its core functions rather than just incorporated into the architecture as with 5G. Furthermore, with increasing concerns over network security and privacy, they emphasised that robust risk

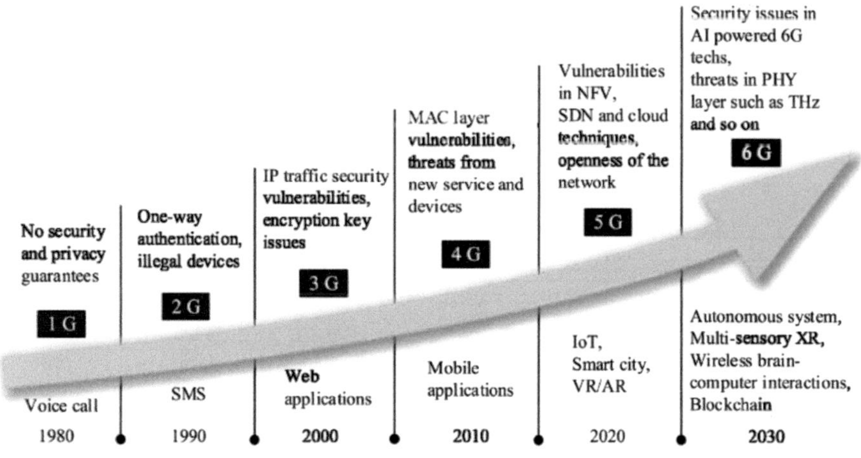

Figure 1.1 1G to 6G evolution.

Table 1.1 Differences between 5G and 6G.

Aspect	5G (fifth generation)	6G (sixth generation)
Speed	Up to 10 Gbps	Expected to offer 100 Gbps or higher
Latency	Below 10 milliseconds	Aims to achieve below 1 millisecond
Bandwidth	Uses frequencies up to 100 GHz	Expected to operate in the terahertz (THz) frequency range
Use cases	Enhanced mobile broadband, ultra-reliable low-latency communications, massive machine-type communications	Advanced applications such as holographic communications, high-fidelity mobile AR/VR, ubiquitous AI-driven applications
Network Infrastructure	Small cell networks supplemented by millimetre-wave spectrum	Combination of terrestrial and non-terrestrial networks (e.g., satellite-based networks) for truly global coverage
Maturity	Being deployed in many countries as of 2023	Still in the conceptual and research phase as of 2023, with potential deployment in the 2030s
Integration	Uses AI in its architecture	Expected to have deeper integration with AI and machine learning for network management, data processing and decision-making

mitigation strategies should be embedded within the architecture. 5G networks, deployed widely by 2023, offer speeds up to 10 Gbps, reduce latency to below 10 milliseconds and utilise frequencies up to 100 GHz. They focus on enhanced mobile broadband, ultra-reliable low-latency communications and massive machine-type communications, relying on small cell networks supplemented by millimetre-wave spectrum. In contrast (Table 1.1), 6G is expected to offer speeds of 100 Gbps or higher and aim for latencies below 1 millisecond, operating in the terahertz (THz) frequency range.

Foreseen use cases for 6G include advanced applications such as holographic communications, high-fidelity mobile AR/VR and ubiquitous AI-driven applications. 6G might utilise a combination of terrestrial and non-terrestrial networks, including satellite-based networks, for truly global coverage and is expected to have a deeper integration with AI and machine learning for network management, data processing and decision-making. As of 2023, 6G remains in the conceptual and research phase, with potential deployment anticipated in the 2030s. In [4], researchers propose four key domains crucial for the evolution of 6G networks:

↣ *Real-time intelligent edge*: The advancement from 5G to 6G networks necessitates a transition towards real-time intelligent edge capabilities, particularly critical for applications like autonomous driving. Although 5G enables the potential for autonomous vehicles, current technology lacks the requisite low latency and real-time intelligence. A 6G network must facilitate interactive AI-powered services, enabling real-time responses in dynamic environments. Additionally, emerging technologies such as visible light communication (VLC) hold promise for enhancing vehicle-to-vehicle communications. However, the integration of machine learning in vehicle networks introduces both advanced security algorithms and new security challenges, underscoring the need for comprehensive risk mitigation strategies.

↣ *Distributed AI*: While 5G networks are geared towards Internet of Things (IoT) compatibility, 6G networks must extend to accommodate the Internet of Everything (IoE). This necessitates a decentralised system capable of intelligent decision-making at various levels. Distributed artificial intelligence will play a crucial role in managing vast datasets distributed across edge devices, ensuring data access, control and privacy while leveraging shared data for enhanced security. However, security concerns such as poisoned model attacks and device-level vulnerabilities underscore the importance of robust security measures and advancements in machine learning models.

↣ *Intelligent radio*: Traditional network architectures have tightly coupled device hardware with transceiver algorithms, limiting adaptability and performance. Intelligent radio, enabled by recent advancements in circuits and antennas, decouples hardware from algorithms, allowing dynamic configuration and optimisation based on hardware capabilities. Software-defined radio and networking techniques facilitate the utilisation of multiple frequency bands and adaptive spectrum sharing, enhancing network flexibility and efficiency. However, challenges such as wideband interference and signal-jamming pose threats to data security, necessitating proactive security measures to predict and mitigate malicious activities.

↣ *3D intercoms*: In the transition to 6G networks, communication capabilities must evolve from two dimensions to three to support diverse applications such as satellite communication, UAV networks and undersea communications. A 3D intercom framework is essential for optimising network resources and mobility management in three-dimensional space. Technologies like THz bands and molecular communication offer promising solutions for long-distance and space-level communication. However, security concerns related to authentication processes and control vulnerabilities highlight the need for robust security protocols to safeguard communication integrity and privacy across 3D intercom networks.

In the following chapters, we will delve into various aspects of the security landscape in 6G networks:

Emerging threat landscape in 6G:

- ↣ We will explore the vulnerabilities posed by quantum computing, including Shor's and Grover's algorithms.
- ↣ AI-driven attacks will be examined, such as adversarial machine learning and attacks on image recognition and text-based systems.
- ↣ Risks associated with decentralised edge computing and threats to IoT and connected devices will be discussed, covering issues like data integrity, supply chain vulnerabilities and regulatory compliance.

Security-preserving techniques in 6G:

- ↣ We will explain quantum key distribution (QKD) and its real-world implementation, including satellite-based QKD.
- ↣ Delve into quantum random number generators (QRNGs), their principles, security properties and applications.
- ↣ Explore post-quantum cryptography and strategies for navigating the transition to fortify 6G against quantum threats.
- ↣ Examine AI-driven threat detection methods, including intrusion detection, security automation and threat intelligence. Discuss the potential evolution of AI-driven cybersecurity toward autonomous systems that can adapt and respond to emerging threats without human intervention.
- ↣ We will also explore regularisation techniques and the concept of intrusion kill chain.

Regulation, policy and ethical considerations:

- ↣ Explore privacy regulations, legal requirements and industry standards aimed at safeguarding user privacy in 6G networks.
- ↣ Ethical considerations surrounding the deployment and use of 6G networks will be addressed, ensuring alignment with regulatory standards and ethical guidelines.
- ↣ Analysing the complexities of determining responsibility in case of security breaches or failures in 6G networks.

- ↣ Examining the role of government policies, regulatory frameworks and standards in shaping security measures for 6G networks.
- ↣ Highlighting the importance of global cooperation and collaboration in addressing emerging threats and vulnerabilities in 6G networks.
- ↣ Delving into strategies for achieving a delicate balance between ensuring robust security measures and protecting user privacy in 6G networks.

Practical applications: Real-world 6G security concrete scenarios and implementations:

- ↣ We will explore secure healthcare IoT, emphasising the integration of wearable smart devices into central health information systems and the security measures necessary to protect sensitive health data.
- ↣ Discuss the security challenges and solutions for autonomous vehicle networks, focusing on communication protocols, data integrity and real-time threat detection.
- ↣ Examine the secure smart grid infrastructure, outlining the potential vulnerabilities and the strategies for safeguarding energy distribution networks against cyberattacks.
- ↣ Delve into the implementation of secure 6G-enabled smart cities, highlighting the integration of various smart services and the comprehensive security framework required to protect them.
- ↣ Analyse the enhancement of supply chain security with 6G, discussing how advanced connectivity can improve transparency, traceability and resilience against cyber threats.
- ↣ Explore the application of 6G technologies in securing Industry 4.0 environments, focusing on the protection of industrial control systems and the prevention of cyber–physical attacks.

The road ahead for shaping a secure 6G future:

- ↣ We will explain the importance of proactive security measures in 6G networks regarding key challenges in 6G security, i.e., (I) quantum computing, (II) AI and machine learning, (III) decentralised edge computing and (IV) IoT and connected devices.
- ↣ We will discuss future prospects for cryptographic advancements, such as AI-driven cybersecurity solutions, blockchain and distributed ledger technologies and privacy-preserving technologies.
- ↣ We will explore research and development directions for 6G, including global cooperation in security research, the role of international

standards organisations in shaping protocols, successful collaboration case studies, interdisciplinary research combining cryptography, AI and network engineering with case studies on outcomes, and the development of testbeds and simulation environments for 6G security testing, emphasising real-world validation and contributions to security research.

↣ Examine policy and regulatory frameworks for 6G, including the importance of proactive policy development for security, case studies on effective policy frameworks from previous generations, ethical implications of advanced security measures in 6G networks, development of governance frameworks to address ethical concerns and case studies on ethical governance in technology deployment.

Finally, we will reflect on the insights gained throughout the exploration of 6G security and privacy. We will discuss the road ahead for shaping a secure 6G future, identifying key challenges and opportunities for further research and development.

References

[1] Ramjee Prasad, Rute C. Sofia, "6G Visions for a Sustainable and People-centric Future: From Communications to Services, the CONASENSE Perspective," River Publishers, 2023.

[2] Ramjee Prasad, Anand Raghawa Prasad, Albena Mihovska, Aarhus University, Nidhi, "6G Enabling Technologies: New Dimensions to Wireless Communication," River Publishers, 2023.

[3] Paulo Sergio Rufino Henrique, Ramjee Prasad, "6G: The Road to the Future Wireless Technologies 2030," River Publishers, 2021.

[4] Minghao Wang, Tianqing Zhu, Tao Zhang, Jun Zhang, Shui Yu, Wanlei Zhou, Security and privacy in 6G networks: New areas and new challenges, Digital Communications and Networks, Volume 6, Issue 3, 2020, pp. 281-291, DOI: 10.1016/j.dcan.2020.07.003.

2

Emerging Threat Landscape in 6G

In the rapidly evolving field of 6G networks, technological advancements are reshaping our future, bringing both opportunities and unforeseen challenges. This chapter serves as a guide through the complex landscape of emerging threats in 6G.

Our focus will be on the novel security challenges defining the 6G era. Quantum computing poses significant threats to network security, requiring careful consideration and robust solutions. Additionally, we will explore the dual role of artificial intelligence in this new landscape – recognising it as both a powerful ally and a potential source of cyber threats.

The narrative then transitions to the interconnected realm of the Internet of Things (IoT), a diverse array of devices that presents a complex landscape. Here, we examine the risks related to data integrity, vulnerabilities within the global supply chain and the balance between regulatory compliance and standardised security measures.

Understanding these inherent risks in the 6G landscape is not just prudent; it is essential. As innovation propels the world forward, malicious actors are poised to exploit vulnerabilities. This chapter is a call to action, highlighting the need to analyse these risks and strengthen the foundation of secure communication.

We delve into the principles of standardisation and international cooperation, which serve as vital tools for building a robust defence against malicious actors. By exploring the strategies used by these entities, we gain insight into their motives and propose proactive measures to counter their threats.

This knowledge not only helps us understand the risks but also guides us toward a future where security and innovation coexist. It envisions communication networks that are resilient against today's challenges while paving the way for tomorrow's advancements.

2.1 Quantum Computing Vulnerabilities

Quantum computation and quantum information mark a paradigm shift in our comprehension of computation and the underlying fabric of the physical universe. This transformative journey has its roots in the early foundations of computer science, particularly the groundbreaking work of Alan Turing. Turing's introduction of the theoretical concept of a programmable computer in 1936, through the formulation of the Turing machine, laid the groundwork for classical computers and gave rise to the Church–Turing thesis.

The Church–Turing thesis, honouring Turing and mathematician Alonzo Church, posits the equivalence between physical computation and the abstract universal Turing machine. This concept underpinned classical computer science, fuelled by the growth anticipated by Gordon Moore's law. However, by the 21st century, the relentless pace of Moore's law faced challenges as classical computing encountered fundamental limitations, particularly when confronted with quantum effects at smaller scales.

The quantum paradigm emerged from the interplay with quantum mechanics, a theory developed in the early 20th century to explain microscopic particle behaviour. David Deutsch's pursuit of connecting physics and computation in 1985 led to the conceptualisation of a universal quantum Computer, capable of simulating any quantum-mechanical system efficiently. This exploration laid the foundation for modern quantum computation.

A pivotal challenge to classical computation arose in the 1970s, with the development of randomised algorithms demonstrating efficiency in solving certain problems. Quantum error-correction codes, inspired by classical counterparts, addressed the impact of noise on quantum states. Peter Shor's 1994 algorithm [1] showcased quantum superiority in solving classically intractable problems like factoring large numbers and discrete logarithms.

The foundational concept in classical computation and information is the bit, while quantum computation and quantum information are grounded in the analogous quantum bit, or qubit. In this exploration, we delve into the properties of single and multiple qubits, drawing comparisons with classical bits. Despite qubits manifesting as physical entities, we initially treat them as abstract mathematical objects, providing a versatile foundation for a general theory of quantum computation and information.

A qubit, akin to a classical bit, possesses a state, represented as $|0\rangle$ or $|1\rangle$ in Dirac notation. Yet, distinctively, a qubit can exist in superpositions, expressed as $|\psi\rangle = \alpha|0\rangle + \beta|1\rangle$, where α and β are complex numbers. This state, a unit vector in a two-dimensional complex vector space, highlights the unique quantum nature. Notably, the inability to directly observe a qubit's state, coupled with probabilistic outcomes upon measurement, underlies the essence of quantum computation and information.

Qubits allow for quantum parallelism, with quantum devices simultaneously occupying various states. A quantum machine's physical state is described by a finite-dimensional Hilbert space, using qubits as quantum memory. A qubit, existing in a two-dimensional Hilbert space $H = C \oplus C$, can be in a superposition state $|\psi\rangle = \alpha|0\rangle + \beta|1\rangle$. For n qubits, wider registers are modelled by $Hn = H \otimes \ldots \otimes H$. Quantum algorithms involve unitary transitions and a sequence of gates from a fixed finite set.

The unusual ability of a qubit to exist in a superposition state challenges classical intuition. While a classical bit is definitively in a state of 0 or 1, a qubit can seamlessly occupy a continuum between $|0\rangle$ and $|1\rangle$ until observed. Measurement collapses the qubit to one of the basis states, with associated probabilities $|\alpha|\wedge 2$ and $|\beta|\wedge 2$ summing to 1. With reference to [2], the Bloch sphere representation (Figure 2.1) provides a geometric insight into a qubit's state, defined by angles θ and ϕ.

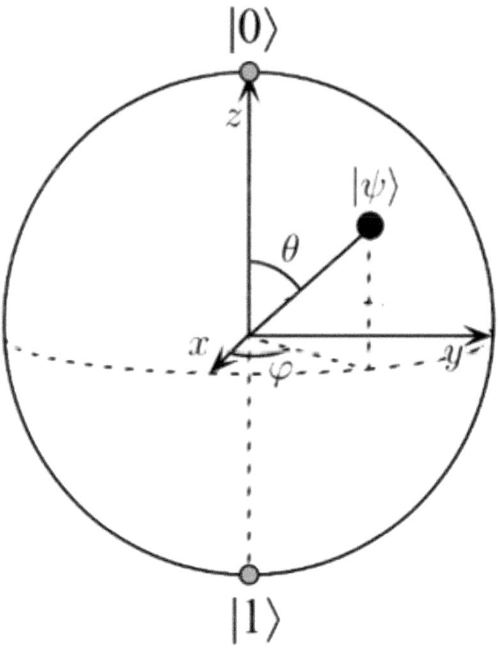

Figure 2.1 Bloch sphere representation of a qubit.

Moving to multiple qubits, the quantum state of a two-qubit system involves complex coefficients for each computational basis state. The Bell state, an entangled state, exemplifies correlated measurement outcomes, showcasing quantum correlations exceeding classical limits. As we expand to systems of n qubits, the vastness of Hilbert space becomes apparent, holding computational potential beyond classical reach.

In essence, qubits, as abstract mathematical entities, allow us to construct a powerful framework for quantum computation and information. Their unique properties, including superposition and entanglement, open avenues for unprecedented computational capabilities. The challenge lies in harnessing this quantum information, understanding the hidden complexities encoded in qubit states and exploring the transformative potential of quantum mechanics in information processing.

Quantum information science, fostering interdisciplinary collaboration, holds the potential for transformative advancements in technology and a deeper understanding of the physical world. The future of quantum computation and quantum information offers the prospect of pushing computational paradigms beyond classical limits.

However, the advent of quantum computing marks a paradigm shift in computational power, presenting both unprecedented opportunities and formidable challenges for the field of cryptography. Quantum computers, leveraging the principles of quantum mechanics, have the potential to revolutionise computational capabilities. However, this quantum leap in processing speed simultaneously poses a significant threat to classical cryptographic algorithms that currently underpin the security of communication systems. Quantum supremacy, a term used to describe the point at which quantum computers surpass the capabilities of the most advanced classical supercomputers, introduces a seismic shift in the security landscape. Classical cryptographic algorithms, such as Rivest–Shamir–Adleman (RSA) and elliptic curve cryptography (ECC), rely on the complexity of certain mathematical problems for their security. Quantum computers, notably through algorithms like Shor's or Grover's algorithms, can efficiently solve mathematical problems that are currently intractable for classical computers. Specifically, Shor's algorithm threatens the foundational principles of widely used public-key cryptographic systems.

There are two quantum methods for breaking the security of the RSA encryption scheme, a fundamental cryptographic algorithm widely used for secure communication between parties like Alice and Bob.

Quantum order-finding attack: In the RSA encryption scheme, Alice generates a public key (e, n) and a private key (d, n). Bob, wanting to send a private message M to Alice, encrypts it using Alice's public key, resulting in (Me mod n). If Eve, equipped with a quantum computer, efficiently performs order-finding, she can deduce a value d' such that (Me)d' $\equiv M$ (mod n). Although Eve does not obtain Alice's exact private key (d, n), she gains enough information (d', n) to decrypt messages intended for Alice.

Quantum factoring attack: In classical RSA, security relies on the difficulty of factoring the product of two large primes ($n = pq$). Alice generates p and q to obtain n. Bob, aware of Alice's public key (e, n), encrypts his message M. Eve, with a quantum computer, efficiently factors $n = pq$ and calculates $\phi(n)$, enabling her to determine the private key d completely. Eve can now decrypt messages intended for Alice using the derived private key.

In both scenarios, Eve, the eavesdropper, exploits quantum algorithms to break the security of RSA. The security of RSA is traditionally based on the assumed computational complexity of classical algorithms for tasks like order-finding and factoring. However, the advent of quantum computers, with their ability to perform these computations exponentially faster, poses a serious threat to the security of RSA, potentially compromising the privacy of communications between Alice and Bob. This underscores the urgency of developing and adopting quantum-resistant cryptographic algorithms.

The potency of quantum computers in efficiently solving specific mathematical problems forms the crux of the looming risks to classical cryptographic algorithms. In the context of 6G networks, these risks manifest through the calculated prowess of quantum computers in tackling problems that are traditionally insurmountable for classical counterparts. Furthermore, quantum computers excel in solving mathematical problems crucial to the security of widely employed encryption methods. Notably, two key mathematical challenges – integer factorisation and discrete logarithms – stand out as prime targets for quantum computational efficiency.

Integer factorisation, the process of decomposing a composite number into its prime factors, is a problem deemed difficult for classical computers, particularly when dealing with large numbers. Quantum computers, through algorithms like Shor's, exhibit an exponential speedup in solving integer factorisation problems, thereby undermining the presumed security of cryptographic systems reliant on the difficulty of this classical problem.

On the other hand, discrete logarithms – fundamental to cryptographic protocols such as Diffie–Hellman key exchange – involve solving for an exponent in modular arithmetic, presenting a classically challenging problem.

Quantum computers have the potential to efficiently solve discrete logarithm problems using algorithms like Shor's, compromising the security foundations of widely used cryptographic mechanisms that rely on the assumed classical complexity of this task.

The security of many contemporary communication systems relies heavily on public-key cryptographic algorithms, with Rivest–Shamir–Adleman (RSA) and elliptic curve cryptography (ECC) being primary examples. The quantum threat magnifies as quantum computers can efficiently unravel the mathematical underpinnings of these algorithms, posing an existential risk to their effectiveness. RSA encryption relies on the difficulty of factoring the product of two large prime numbers. The efficiency of quantum algorithms in integer factorisation challenges the classical complexity of RSA, potentially rendering it susceptible to rapid decryption by quantum adversaries. ECC leverages the difficulty of solving discrete logarithms on elliptic curves for its security. Quantum computers, with their prowess in solving discrete logarithms, pose a direct threat to the security assumptions that underlie ECC, rendering it vulnerable to quantum attacks.

The emergence of quantum computing poses a profound challenge to the security foundations of classical cryptography. In this paradigm shift, quantum attacks threaten the robustness of classical cryptographic systems, emphasising the need for a comprehensive understanding of vulnerabilities and the quest for quantum-resistant alternatives. In the realm of classical cryptography, public-key systems face imminent threats from quantum algorithms. The breakthrough algorithms for factoring and discrete logarithms, spearheaded by Shor in 1994, usher in a new era of vulnerabilities. Systems like RSA, Diffie–Hellman, and elliptic curve cryptography, once stalwarts of secure communication, succumb to the efficiency of quantum attacks. The crux of the matter lies in the hidden subgroup problem (HSP), a linchpin of quantum algorithms. As classical cryptographic systems rely on the presumed computational difficulty of specific number-theoretic problems, quantum computers disrupt this landscape with exponential speedups for solving problems related to the HSP. Classical cryptosystems, such as RSA and Diffie–Hellman, find their security compromised in the face of efficient quantum algorithms. The vulnerability assessment of classical cryptosystems against quantum attacks reveals a pressing need for quantum-resistant alternatives. While some systems, like lattice-based cryptography and McEliece encryption, remain unbroken, their practical adoption is hindered by inefficiencies. As quantum computers loom on the horizon, the cryptographic community faces the formidable task of identifying secure replacements for classical cryptosystems. The efficiency of these replacements, coupled with resilience against quantum attacks, emerges as a critical focus in the pursuit of post-quantum cryptography. This ongoing exploration heralds a new era in secure communication, navigating the challenges posed by quantum adversaries.

2.1.1 Shor's algorithm

Shor's algorithm, proposed by mathematician Peter Shor in 1994 [1], is a quantum algorithm designed to efficiently factor large integers. Factoring large integers into their prime factors is a problem that has been traditionally considered hard for classical computers, especially when dealing with very large numbers. The difficulty of factoring large numbers forms the basis of widely used cryptographic systems, such as RSA. The algorithm is divided into two main parts: a classical reduction of the factoring problem to the order-finding problem and a quantum algorithm to solve the order-finding problem.

In the first part, the goal is to factorise an odd composite number N into two nontrivial integers p and q. We assume N is odd as, using Euclid's algorithm, it can be efficiently determined whether N is even. If it is, 2 is a trivial factor. Next, efficient classical algorithms are used to check if N is a prime power. Then, choose a random integer a between 2 and $N - 1$ and use the Euclidean algorithm to compute the greatest common divisor (gcd) of a and N. If $\gcd(a, N) \neq 1$ then $\gcd(a, N)$ is a nontrivial factor of N. If, on the contrary, $\gcd(a, N) = 1$, run the quantum subroutine to find the order r of a modulo N. Then, if r is odd, restart the algorithm. Otherwise, compute $d = \gcd(N, ar/2 + 1)$. If $d \neq 1$, d is a nontrivial factor of N, and the other factor is N/d.

In the quantum order-finding subroutine, given coprime integers a, N, find the order r of a modulo N, where r is the smallest positive integer such that $ar \equiv 1 \pmod N$. Use quantum phase estimation with a unitary operator U representing the operation of multiplying by a (modulo N). Then, utilise two registers, the second one having n qubits, where n is the smallest integer such that $N \leq 2n$. Apply quantum phase estimation to find a random integer of the form $j/r \cdot 22n + 1$. Use the continued fractions algorithm to extract the period r from the measurement outcomes. Run the quantum subroutine multiple times to obtain a list of fraction approximations. Take the least common multiple of their denominators to recover the order r with high probability.

The most time-consuming part of Shor's algorithm is quantum modular exponentiation, which involves implementing circuits for reversible gates. The current practical approach mimics conventional arithmetic circuits with reversible gates, such as ripple-carry adders. Quantum Fourier transforms and classical pre-/post-processing are faster in comparison. The bottleneck arises because quantum modular exponentiation requires a significant number of gates. Shor's algorithm for the discrete logarithm problem involves solving the hidden subgroup problem in an abelian group. The algorithm utilises a group homomorphism and a quantum circuit involving Hadamard gates and quantum Fourier transforms.

With reference to [1], Shor's algorithm (Figure 2.2) starts by employing a quantum version of the classical Fourier transform, known as the quantum Fourier transform (QFT). This quantum algorithm allows for the efficient evaluation of the discrete Fourier transform, a task that is classically hard for large datasets. One of the crucial steps in Shor's algorithm is the ability to efficiently find the period of a function. Shor achieves this by using the QFT to find the period of a modular exponentiation function. In summary, Shor's algorithm combines classical and quantum components to efficiently factorise large integers and solve discrete logarithm problems, leveraging the unique capabilities of quantum computation for specific mathematical operations.

Shor's algorithm, as a quantum algorithm, can factorise large numbers exponentially faster than classical algorithms, compromising the security of traditional public-key cryptography. In classical computing, factoring large numbers into their prime components is recognised as a computationally intensive task. Classical algorithms, such as the general number field sieve

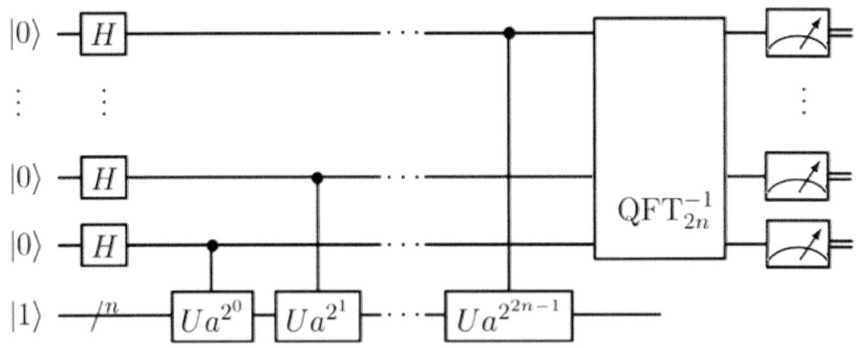

Figure 2.2 Quantum subroutine in Shor's algorithm.

(GNFS), have been the traditional tools for integer factorisation but exhibit polynomial time complexity. Shor's algorithm dramatically alters the landscape of factorisation. Quantum computers equipped with Shor's algorithm demonstrate an exponential speedup compared to classical algorithms when confronted with the challenge of factoring large numbers. Aforementioned RSA, a widely used public-key cryptographic algorithm, hinges on the difficulty of factoring the product of two large prime numbers. Shor's algorithm, with its quantum efficiency in factorisation, undermines the classical complexity that forms the basis of RSA's security, potentially enabling rapid decryption of RSA-encrypted communications. Similarly, ECC, another cornerstone of public-key cryptography, relies on the complexity of solving discrete logarithms on elliptic curves. Shor's algorithm's prowess in efficiently solving discrete logarithms poses a direct threat to ECC, compromising the security assumptions that underpin its effectiveness. Furthermore, many widely used cryptographic protocols, such as Diffie–Hellman key exchange, rely on the difficulty of certain mathematical problems, including factoring. Shor's algorithm could potentially break these protocols, compromising the security of communication.

The impact of Shor's algorithm is contingent on the development of practical quantum computers. As of now, large-scale, fault-tolerant quantum computers capable of running Shor's algorithm efficiently do not exist. However, researchers are working on building more powerful quantum computers, and this has prompted a push for quantum-resistant cryptographic algorithms. Shor's algorithm introduces a palpable threat to the security foundations of traditional public-key cryptography, which relies on the presumed computational complexity of certain mathematical problems. Understanding the implications of Shor's algorithm prompts the exploration of quantum-resistant cryptographic alternatives to safeguard data confidentiality. By virtue of its quantum speedup, it transforms problems deemed impossible into ones that quantum computers can solve efficiently. In the context of 6G networks, where secure communication is paramount, the implications are profound. The compromise of traditional public-key cryptographic algorithms raises critical concerns about the confidentiality and integrity of data transmitted over 6G networks.

Countermeasures against the potential impact of Shor's algorithm include the development and deployment of quantum-resistant cryptographic algorithms, ensuring the resilience of communication systems in the face of evolving threats.

2.1.2 Grover's algorithm

Grover's algorithm, proposed by Lov Grover in 1996 [3], is a quantum algorithm that offers a significant speedup for certain types of search problems. Specifically, Grover's algorithm can be employed to search an unsorted database of N items in approximately $\sqrt{N}$ iterations, as opposed to the classical brute-force search that requires N iterations. This quadratic speedup has profound implications for cryptography, particularly in the context of symmetric key cryptography.

Grover's algorithm leverages the concept of amplitude amplification to increase the probability of finding the correct solution. It uses a series of quantum operations, including quantum gates and phase inversions, to enhance the amplitude of the correct solution while diminishing the amplitudes of incorrect solutions. Classically, searching an unsorted database requires checking each item one by one, leading to a linear time complexity of $O(N)$. Grover's algorithm reduces this time complexity to approximately $O(\sqrt{N})$, which represents a quadratic speedup. This is particularly relevant for cryptographic applications where the search space corresponds to potential cryptographic keys.

With reference to [3], Grover's algorithm (Figure 2.3) has direct implications for symmetric key cryptography, where the security of the cryptographic system relies on the difficulty of searching through the space of possible keys. With Grover's algorithm, the time required to perform a brute-force search for the correct key is reduced to approximately $\sqrt{N}$. To maintain the same level of security, the key length may need to be doubled. As a general guideline, if a symmetric key algorithm is considered secure against classical brute-force attacks with a certain key length, the same level of security would require doubling the key length to resist attacks leveraging Grover's algorithm. For example, a 128-bit key in a classical context might be equivalent to a 256-bit key in the quantum context.

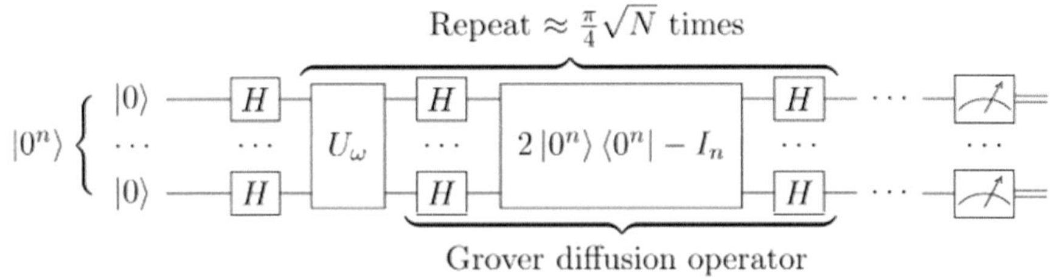

Figure 2.3 Grover's quantum circuit representation of Grover's algorithm.

Table 2.1 Current security status of classical cryptosystems concerning quantum algorithms.

Cryptosystem	Broken by quantum algorithms?
RSA public-key encryption	✓
Diffie–Hellman key-exchange	✓
Elliptic curve cryptography	✓
Buchmann–Williams key-exchange	✓
Algebraically homomorphic	✓
McEliece public-key encryption	X
NTRU public-key encryption	X
Lattice-based public-key encryption	X

One straightforward mitigation strategy is to double the key length in symmetric key cryptographic algorithms to counter the quadratic speedup introduced by Grover's algorithm. This approach can provide a transitional solution while organisations work on adopting quantum-resistant cryptographic techniques. Ultimately, to address the full spectrum of quantum threats, organisations may need to transition to cryptographic algorithms that are specifically designed to be secure against quantum attacks, such as those based on lattice cryptography, hash-based cryptography or code-based cryptography.

In summary, Grover's algorithm introduces a paradigm shift in the search capabilities of quantum computers, impacting symmetric key cryptography by potentially reducing the effective key length. This underscores the importance of considering quantum-resistant cryptographic strategies to ensure the long-term security of information in a quantum computing landscape. Table 2.1 shows the current status of security of classical cryptosystems in relation to quantum algorithms.

2.2 AI-driven Attacks

Navigating the intricate landscape of AI-driven attacks requires a deep and nuanced exploration, demanding a comprehensive understanding of adversarial techniques, the nuanced challenges embedded in defence strategies and the intricate ethical considerations inherent in the deployment of AI for security. As the technological landscape rapidly evolves, adversaries operating in the AI realm employ a spectrum of sophisticated techniques, each with its unique implications for compromising the integrity of AI systems. This multifaceted understanding is crucial for anticipating and mitigating the myriad threats that arise in the ever-expanding domain of artificial intelligence security.

In this dynamic landscape, where the intersection of AI and cybersecurity presents both opportunities and challenges, a thorough examination of adversarial techniques becomes paramount. Adversaries strategically manipulate machine learning systems, exploiting vulnerabilities in algorithms or poisoning datasets to influence model outputs, necessitating a vigilant approach to fortify AI systems against unauthorised interference. Crafting adversarial examples, especially in the realm of image recognition, involves subtle modifications to inputs, which can significantly impact the reliability of AI models. Simultaneously, the vulnerabilities associated with reading comprehension systems highlight the need to grapple with deceptive input data, ensuring the accuracy and reliability of natural language processing systems. The transferability of adversarial samples across multiple machine learning models adds another layer of complexity, emphasising the importance of recognising and addressing this characteristic for developing robust defences.

Amidst these adversarial intricacies, anticipating and mitigating AI-driven attacks requires dynamic defence strategies that can adapt to evolving threats. Proactive monitoring, anomaly detection and swift responses are indispensable components of an effective defence posture. Additionally, the development of robust model architectures that can identify and discard adversarial inputs, while maintaining accurate predictions under normal circumstances, contributes to the overall resilience of AI systems. Ethical considerations, including fairness, transparency and accountability, are integral to AI security, ensuring that unintended biases and discriminatory outcomes are minimised in the deployment of AI technologies for security purposes.

In this ever-evolving technological landscape, the fusion of ethical AI deployment, dynamic defence strategies and a profound understanding of adversarial techniques constitutes the foundation for organisations seeking to navigate the challenges posed by AI-driven attacks successfully. The adversaries in the AI landscape employ various techniques to compromise the integrity of AI systems. These techniques include manipulating machine learning systems, crafting adversarial examples to mislead AI models (especially in image recognition), targeting reading comprehension systems with deceptive input data and exploring the transferability of adversarial samples across multiple machine learning models. Understanding these techniques is crucial for anticipating and mitigating AI-driven attacks. By addressing these aspects comprehensively, stakeholders can cultivate a resilient and secure environment in the realm of artificial intelligence and cybersecurity.

2.2.1 Adversarial machine learning

Adversarial machine learning constitutes a paradigm where attackers strategically exploit vulnerabilities inherent in AI models to generate misleading outputs. At its core, this concept hinges on the manipulation of an AI model's decision-making process by introducing subtle, carefully crafted perturbations into input data. These imperceptible alterations, often imperceivable to the human eye, are strategically designed to mislead the model and force it into producing incorrect or unintended results. Understanding and addressing these vulnerabilities are crucial for ensuring the robustness and reliability of AI systems across diverse applications.

Adversarial machine learning constitutes an established domain, extending beyond exclusive relevance to deep neural networks. In 2006, Barreno et al. authored the paper 'Can Machine Learning Be Secure?' [5], which delved into adversarial attacks, presenting potential defences against them. During this period, the pinnacle of machine learning featured support vector machines (SVMs) and random forests (RFs). Notably, research demonstrated the susceptibility of both SVMs and RFs to adversarial attacks. The landscape shifted with the ascension of deep neural networks' popularity around 2012. Initial optimism suggested that these highly non-linear models might exhibit reduced vulnerability to adversarial attacks. However, such aspirations were diminished by revelations from researchers such as Goodfellow et al. [6] Contrary to early expectations, deep neural networks have proven vulnerable to adversarial attacks, akin to their predecessors. Biggio and Roli's 2017 paper, 'Wild Patterns: Ten Years After the Rise of Adversarial Machine Learning' [7] gives a comprehensive exploration of the historical trajectory of adversarial attacks. Classi?cation of adversarial attacks from different perspectives is as follows.

Perspective #1: Available knowledge of the model

- ↣ *White-box attack (full knowledge)*: In this form of adversarial attack, the attacker possesses comprehensive information about the model, including its architecture, individual layer parameters and the training dataset. While this scenario is valuable for understanding the impact of adversarial perturbations caused by internal parameters, it is primarily useful for academic research purposes due to its lack of practical applicability in real-world situations. It allows for a worst-case evaluation of learning algorithm security, providing upper bounds on potential performance degradation during an attack.

- *Grey-box attack (limited knowledge)*: In this type of adversarial attack, the adversary has partial knowledge of the model, such as its architecture and/or some layer parameters. This scenario helps illuminate the relationship between the feature extractor (often a convolution network) and the classifier (typically a fully connected network). Understanding this relationship is beneficial for tasks like transfer learning. However, grey-box attacks are often considered more potent and transferable than white-box attacks. Like white-box attacks, their real-world utility is constrained, mainly serving academic and research purposes.
- *Black-box attack (minimal knowledge)*: In this adversarial attack, the attacker has no information about the model. The model only reveals the output of the neural network, knowing none of its parameters or any layer details. A more stringent form of this is a no-model attack, where there is no information from the model, neither input nor output. This type of attack is particularly significant in the classification, requiring minimal information and exhibiting scalability to the real world. However, its potential for scalability raises ethical concerns, as some attacks could be misused in applications. Despite this, many black-box attacks tend to be slower than their white-box and grey-box counterparts, limiting their scalability.

Perspective #2: Model output

- *Score-based attack*: In this type of adversarial attack, the attacker is aware of the probabilities or soft-labels associated with each class predicted by the model, denoted as $g(x)$.
- *Decision-based attack*: In this adversarial strategy, the attacker possesses information solely about the model's decision, specifically the predicted class or $\text{argmax}[g(x)]$.

Perspective #3: Attack goal (objective)

- *Untargeted (error-generic) attack*: This adversarial approach aims to misguide a neural network model into classifying any incorrect class. Formally, the goal is to minimise $g(x + \epsilon)C$ subject to ϵ, where $g(x)C$ represents the soft-label for the correct class. This type of attack focuses solely on misclassification, providing limited insights into the reasons behind it. It sheds light on challenges related to representation space quality and the intricate, non-smooth decision boundaries of neural networks in higher dimensions.

↣ *Targeted (error-specific) attack*: In this adversarial strategy, the adversary's objective is to guide the model into classifying a specific class other than the actual one. Formally, the goal is to maximise $g(x + \epsilon)T$, subject to ϵ, where $g(x)T$ is the soft-label for the target class. Targeted attacks are more challenging than untargeted ones as they focus on a particular class, aiding in understanding primary patterns. However, these attacks typically have a lower success rate, making generalisation across datasets difficult.

Perspective #4: Perceivability of adversarial samples

↣ In a perceivable (visible) adversarial attack, alterations are easily noticeable, being apparent to human perception. This may include the addition of an adversarial patch, input deformation or other modifications. This approach highlights the contrast between human and machine learning. Unlike humans who focus on the object, machine learning can be misled by disruptions in patterns, leading to misclassification. The use of visible attacks, however, limits real-world applicability as they are easily detectable and can be promptly corrected.

↣ In an imperceptible (invisible) adversarial attack, the perturbation remains hidden from human senses. This typically involves adding digital noise to the input, which is undetectable to humans. This type of attack contributes to an understanding of the model's fragility and illuminates the decision boundary. Simultaneously, from a security perspective, these attacks pose a significant threat as they operate without observation. The model, relying on human observation, remains unaware of the input manipulation.

Perspective #5: Format of adversarial samples

↣ In a digital adversarial attack, the adversary focuses on compromising digital assets such as images, videos or files. This approach, commonly seen in academic research, allows for a broad selection of formats and ease in crafting perturbations. While often explored for understanding neural network vulnerabilities, digital attacks pose a real threat to deployed models, making digital assets vulnerable to cyber hacking.

↣ In a physical adversarial attack, the adversary targets real-world objects. This form of attack may include actions like manipulating stop signs or altering lane markings. Some attacks may require larger, coarser patterns and involve the digitisation of physical objects using sensors, potentially sacrificing finer details. Despite limitations such as the need for physical objects and more challenging attack perturbations, physical assaults pose a significant security threat to various real-world applications.

Perspective #6: Attack scope

- In an individual adversarial attack, the focus is on finding perturbations that, when added to specific samples, lead to misclassification. Each input sample undergoes optimisation, shedding light on the breakdown of patterns and textures in images. However, due to the distinct nature of each input sample, generalising and understanding the perturbation become challenging. This form of attack mainly provides insights into robustness and offers limited understanding of the existence of adversarial samples.
- In a universal adversarial attack, the goal is to identify a perturbation that, when added to original samples, misclassifies a majority of them. Optimisation occurs for the entire dataset, uncovering the universal perturbation (ϵ) affecting various input samples. This type of attack is instrumental in understanding the network's global vulnerability, revealing weaknesses in input accessibility. Additionally, it aids in comprehending the transferability of adversarial samples.

Perspective #7: Attacking strategy

- *Data poisoning attack*: The adversary typically schematises during model training, aiming to inject perturbations into the training data. The objective is to deceive the model into misclassifying non-perturbed samples during testing. Backdoor attacks, a subset of data-poisoning attacks, involve imprinting triggers on a few training samples, altering their labels during training and causing misclassification during inference. While effective during model exposure in training, this strategy becomes less practical for real-world attacks when the trained model is deployed. Nevertheless, it provides valuable insights into training biases, aiding in understanding the decision boundary and representation space of the model. Notably, this type of attack proves effective against continual learning and reinforcement learning models, where the model learns based on outcomes. A case study illustrating this concept is observed in the Twitter chatbot 'Tay' launched by Microsoft in 2016 [8]. The concept was to initiate conversations with users and gather playful interactions. However, malicious internet users, characterised as trolls, began providing vulgar and offensive tweets, leading to the chatbot responding with increasingly offensive content [9].

↣ *Evasive manoeuvre*: The adversary typically collaborates when the model is already trained. The objective is to identify perturbations for the testing data, causing the neural network model to misclassify them. This trial-and-error attack involves the adversary's attempt to find perturbations without prior knowledge of their impact on misclassification. The success of this attack relies on compromising the integrity of the testing data. Most proposed attacks fall under this category, making it a common approach for adversarial manipulation.

↣ *Extraction tactic*: The extraction adversarial attack occurs after the model has been deployed, aiming to retrieve the neural network model parameters or functionality. The attack relies on compromising the confidentiality of the model to recover private learned features. Extraction attacks include attempts to extract both model parameters and functionality, exemplified by Copycat CNN (convolutional neural network) [10], and Knock-off Nets [11]. Copycat CNN refers to an adversarial attack technique where an adversary creates a neural network that mimics the behaviour of the targeted model. The objective is to imitate the functionality of the original model without necessarily replicating its parameters. By observing the responses of the target model to various inputs, the adversary trains a copycat CNN to approximate the decision-making process of the original model. This type of attack aims to extract the learned features and decision boundaries of the target model without directly accessing its internal parameters. Knock-off Nets is an adversarial attack technique where an adversary attempts to replicate the functionality of a target neural network without explicitly copying its parameters. Instead of directly mimicking the internal weights of the target model, Knock-off Nets focus on understanding the decision boundaries and learned features. The goal is to create a substitute neural network that can produce similar outputs to the original model for a given set of inputs. This type of attack aims to extract the essential characteristics of the target model without relying on a direct transfer of its parameters.

↣ *Model poisoning manoeuvres*: The adversary straightforwardly replaces the legitimate model with an adversarial one. This traditional cyberattack involves substituting the model file, usually containing weights, with another potentially malicious one.

Perspective #8: Optimisation strategy

↣ *Gradient-based attack*: The adversary utilises gradients and/or back-propagation to calculate the perturbation needed for the original sample to be misclassified. Examples of such attacks include the fast gradient sign method (FGSM) [6] and projected gradient descent (PGD) attack [12]. FGSM is a popular and simple adversarial attack technique in the field of machine learning and deep learning. FGSM perturbs input data by adding small, carefully crafted perturbations based on the gradient of the loss function with respect to the input. The key idea is to maximise the loss to cause misclassification without necessarily understanding the detailed parameters of the target model. The formula for generating an adversarial example using FGSM is:

$$\text{Adversarial Example} = \text{Input} + \epsilon \cdot \text{sign}(\nabla\text{InputLoss}(\text{Model}(\text{Input}), \text{True Label})),$$

where Input is the original input data, ϵ is a small constant representing the magnitude of the perturbation, sign$(\cdot)$ is the signum function, and ∇InputLoss(Model(Input), True Label) is the gradient of the loss function with respect to the input. The resulting perturbed input is then used to fool the model into making incorrect predictions while appearing visually similar to the original input to the human eye. FGSM is known for its efficiency and effectiveness, making it a foundational technique in adversarial machine learning research. PGD attack is an iterative optimisation technique used in adversarial attacks against machine learning models. It aims to generate adversarial examples by perturbing the input data in a way that causes misclassification. In each iteration of PGD, the input data is modified slightly based on the gradient of the loss function with respect to the input. The perturbation is then projected onto a constrained set (e.g., within a specified ϵ-ball around the original data) to ensure that the adversarial example remains close to the original data in a defined metric space. This process is repeated for multiple iterations to enhance the effectiveness of the attack. PGD is a stronger and more robust form of attack compared to single-step methods like the FGSM because it considers multiple steps, making it harder for the model to defend against the adversarial perturbations.

↣ *Evolutionary strategy-based attack*: The adversary employs evolutionary strategy-based optimisation, such as differential evolution (DE) [13] and covariance matrix adaptation evolution strategy (CMA-ES) [14], to search for the adversarial perturbation ϵx. DE utilises differences between candidate solutions, while CMA-ES adapts a covariance matrix to guide the search. This approach is particularly useful for black-box attacks, where information about the model is not present, and optimisation cannot rely on backpropagating gradients. Examples of this attack include the One-Pixel attack [15] and Threshold attack [16]. In One-Pixel attack, the adversary modifies just a single pixel in an input image to cause misclassification by the model. Despite the minimal perturbation, the attack exploits the model's vulnerability, highlighting the sensitivity of machine learning systems to small, strategically placed changes in input data. In Threshold attack, the adversary manipulates the input data to cross a decision threshold of a machine learning model. The goal is to make small changes to the input, often near the decision boundary, causing the model's output to switch from one class to another. This attack exploits the model's sensitivity to minor variations around decision boundaries, demonstrating potential vulnerabilities in the model's robustness.

Perspective #9: Perturbation constraints

- In distance metrics-based constraint attack, the adversary limits the perturbation search for the input by considering the distance from the original sample. Different distance norms, such as L0, L1, L2 and L8, are employed to create various types of attacks. The perturbation ϵx is constrained based on the chosen distance norm (p), ensuring $|\epsilon x|p$ is below a specified threshold.
- On the other hand, geometric transformations based constraint attack relies on geometric transformations of the original input to misclassify the model. Spatial transformations like affine and rotations, even if used as augmentations during model training, can lead to misclassifications. Colour-channel permutation is another technique affecting the model's performance and can be employed as an adversarial attack.

Perspective #10: Intent

- In Intended attack, the adversary intentionally seeks to misclassify the model through perturbations with malicious intent.
- Conversely, Unintended attack refers to misclassifications resulting from various unintended failures during training or inference. An example is reward hacking, where discrepancies between the specified reward received by the model and the true intended reward lead to peculiar behaviour in reinforcement learning systems.

Perspective #11: Influence

- ↣ In Causative attack, the adversary can manipulate both training and testing data.
- ↣ On the other hand, in Exploratory attack, the adversary is limited to manipulating only the testing data.

The crux of adversarial attacks lies in understanding the vulnerabilities of machine learning models, particularly neural networks, which are susceptible to subtle modifications in input patterns. By leveraging optimisation techniques, attackers can identify and exploit the sensitivities of a model's decision boundaries, causing it to misclassify or misinterpret data. This strategic manipulation is not confined to specific domains; it spans image recognition, natural language processing and various AI applications.

In image recognition, for instance, adversaries can introduce minimal perturbations to an image – imperceptible to human observers – leading an AI model to misclassify the object within the image. Similarly, in natural language processing, attackers may subtly alter words or phrases in a text to deceive language models.

2.2.2 Adversarial attacks on image recognition

Adversarial attacks on image recognition represent a sophisticated manipulation of AI models, particularly neural networks, through the use of gradient-based methods. In this context, attackers exploit the underlying mathematical principles of machine learning models, seeking to subtly alter the features of input images in a way that induces misclassification. A brief history of adversarial attacks and images is given in Figure 2.4.

Gradient-based attacks leverage the gradients of a neural network concerning its loss function with respect to the input image. These gradients, representing the sensitivity of the model to changes in the input, are utilised by attackers to identify the most impactful modifications that will lead to a misclassification. The perturbations introduced through this method are often imperceptible to the human eye but can have a profound impact on the model's decision-making process. The exemplar illustration of an adversarial attack, as according to [6], is presented in Figure 2.5. On the left, we observe our original input image, accurately identified by our neural network as a 'panda' with a confidence of 57.7%. In the middle, there is a noise vector that, to the human observer, seems random. Nevertheless, it is anything but random. The pixel values in the noise vector are determined by 'the sign of

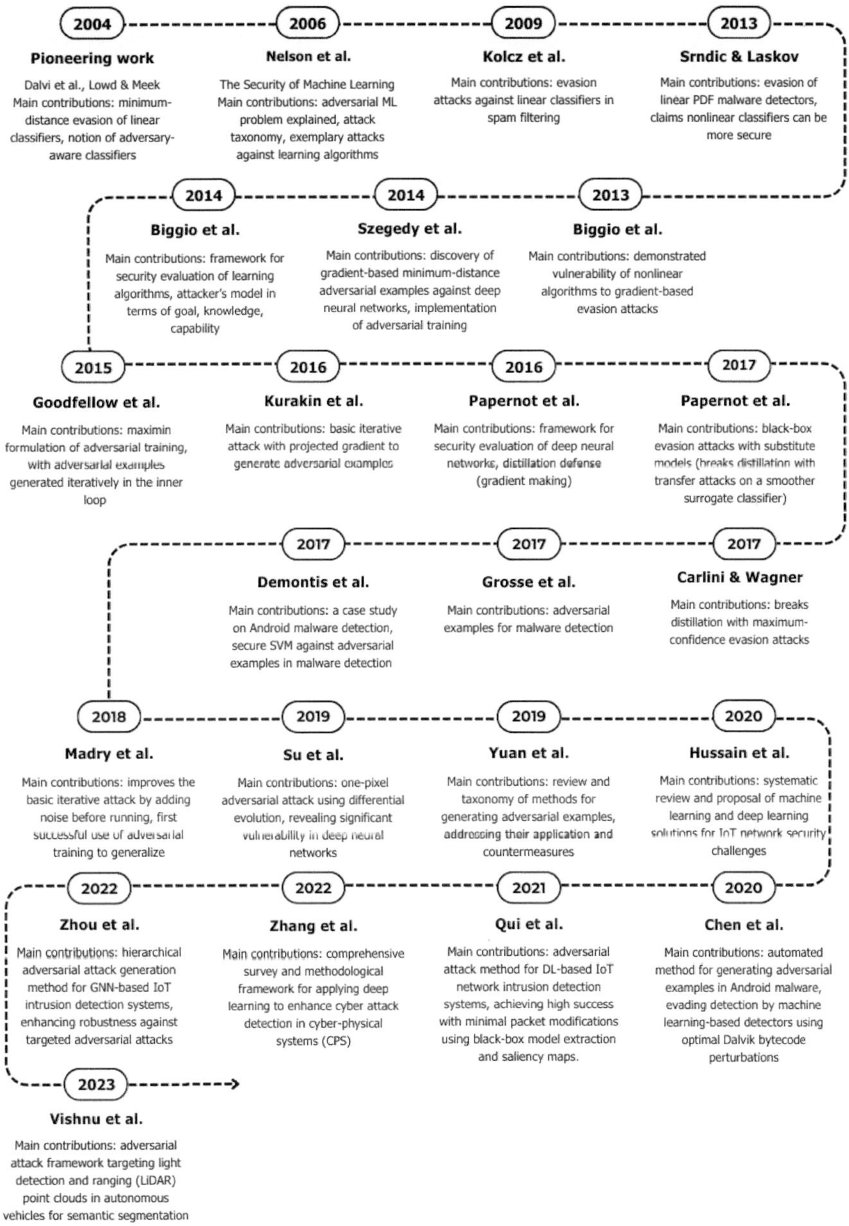

Figure 2.4 A timeline of adversarial machine learning and security of deep neural network publications.

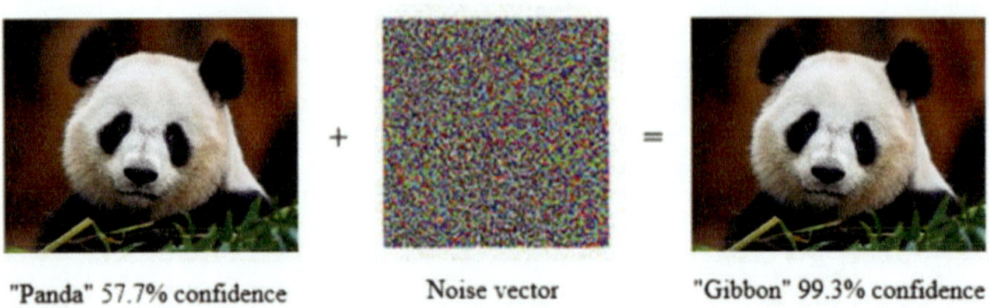

Figure 2.5 Executing an adversarial attack involves taking an initial input image (on the left), intentionally introducing a noise vector to perturb it (in the middle). This deliberate perturbation compels the neural network to misclassify the input image, leading to an inaccurate classification outcome, potentially with significant repercussions (depicted on the right).

the elements of the gradient of the cost function with respect to the input image' [17]. This noise vector is then added to the input image, resulting in the output (depicted on the right) in Figure 2.5. To our eyes, this image seems indistinguishable from the original; however, our neural network now categorises the image as a 'gibbon' (a small ape, akin to a monkey) with a confidence level of 99.7%.

A classic example of gradient-based attacks is the fast gradient sign method (FGSM), where perturbations are generated by taking the sign of the gradient of the loss function with respect to the input image. This results in a perturbed image that, when added to the original, causes the model to misclassify the perturbed image. Iterative methods, such as the iterative FGSM, extend this concept by applying the process iteratively to amplify the impact of perturbations.

The consequences of gradient-based attacks in image recognition are significant. A seemingly innocuous image, when subject to carefully crafted perturbations, can be misinterpreted by the model, leading to incorrect classifications. This has implications in various domains, including security systems relying on image recognition for authentication or surveillance.

Countermeasures against gradient-based attacks involve the incorporation of adversarial training during the model's learning phase. By exposing the model to both standard and adversarial examples during training, the model learns to be more resilient to these subtle manipulations. Additionally, research is ongoing to develop regularisation techniques and architecture modifications that enhance the robustness of image recognition models against adversarial attacks.

Understanding and mitigating gradient-based attacks are crucial for bolstering the reliability and security of image recognition systems. As AI continues to permeate various aspects of daily life, from facial recognition in smartphones to surveillance applications, addressing vulnerabilities to adversarial manipulation becomes paramount for ensuring the integrity of AI-based image recognition.

2.2.3 Text-based adversarial attacks

Text-based adversarial attacks represent a sophisticated manipulation of natural language processing (NLP) models, focusing on the strategic modification of word embeddings to deceive text-based classifiers. In this realm, attackers exploit the fundamental structure of language representations within machine learning models, aiming to introduce subtle alterations that lead to misclassification or misinterpretation.

Word embeddings, which capture semantic relationships between words in vector spaces, are foundational to many NLP models. Adversaries target these embeddings, seeking to manipulate the semantic context in a way that deceives the model's understanding of the input text.

One common method of manipulation involves perturbing the word embeddings of specific terms within a text. The objective is to generate a modified text that appears almost identical to the original to human observers but leads the NLP model to produce incorrect or unintended results. Adversaries can leverage optimisation techniques to identify the most effective modifications to word embeddings. These alterations, often imperceptible to human readers, prompt the model to make erroneous predictions or classifications.

An example of a text-based adversarial attack involves slight changes in the wording of a sentence, leading a sentiment analysis model to misinterpret the sentiment expressed. By manipulating word embeddings, attackers can trick the model into assigning a positive sentiment to a negative statement or vice versa.

TextAttack [18] is a Python library reshaping NLP model robustness research. Adversarial examples are inputs crafted to deceive machine learning models, with TextAttack specifically addressing adversarial perturbations – alterations to benign inputs causing misclassification. In NLP, adversarial attacks involve generating perturbations through an iterative process, aiming to fool models. TextAttack breaks this process into stages with

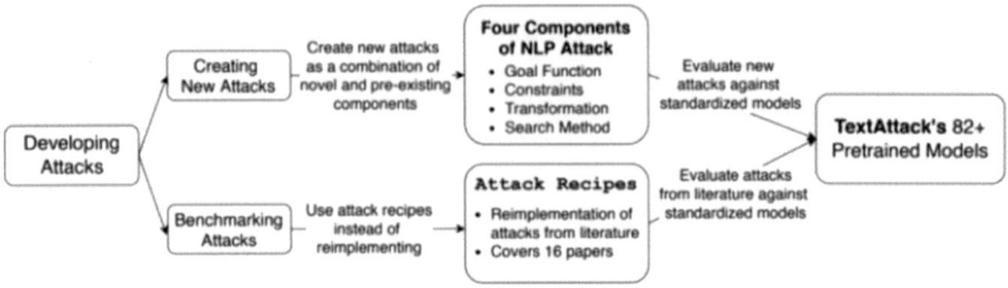

Figure 2.6 TextAttack – developing attacks.

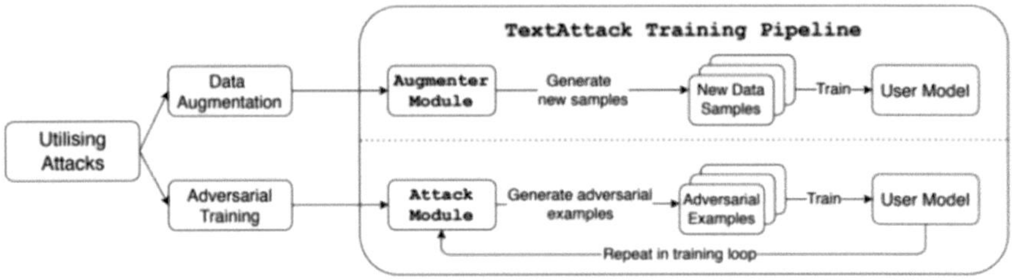

Figure 2.7 TextAttack – utilising attacks.

interchangeable components, measuring model robustness through attack success rates and after-attack accuracy. Referring to [18], Figure 2.6 provides an overview of the primary functionalities of TextAttack related to attack development, while Figure 2.7 illustrates how these attacks are utilised.

Results from TextAttack's DeepWordBug attack on an LSTM (long short-term memory) model reveal both successes and failures, highlighting the nuanced nature of adversarial attacks. The attacks are further categorised based on visual and semantic similarity, as referring to [18] and shown in Table 2.2, emphasising the need for diverse adversarial strategies. TextAttack, with its components for goal function, constraints, transformation and search method, aims to facilitate comprehensive research on adversarial examples in NLP.

Countermeasures against text-based adversarial attacks include developing NLP models with enhanced robustness to subtle semantic alterations. Researchers are exploring methods such as adversarial training, where models are exposed to both standard and adversarial examples during training, enabling them to learn more resilient representations.

The implications of text-based adversarial attacks are broad, affecting applications ranging from spam filters and sentiment analysis tools to more critical systems like automated content moderation and information

Table 2.2 Two varying notions of adversarial examples in NLP are exemplified. These outcomes were produced utilising TextAttack on an LSTM model trained on the sentiment classification dataset from Rotten Tomatoes Movie Reviews. These instances represent authentic adversarial examples, crafted through the application of the DeepWordBug and TextFooler attacks.

Original input	Connoisseurs of Chinese film will be pleased to discover that Tian's meticulous talent has not withered during his enforced hiatus.	Prediction: Positive (77%)
Adversarial example (visually similar)	Vonnoisseurs of Chinese film will be pleased to discover that Tian's meticulous talent has not withered during his enforced hiatus.	Prediction: Negative (52%)
Adversarial example (semantically similar)	Connoisseurs of Chinese footage will be pleased to discover that Tian's meticulous talent has not withered during his enforced hiatus.	Prediction: Negative (54%)

extraction. As NLP models become integral to various technologies and services, addressing vulnerabilities to adversarial manipulation is essential for maintaining the reliability and security of these systems.

2.2.4 Transferability of adversarial attacks

Researchers have identified the transferability of adversarial attacks [19], meaning that an attack crafted for one model can often be effective against different models, even those with distinct architectures. This generalisation of adversarial attacks underscores the broad-reaching implications and challenges in fortifying AI systems against manipulation.

The concept of transferability in adversarial attacks introduces a fascinating and concerning phenomenon where adversarial examples crafted for one machine learning model can effectively deceive other models, even those with different architectures. This phenomenon underscores the challenges in fortifying models against adversarial manipulation, as successful attacks on one system can potentially generalise to compromise a broader range of models.

At the core of transferability lies the idea that the perturbations introduced to manipulate one model's decision boundaries exhibit a degree of universality. Adversarial examples, carefully crafted to exploit vulnerabilities in one model's structure, often retain their efficacy when applied to other models. This phenomenon persists even when the target models employ different architectures, datasets or training methodologies.

One of the driving forces behind transferability is the shared vulnerabilities across various machine learning models. Adversarial attacks typically exploit inherent blind spots or non-robust features in the decision-making process, and these vulnerabilities can transcend the specifics of individual models. This poses a significant challenge for developers aiming to secure their models against adversarial manipulation, as defences must contend with the potential cross-model impact of a successful attack.

Transfer learning, a technique where a model trained on one task is adapted to perform other related tasks, can inadvertently exacerbate the transferability of adversarial attacks. Models that share knowledge or features through transfer learning may inherit vulnerabilities, making them susceptible to similar adversarial manipulations.

Addressing the issue of transferability requires a holistic understanding of the common vulnerabilities exploited by adversarial attacks. Developing defences that are robust across different model architectures, training datasets and applications is essential. Adversarial training, where models are exposed to both standard and adversarial examples during training, is one approach to enhance the overall robustness of models and mitigate the transferability of attacks.

The significance of transferability extends beyond individual model security; it has implications for the broader field of machine learning security. As machine learning models become increasingly integrated into diverse applications, from image recognition to natural language processing, comprehending and mitigating transferability is pivotal for establishing a robust defence against adversarial manipulation across the entire machine learning landscape.

2.2.5 Real-world implications

The real-world implications of adversarial machine learning pose critical challenges, especially in security-critical applications where the consequences of misclassification or manipulation can have profound effects. Analysing the security implications provides insights into the potential risks associated with deploying machine learning systems in domains such as autonomous vehicles, healthcare diagnostics and financial systems.

Adversarial attacks on object detection algorithms in autonomous vehicles can lead to misinterpretation of road signs, obstacles or other vehicles. This could result in dangerous behaviours, accidents or even malicious traffic manipulation. Compromised autonomous vehicle systems could pose significant threats to public safety, impacting not only the occupants of the vehicles but also pedestrians and other drivers on the road. For example, in [20], by placing carefully crafted stickers on road signs, researchers could cause misinterpretation by the vehicle's vision system, potentially leading to incorrect navigation decisions impacting the performance of object detection systems in self-driving cars.

Adversarial attacks on medical image classification systems may lead to misdiagnosis or incorrect treatment recommendations. Attackers could manipulate medical images subtly, affecting the accuracy of disease detection. Misdiagnosis in healthcare could have severe implications for patients, resulting in delayed or inappropriate treatment plans. Patient safety and the integrity of medical diagnoses are at stake. Finlayson et al. [21] explore the vulnerabilities in medical image classification systems and the potential impact on diagnosis and treatment.

Adversarial attacks on fraud detection models in financial systems can lead to the evasion of detection mechanisms. Attackers may manipulate transaction data to conduct fraudulent activities without triggering alarms. Compromised fraud detection can result in financial losses for individuals and institutions. The integrity of financial transactions and the trust in secure online transactions may be undermined.

Adversarial attacks designed in one domain may have unforeseen consequences when transferred to another. Attacks crafted in a controlled environment might generalise to security-critical applications. The cross-domain impact of adversarial attacks introduces an additional layer of complexity, requiring comprehensive security measures that consider the interconnectedness of various applications and domains.

Adversarial attacks underscore the challenge of making machine learning models robust in dynamic, real-world environments. Models designed and trained in controlled settings may struggle when exposed to the complexity and variability of the real world. Lack of robustness increases the susceptibility of machine learning systems to manipulation, leading to security vulnerabilities. Ensuring models can handle real-world scenarios is crucial for the reliability of security-critical applications.

Adversarial attacks may exploit biases in machine learning models, leading to unfair or discriminatory outcomes. The ethical considerations surrounding adversarial machine learning involve not only technical vulnerabilities but also the potential for social harm. Unintended biases in security-critical applications can exacerbate existing inequalities, affecting individuals' rights, privacy, and access to services.

The real-world implications of adversarial machine learning on security-critical applications are extensive and multifaceted. Understanding the security risks is imperative for developing robust and resilient machine learning systems that can withstand adversarial challenges in diverse and complex environments. As machine learning continues to play an increasingly integral role in various sectors, addressing these implications is essential for ensuring the safety, reliability and ethical use of advanced technologies.

2.3 Decentralised Edge Computing Risks

In the rapidly evolving landscape of 6G networks, the promise of transformative capabilities hinges on the foundational paradigm of decentralised edge computing. As we navigate the intricate web of technological advancements, it becomes apparent that the decentralised architecture at the network edge is not merely a component; it is the linchpin shaping the very fabric of 6G's potential.

To comprehend the essence of decentralised edge computing, it is imperative to first grasp the unfolding narrative of 6G networks. Beyond the incremental improvements of its predecessors, 6G represents a quantum leap in connectivity, ushering in an era where the convergence of technologies propels us into uncharted territories. With promises of unprecedented speed, ultra-low latency and ubiquitous connectivity, 6G is poised to redefine the boundaries of what is conceivable in the realm of telecommunications.

At the heart of this transformative journey lies the pivotal role of decentralised edge computing. No longer confined to centralised data processing hubs, computing capabilities are distributed to the very edge of the network. This decentralised paradigm is not merely an architectural shift; it is a strategic imperative that empowers applications and services with real-time processing, minimising latency and enhancing overall system efficiency. The network edge, once a boundary, now emerges as a dynamic frontier where data is not just transmitted but processed, analysed and acted upon instantaneously.

Decentralised edge computing, with its emphasis on real-time processing at the edge of the network, demands a nuanced exploration of the security challenges it introduces. While it holds great promise in enhancing performance, efficiency and enabling new applications, it also brings along its share of risks and challenges, particularly in terms of security. The key aspects to consider are:

- ↣ *Data privacy and security*: With data being processed and stored closer to the point of origin (i.e., the edge devices), there are concerns regarding data privacy and security. Edge devices may not have the same level of security measures as centralised data centres, making them more susceptible to breaches and unauthorised access. Edge computing involves processing data as close to the source as possible, which means that sensitive information may reside on devices located at the network's edge. This proximity to data sources poses unique challenges for ensuring data privacy and security. Unlike centralised data centres, where security measures can be more tightly controlled, edge devices may be deployed in diverse environments with varying levels of physical security. Furthermore, many edge devices, such as IoT sensors, drones and autonomous vehicles, have limited computing resources and may lack robust security features compared to traditional servers in centralised data centres. These devices are often designed with a focus on efficiency and cost-effectiveness rather than comprehensive security measures, making them more vulnerable to attacks. Additionally, the distributed nature of edge computing means that sensitive data could be spread across various locations, increasing the potential attack surface. Decentralised edge computing expands the attack surface by distributing computing resources across various locations. Attackers may exploit vulnerabilities in individual edge devices or compromise communication channels between edge nodes, leading to unauthorised access to sensitive data. The distributed nature of edge computing also makes it challenging to monitor and defend against attacks effectively.
- ↣ *Network vulnerabilities*: Decentralised edge computing relies heavily on network connectivity to facilitate communication between edge devices and centralised servers. Any vulnerabilities in the network infrastructure, such as routers, switches, and communication protocols, could compromise the security of the entire system. Attackers may exploit these vulnerabilities to intercept, manipulate or disrupt communication channels, leading to unauthorised access to sensitive data or denial of service attacks. Attackers could exploit weaknesses in the communication channels between edge devices and centralised servers, leading to data interception, manipulation or denial of service attacks. One of the primary concerns in decentralised edge computing is the risk of man-in-the-middle (MITM) attacks, where an attacker intercepts communication between edge devices and centralised servers. By impersonating

either the edge device or the server, the attacker can eavesdrop on sensitive information, modify data packets or inject malicious code into the communication stream. MITM attacks pose a significant threat to data privacy and integrity in decentralised edge computing environments. Inadequately secured communication channels between edge devices and centralised servers may expose data to interception by unauthorised parties. Attackers can capture data packets traversing the network and extract sensitive information, such as credentials, personally identifiable information (PII) or proprietary data. Moreover, attackers may tamper with data packets to modify or manipulate the content, leading to inaccurate results or compromised decision-making processes. Decentralised edge computing networks are also susceptible to denial of service (DoS) attacks, where attackers flood the network with a high volume of traffic or malicious requests to disrupt normal operations. By overwhelming network resources or exhausting bandwidth capacity, DoS attacks can render edge devices and centralised servers inaccessible, causing service disruptions and downtime. Protecting against DoS attacks requires implementing robust network defences and traffic filtering mechanisms. Securing data in transit between edge devices and centralised servers is essential for maintaining data privacy and integrity. Encryption protocols such as TLS (transport layer security) or VPNs (virtual private networks) can help protect data against interception and eavesdropping during transmission. However, implementing encryption on resource-constrained edge devices may pose performance challenges and require careful optimisation to balance security and efficiency. Continuous monitoring of network traffic and behaviour analysis is critical for detecting and mitigating potential security threats in decentralised edge computing environments. Intrusion detection systems (IDS) and intrusion prevention systems (IPS) can help identify suspicious activities, unauthorised access attempts or anomalies in network behaviour, enabling timely response and mitigation actions. Securing network connectivity and data transmission in decentralised edge computing environments requires a comprehensive approach that encompasses both technical solutions, such as encryption and network monitoring tools, and proactive security measures, such as vulnerability assessments and patch management. Collaboration between network operators, cybersecurity professionals and system administrators is essential to develop and implement effective strategies for mitigating network vulnerabilities and safeguarding data privacy and integrity in decentralised edge computing deployments.

↣ *Device security*: Edge devices, including IoT sensors, gateways and edge servers, may be susceptible to malware and ransomware attacks. Malicious actors can exploit vulnerabilities in device firmware or software to install malware, which can compromise the device's functionality, steal sensitive data or disrupt operations. Ransomware attacks, where attackers encrypt device data and demand payment for decryption, pose a significant threat to the availability and integrity of edge computing systems. Edge devices deployed in uncontrolled environments are vulnerable to physical tampering and compromise. Attackers may gain physical access to devices, either through theft or unauthorised access, and tamper with hardware components or install malicious software. Physical security measures, such as tamper-evident seals, locks and secure enclosures, are essential for protecting edge devices from unauthorised access and tampering. Many edge devices are designed with a focus on cost-effectiveness and efficiency, resulting in limited security features and capabilities. These devices may lack robust authentication mechanisms, encryption support or secure boot processes, making them more vulnerable to exploitation by malicious actors. Additionally, firmware and software updates for edge devices may be infrequent or non-existent, leaving devices exposed to known vulnerabilities. Decentralised edge computing ecosystems typically consist of a diverse range of devices from different manufacturers, running various operating systems and software platforms. Managing the security of such a heterogeneous environment becomes challenging, as each device may require different security measures and updates. Ensuring uniform security protocols across the entire ecosystem is difficult, given the scale and diversity of edge devices deployed. Securing edge devices requires the ability to remotely manage and monitor device health, security status, and software updates. However, managing a large number of geographically distributed edge devices poses logistical challenges, particularly concerning connectivity, bandwidth and latency. Implementing remote management tools, over-the-air (OTA) updates and centralised monitoring systems can help streamline device security management in decentralised edge computing environments. Effective device security also requires comprehensive lifecycle management practices, including provisioning, configuration, monitoring and decommissioning of edge devices. Ensuring that devices are securely provisioned with appropriate access credentials, configured according to security best practices and regularly audited for security compliance is essential for mitigating security risks throughout the device lifecycle. Addressing these challenges requires a concerted effort from device manufacturers, network operators, system integrators and cybersecurity professionals to develop and implement robust security measures for edge devices in decentralised computing environments. This includes incorporating security-by-design principles into device development, establishing secure communication protocols, implementing access control mechanisms and continuously monitoring and updating device security to adapt to evolving threats. Collaboration and information sharing among stakeholders are essential for enhancing device security and ensuring the integrity and resilience of decentralised edge computing deployments.

↣ *Authentication and access control*: Decentralised edge computing environments are characterised by a distributed architecture with numerous edge devices and services scattered across different locations. Managing authentication and access control in such complex environments presents challenges in terms of ensuring consistent enforcement of security policies, maintaining visibility into access activities and synchronising user credentials and permissions across decentralised nodes. Weak authentication mechanisms or improper access control policies can expose decentralised edge computing environments to the risk of unauthorised access and data breaches. Without robust authentication mechanisms in place, malicious actors may exploit vulnerabilities to gain unauthorised entry into edge devices or services, leading to data theft, tampering or disruption of operations. In decentralised edge computing environments, it is essential to implement granular access control policies to ensure that users and devices have access only to the resources and data necessary for their roles and responsibilities. Role-based access control (RBAC) enables organisations to define and enforce access policies based on users' roles, granting permissions according to their specific job functions and responsibilities. This helps minimise the attack surface and mitigate the risk of privilege escalation attacks. Multi-factor authentication (MFA) adds an extra layer of security by requiring users to provide multiple forms of verification, such as passwords, biometric data, smart cards or one-time codes, to access edge resources. Implementing MFA strengthens authentication mechanisms and helps prevent unauthorised access, even if user credentials are compromised or stolen. Deploying secure authentication protocols, such as OAuth, OpenID Connect or SAML, helps facilitate secure authentication and single sign-on (SSO) capabilities in decentralised edge computing environments. These protocols enable users to authenticate once and access multiple edge services seamlessly, while ensuring that authentication credentials are transmitted securely over the network. Centralised identity and access management (IAM) solutions provide a centralised platform for managing user identities, authentication and access control policies across decentralised edge computing environments. IAM solutions offer features such as user provisioning, authentication policy enforcement, access control management and audit trail logging, enabling organisations to maintain visibility and control over user access activities. Implementing continuous monitoring and auditing mechanisms helps organisations detect and respond to unauthorised access attempts, anomalous behaviour and security incidents in real time. By monitoring user access activities, logging authentication events and performing regular audits of access control configurations, organisations can identify security gaps, enforce compliance with security policies and mitigate risks effectively. In summary, managing authentication and access control in decentralised edge computing environments requires a combination of robust authentication mechanisms, granular access control policies, secure authentication protocols, centralised IAM solutions and continuous monitoring and auditing practices. By implementing these best practices, organisations can enhance security, protect sensitive data and mitigate the risk of unauthorised access in decentralised edge computing deployments.

↣ *Data integrity and trustworthiness*: As data is processed and transmitted across distributed edge nodes, maintaining data integrity becomes paramount. Data processed at the edge is susceptible to tampering and manipulation by malicious actors or compromised edge nodes. Any unauthorised alterations to data can lead to inaccurate results, compromised decision-making processes and potentially severe consequences, especially in critical applications such as healthcare, finance or autonomous systems. Establishing mechanisms for data validation is essential for ensuring the integrity and trustworthiness of data processed at the edge. This involves verifying the authenticity, completeness and correctness of data through cryptographic techniques, digital signatures, checksums or hash functions. By validating data integrity at each stage of processing, organisations can detect and mitigate unauthorised modifications or discrepancies. Securing data transmission between edge nodes is critical for maintaining data integrity and preventing unauthorised interception or tampering. Encryption protocols, such as TLS (transport layer security) or IPsec (internet protocol security), can help protect data against eavesdropping, interception, and tampering during transmission over insecure networks. Implementing end-to-end encryption ensures that data remains confidential and unaltered throughout its journey across distributed edge nodes. Deploying trusted computing platforms and hardware-based security mechanisms can enhance the trustworthiness of edge nodes and protect against unauthorised access or tampering. Trusted execution environments (TEEs), such as Intel SGX (Software Guard Extensions) or ARM TrustZone, provide secure enclaves for executing sensitive computations and storing cryptographic keys, ensuring that data remains secure even if the underlying platform is compromised. Leveraging immutable data storage solutions, such as blockchain or distributed ledger technology (DLT), can help maintain the integrity and auditability of data processed at the edge. By recording data transactions in a tamper-evident and transparent manner, blockchain-based systems enable organisations to verify the authenticity and integrity of data, mitigate the risk of data manipulation and establish trust among distributed edge nodes. Implementing robust data lifecycle management practices is essential for ensuring data integrity throughout its lifecycle, from generation and processing at the edge to storage and archival. This includes implementing data validation checks, version control mechanisms, access controls and audit trails to track data changes, enforce data integrity policies and detect anomalies or unauthorised modifications. Finally, implementing continuous monitoring and auditing mechanisms helps organisations detect and respond to potential threats or anomalies that may compromise data integrity. By monitoring data access activities, auditing data transactions and performing regular integrity checks, organisations can identify and mitigate security risks, enforce compliance with data integrity policies and maintain the trustworthiness of data processed at the edge. Thus, ensuring data integrity and trustworthiness in decentralised edge computing environments requires a combination of technical solutions, secure communication protocols, trusted computing platforms, immutable data storage solutions, robust data lifecycle management practices and continuous monitoring and auditing mechanisms. By implementing these strategies, organisations can mitigate the risk of data tampering, protect sensitive information and maintain the integrity of systems and applications in decentralised edge computing deployments.

↣ *Compliance and regulatory challenges*: Decentralised edge computing may introduce compliance and regulatory challenges, particularly concerning data sovereignty and jurisdictional issues as it involves processing and storing data across distributed edge nodes, which may span multiple jurisdictions with varying data protection laws and regulations. Determining the applicable legal framework for data residency, storage and transfer becomes challenging when data traverses geographical boundaries. Organisations must navigate complex jurisdictional issues and ensure compliance with applicable laws and regulations in each jurisdiction where data is processed or stored. Data processed at the edge may be subject to specific regulatory requirements governing data protection, privacy, security and confidentiality. Regulations such as the GDPR in the European Union (EU) or the HIPAA in the United States impose stringent requirements on organisations for the collection, processing, storage and transfer of personal and sensitive data. Ensuring compliance with these regulations in decentralised edge computing environments requires careful consideration of data governance, risk management and security practices. Some jurisdictions have data residency and localisation laws that mandate data to be stored within the geographical boundaries of the jurisdiction or restrict the transfer of data across borders. Decentralised edge computing, which distributes data processing and storage across multiple locations, may pose challenges in complying with these requirements. Organisations must assess the impact of data residency and localisation laws on their edge computing deployments and implement measures to ensure compliance while maintaining operational efficiency. Regulatory compliance often requires organisations to implement specific security and privacy safeguards to protect personal and sensitive data from unauthorised access, disclosure or misuse. In decentralised edge computing environments, where data is processed and stored closer to the point of origin, ensuring the confidentiality, integrity and availability of data becomes paramount. Organisations must implement robust security measures, such as encryption, access controls, data anonymisation and audit trails, to safeguard data and demonstrate compliance with regulatory requirements. Transferring data between edge nodes and centralised servers or across different jurisdictions may raise concerns regarding data privacy, security and compliance. Organisations must select appropriate data transfer mechanisms, such as secure communication protocols, data encryption and data masking techniques, to ensure that data is transmitted securely and in compliance with regulatory requirements. Failure to comply with applicable regulations, such as GDPR or HIPAA, can result in severe consequences, including fines, legal penalties, regulatory sanctions and damage to the organisation's reputation. Non-compliance with data protection laws may also lead to loss of customer trust, erosion of brand reputation and potential legal liabilities. Therefore, organisations must prioritise compliance efforts and adopt a proactive approach to managing regulatory risks in decentralised edge computing deployments. Thus, navigating compliance and regulatory challenges in decentralised edge computing requires organisations to address issues related to data sovereignty, jurisdictional differences, regulatory requirements, data residency laws, security and privacy safeguards, data transfer mechanisms and the risk of non-compliance. By implementing robust data governance practices, security controls, and compliance frameworks, organisations can mitigate regulatory risks and ensure that their edge computing deployments comply with applicable laws and regulations while delivering value to stakeholders.

Addressing these security risks inherent in decentralised edge computing demands a comprehensive strategy that incorporates robust encryption protocols, secure authentication mechanisms, continuous monitoring and auditing, regular security updates and patches and clear policies for data handling and access control. This holistic approach is crucial for safeguarding sensitive data, protecting against cyber threats and ensuring the integrity and trustworthiness of decentralised edge computing environments. Moreover, collaborative efforts among stakeholders, including network operators, device manufacturers, software developers and regulatory bodies, are paramount to effectively mitigate security risks and unlock the full potential of decentralised edge computing in the era of 6G networks. By working together to address security challenges and implement best practices, stakeholders can enhance the resilience, reliability and security of decentralised edge computing deployments, enabling organisations to leverage the transformative capabilities of 6G networks while maintaining trust and compliance with regulatory requirements.

2.4 Threats to IoT and Connected Devices

In the interconnected world of the Internet of Things (IoT), where devices seamlessly communicate and collaborate to enhance efficiency, productivity and convenience, the proliferation of connected devices brings forth unprecedented opportunities. From smart homes and wearable gadgets to industrial sensors and autonomous vehicles, IoT technologies promise to revolutionise various aspects of our lives and industries. However, amidst this paradigm shift towards interconnectedness, a stark reality emerges: the inherent vulnerabilities of IoT and connected devices expose them to a myriad of threats, ranging from malicious intrusions to data breaches. In the ever-evolving landscape of IoT security, there are emerging threats that pose significant challenges to the integrity and resilience of connected devices.

Ransomware attacks targeting IoT devices have been on the rise, with cybercriminals exploiting vulnerabilities in connected gadgets to encrypt data or disrupt operations, demanding ransom payments for decryption keys. One prominent example is the 'Mirai botnet' [22] attack in 2016, which targeted IoT devices such as routers, cameras and DVRs, exploiting default credentials to infect and control millions of devices. The attackers then used this massive botnet to launch distributed denial-of-service (DDoS) attacks, disrupting internet services for major websites and online services worldwide. Another notable incident is the 'WannaCry' [23] ransomware attack in 2017, which exploited a vulnerability in Windows systems to spread rapidly across networks, encrypting files and demanding ransom payments for decryption. One more recent example of an IoT ransomware attack is the 'Sodinokibi' (also known as 'REvil') [24] ransomware, which targeted a managed service provider (MSP) in 2019. The attack compromised the MSP's infrastructure, allowing the ransomware to spread to its clients' systems, including IoT devices such as security cameras and networked printers. The attackers demanded ransom payments in cryptocurrency in exchange for decrypting the encrypted files and restoring access to the compromised systems. This incident highlighted the interconnected nature of IoT ecosystems and the potential ripple effects of ransomware attacks across multiple organisations and devices. While these incidents may not have exclusively targeted IoT devices, they underscore the potential impact of ransomware attacks on connected systems and the need for robust security measures to protect against such threats.

With the proliferation of artificial intelligence (AI) and machine learning (ML) technologies, cybercriminals are increasingly leveraging AI-powered attacks to target IoT and connected devices [25]. AI algorithms are used to automate and enhance cyberattack techniques, such as generating sophisticated malware variants, evading detection or orchestrating large-scale botnet attacks. One example of an AI-driven cyberattack on IoT ecosystems that has occurred is the use of deep fake audio to manipulate voice-controlled IoT devices. In this instance, researchers demonstrated how AI-generated audio clips could deceive voice assistants like Amazon Alexa or Google Assistant into executing unauthorised commands. By crafting synthetic voice commands that mimic the owner's voice, attackers could instruct IoT devices to perform actions such as unlocking smart locks, making unauthorised purchases or accessing sensitive information. This demonstration highlighted the potential security vulnerabilities inherent in voice-controlled IoT devices and raised concerns about the susceptibility of AI-based systems to manipulation. While this example may not represent a large-scale cyberattack, it underscores the need for robust security measures to protect against AI-driven threats to IoT ecosystems. As AI technologies continue to evolve, the risk of sophisticated AI-driven cyberattacks targeting IoT devices is likely to increase, necessitating proactive measures to mitigate such risks and safeguard IoT deployments.

The rollout of 5G/6G networks introduces new opportunities for innovation and connectivity but also brings new security challenges. This includes potential vulnerabilities in 5G/6G infrastructure, protocols and IoT devices connected to 5G/6G networks. Security risks are associated with network slicing, virtualised network functions, edge computing and the increased attack surface presented by the proliferation of IoT devices in a 5G/6G environment.

A systematic exploration of the threats facing IoT and connected devices given below serves as a foundation for comprehending the underlying risks and implications.

2.4.1 Device proliferation and diversity

Analysing the security implications of the vast array of IoT devices in 6G networks requires a comprehensive understanding of the diverse landscape of connected devices and the associated risks they pose. With the proliferation of IoT devices in 6G networks, ranging from consumer electronics and industrial sensors to medical devices and autonomous vehicles, the attack surface expands exponentially, presenting numerous security challenges. One significant security implication is the heterogeneity and diversity of IoT devices, each with its unique hardware, software and communication protocols. This diversity complicates security management, as different devices may have varying levels of security features, vulnerabilities and update mechanisms. Securing diverse devices in IoT ecosystems within 6G networks presents a multitude of challenges stemming from the heterogeneous nature of these devices. One significant challenge is the wide spectrum of hardware, software and communication protocols employed by IoT devices. Each device type may have its unique security features, vulnerabilities and update mechanisms, making it challenging to implement standardised security measures across the entire IoT ecosystem. Additionally, the sheer volume and diversity of IoT devices can overwhelm traditional security management systems, complicating the task of monitoring, managing, and securing these devices effectively. Moreover, the resource constraints inherent in many IoT devices pose additional challenges to implementing robust security measures. Resource-constrained devices, such as sensors and actuators, may lack the computational power, memory or energy resources to support advanced security functionalities, such as encryption, secure authentication or secure software updates. As a result, these devices are often more susceptible to exploitation by adversaries, increasing the overall security risk within the IoT ecosystem. Furthermore, legacy IoT devices with outdated firmware or unsupported software may remain in operation, posing security risks due to unpatched vulnerabilities and lack of security updates. Another security concern is the scale and volume of IoT deployments in 6G networks, which can overwhelm traditional security mechanisms and monitoring tools. The sheer number of interconnected devices increases the likelihood of cyberattacks, such as botnets, distributed denial-of-service (DDoS) attacks, and reconnaissance activities targeting vulnerable devices. Furthermore, the dynamic nature of IoT environments, with devices frequently joining or leaving the network, introduces challenges for maintaining security posture and enforcing security policies consistently. The transient nature of device connections and interactions complicates identity management, access control and threat detection efforts, making it difficult to detect and respond to security incidents in real time. Additionally, the inherent resource constraints of IoT devices, including limited processing power, memory and battery life, pose challenges for implementing robust security measures. Resource-constrained devices may lack the computational capabilities to support advanced encryption algorithms, secure authentication mechanisms or secure software updates, making them susceptible to exploitation by adversaries. Furthermore, the interconnectivity and interdependence of IoT devices in 6G networks introduce complex attack vectors and potential cascading effects. A compromise of one IoT device could lead to the compromise of other interconnected devices or critical infrastructure components, amplifying the impact of security incidents. To address these security implications, organisations deploying IoT devices in 6G networks must adopt a multi-layered approach to security, encompassing device-level security measures, network security controls and security monitoring capabilities. This includes implementing strong authentication mechanisms, encryption protocols and access controls to protect IoT devices from unauthorised access and data breaches. Standardised security protocols play a crucial role in ensuring the security and interoperability of diverse IoT devices within 6G networks. Standardised security protocols provide a common framework for implementing security measures across different device types, enabling interoperability, compatibility and seamless integration within the IoT ecosystem. By adhering to standardised security protocols, organisations can establish a baseline of security requirements and best practices that all IoT devices must meet, regardless of their specific hardware or software characteristics. Standardised security protocols also facilitate collaboration and information sharing among industry stakeholders, enabling the development of common security standards, guidelines and certification programs. This collaborative approach fosters a more cohesive and coordinated response to emerging security threats, promoting the adoption of security-by-design principles and proactive risk management practices throughout the lifecycle of IoT devices. Furthermore, standardised security protocols enhance transparency and accountability in the IoT ecosystem by enabling device manufacturers to demonstrate compliance with industry-recognised security standards and certifications. This helps build trust and confidence among consumers, businesses and regulatory authorities, fostering adoption and deployment of IoT devices with confidence in their security and reliability. The challenges associated with securing diverse devices in IoT ecosystems within 6G networks necessitate the adoption of standardised security protocols. By providing a common framework for implementing security measures and fostering collaboration among industry stakeholders, standardised security protocols play a vital role in mitigating security risks, enhancing interoperability and ensuring the security and resilience of connected ecosystems in the next generation of wireless technology. Additionally, organisations should regularly update and patch IoT devices to address known vulnerabilities and mitigate security risks. Enhanced network segmentation and traffic monitoring can help isolate compromised devices and prevent lateral movement of attackers within the network. Moreover, organisations should invest in security awareness training for users and stakeholders involved in IoT deployments to promote cybersecurity best practices and mitigate the risk of human error or negligence. Collaborative efforts between industry stakeholders, standards bodies and regulatory authorities are essential to develop and enforce security standards and best practices for IoT devices in 6G networks, ensuring the security and resilience of connected ecosystems in the next generation of wireless technology.

2.4.2 Data integrity and privacy concerns

Exploring the potential risks related to data integrity and privacy in IoT ecosystems within 6G networks reveals a complex landscape of challenges that must be addressed to ensure the security and trustworthiness of connected systems. One significant risk is the potential for unauthorised access or tampering with sensitive data collected and transmitted by IoT devices. As IoT devices often collect vast amounts of personal, sensitive or proprietary data, such as health information, location data or industrial telemetry, any compromise of data integrity or privacy can have severe consequences for individuals, businesses and society as a whole. Additionally, the distributed nature of IoT ecosystems and the interconnectedness of devices increase the risk of data breaches, data leaks or unauthorised data access. Vulnerabilities in IoT devices, communication channels or cloud-based services can be exploited by malicious actors to intercept, manipulate or exfiltrate sensitive data, leading to privacy violations, identity theft or financial fraud. Moreover, the lack of standardised security protocols and best practices for securing IoT devices exacerbates the risk of data integrity and privacy breaches. Many IoT devices lack built-in security features, such as encryption, access control or secure authentication mechanisms, making them vulnerable to exploitation by adversaries. Furthermore, the fragmented regulatory landscape governing data privacy and security in different jurisdictions adds complexity to compliance efforts and may leave gaps in protection for IoT data. To mitigate the risks related to data integrity and privacy in IoT ecosystems, organisations must adopt a multi-layered approach to security that encompasses device-level security measures, network security controls, and data protection mechanisms. This includes implementing strong encryption algorithms, secure authentication mechanisms, and access controls to protect data both at rest and in transit. Additionally, organisations should implement robust identity and access management (IAM) policies to ensure that only authorised users and devices can access sensitive data. Furthermore, organisations should prioritise data minimisation and anonymisation strategies to limit the collection and retention of unnecessary or sensitive data by IoT devices. By adopting privacy-enhancing technologies and anonymisation techniques, organisations can reduce the risk of data exposure and mitigate privacy concerns associated with IoT deployments. Moreover, organisations should conduct regular security assessments, vulnerability scans, and penetration testing of IoT devices and infrastructure to identify and remediate security weaknesses proactively. By continuously monitoring for security incidents and anomalies, organisations can detect and respond to data integrity and privacy breaches promptly, minimising the impact on individuals and organisations. Finally, collaboration among industry stakeholders, standards bodies, and regulatory authorities is essential to develop and enforce comprehensive data privacy and security regulations that address the unique challenges posed by IoT ecosystems. By establishing clear guidelines, standards, and accountability mechanisms, organisations can build trust and confidence in IoT deployments and ensure the protection of data integrity and privacy in an increasingly interconnected and digitised world. End-to-end encryption and privacy-preserving techniques are paramount to safeguard sensitive information transmitted through connected devices within 6G networks. End-to-end encryption ensures that data is encrypted at the source device and remains encrypted until it reaches the intended recipient, protecting it from unauthorised access or interception by malicious actors. By encrypting data throughout its entire journey across IoT ecosystems, end-to-end encryption mitigates the risk of data breaches, data leaks, or unauthorised data access, thereby preserving the confidentiality and integrity of sensitive information. Furthermore, privacy-preserving techniques, such as differential privacy, homomorphic encryption, and secure multi-party computation, offer additional layers of protection for sensitive data transmitted through connected devices. These techniques allow data to be analysed, processed, or shared without compromising individual privacy or revealing sensitive information. For example, differential privacy adds noise to aggregated data to prevent the identification of individual data points, while homomorphic encryption allows computations to be performed on encrypted data without decrypting it, preserving data confidentiality. Implementing end-to-end encryption and privacy-preserving techniques requires collaboration among device manufacturers, network operators, and service providers to integrate robust encryption algorithms, cryptographic protocols, and privacy-enhancing technologies into

IoT devices and infrastructure. By adopting industry-standard encryption protocols, such as Transport Layer Security (TLS) or Datagram Transport Layer Security (DTLS), organisations can ensure secure communication between IoT devices and cloud-based services, preventing unauthorised interception or tampering of data. Moreover, organisations should prioritise the use of secure key management practices to generate, distribute, and manage encryption keys used for end-to-end encryption. Strong encryption keys, combined with proper key management policies and procedures, are essential to maintaining the confidentiality and integrity of encrypted data and preventing unauthorised access to sensitive information. Additionally, organisations should implement privacy-by-design principles when designing and deploying IoT solutions, embedding privacy-enhancing features and controls into the design and architecture of connected devices and applications. By integrating privacy controls, such as data anonymisation, pseudonymisation, and user consent mechanisms, organisations can empower individuals to control their personal data and mitigate privacy risks associated with IoT deployments. Finally, organisations should educate users, stakeholders, and employees about the importance of data privacy and security best practices in IoT environments. By raising awareness about the risks of data breaches, unauthorised data access, and privacy violations, organisations can promote a culture of security awareness and empower individuals to take proactive steps to protect sensitive information transmitted through connected devices. Thus, end-to-end encryption and privacy-preserving techniques are essential components of a comprehensive security strategy to safeguard sensitive information transmitted through connected devices within 6G networks. By integrating robust encryption algorithms, cryptographic protocols, and privacy-enhancing technologies into IoT devices and infrastructure, organisations can ensure the confidentiality, integrity and privacy of data in an increasingly interconnected and digitised world.

2.4.3 Supply chain vulnerabilities

A supply chain attack, also known as a 'value chain' breach, happens when cyberattackers breach your system via an external partner with access to your data and systems. It is typical for a company to work with numerous third-party suppliers, as this interconnectedness fuels our economy. However, while the integration of supply chains streamlines business operations, it also introduces significant risks (Figure 2.8). The strength of a chain is determined by its weakest link. Regrettably, for many organisations, this vulnerability may

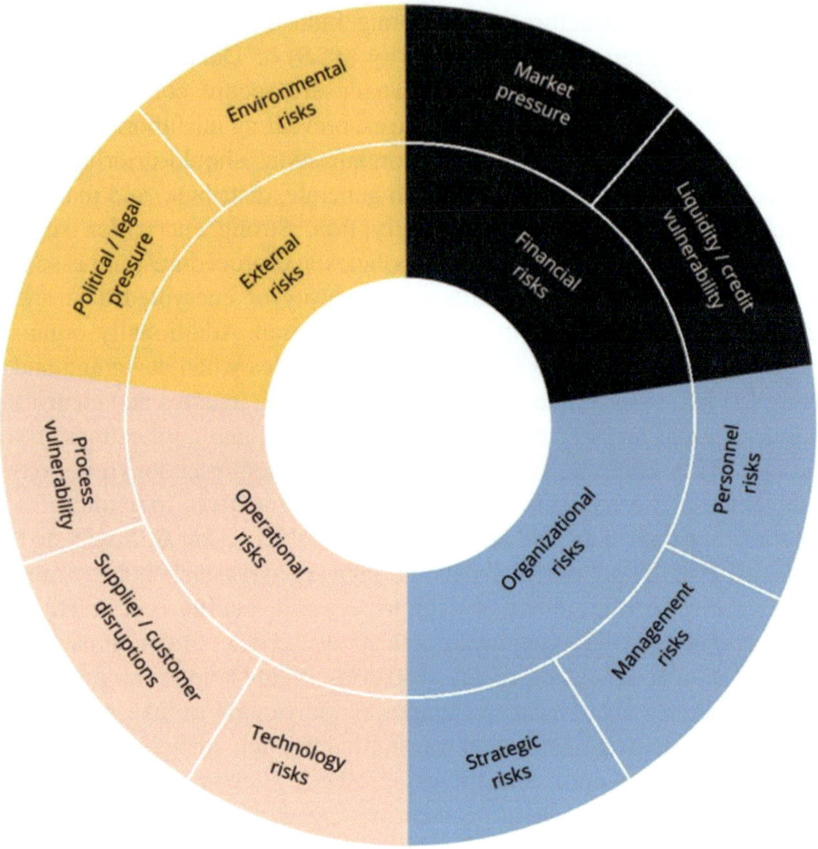

Figure 2.8 Supply chain risks.

lie within a third-party supplier over which they exert limited control. In an era defined by heightened connectivity, the digital interdependence between companies and their partners is established from the onset of contractual agreements. Consequently, irrespective of the robustness of internal security measures, the level of safety is contingent upon the resilience of the most vulnerable vendor. This is a prevailing reality that businesses must confront in the present era and beyond.

The SolarWinds cyberattack, discovered in December 2020, is one of the most significant cybersecurity incidents in recent history. It involved the infiltration of SolarWinds' Orion software, a widely used network management tool, by a sophisticated threat actor, suspected to be a Russian state-sponsored group known as APT29, or Cozy Bear. The attackers inserted malicious code, dubbed Sunburst or Solorigate, into legitimate software updates distributed to SolarWinds' customers. As a result, approximately 18,000 organisations worldwide unknowingly installed the compromised updates, granting the attackers access to their networks. Once inside the networks, the attackers conducted reconnaissance, exfiltrated sensitive information, and potentially planted additional malware to maintain persistence. The attack went undetected for months, allowing the threat actors to carry out extensive espionage and espionage-related activities. The SolarWinds breach marked a concerning shift in supply chain attacks, setting a new standard for infiltration tactics. What made it particularly alarming was its ability to exploit a hybrid infrastructure model, seamlessly blending on-premise and Cloud-based networks. By initially compromising internal systems, the attackers gained access to Cloud servers without triggering suspicion. This strategic approach capitalised on the growing trend towards hybrid cloud adoption, which has accelerated due to the pandemic-driven shift towards flexible work arrangements. As of June 2020, approximately 58% of businesses globally were embracing hybrid cloud strategies, a number expected to rise significantly in the wake of evolving workplace dynamics. Consequently, this breach exposed the vulnerability of businesses across various sectors to similar sophisticated attacks. The SolarWinds attack highlighted the vulnerability of software supply chains and the potential for widespread damage resulting from a single breach. It also underscored the sophistication and persistence of modern cyber threats, as well as the challenges organisations face in defending against such attacks. The incident prompted heightened scrutiny of cybersecurity practices, supply chain security and threat detection capabilities across both the public and private sectors. It also sparked calls for improved information sharing, collaboration and regulatory measures to enhance cybersecurity resilience and mitigate the risk of future attacks.

Supply chain vulnerabilities refer to weaknesses or risks within the interconnected network of suppliers, manufacturers and distributors involved in the production and distribution of goods or services. These vulnerabilities can include supply chain disruptions, counterfeit components, malicious actors infiltrating the manufacturing process and inadequate security practices among suppliers or subcontractors. Such vulnerabilities can compromise the integrity, security and reliability of products or services, posing risks to organisations and end-users. Examining the vulnerabilities introduced by the global supply chain in manufacturing IoT devices for 6G networks reveals a complex landscape of security risks that organisations must address to ensure the integrity and resilience of connected systems. One significant vulnerability stems from the reliance on a global network of suppliers, manufacturers and subcontractors involved in the production of IoT devices. This interconnected supply chain increases the risk of malicious actors infiltrating the manufacturing process to introduce counterfeit components, malicious firmware or hardware backdoors into IoT devices, compromising their security and functionality. Moreover, the complexity and opacity of the supply chain make it challenging for organisations to trace the origin and authenticity of components used in IoT devices. Substandard or counterfeit components sourced from untrusted suppliers may contain vulnerabilities or malicious code that can be exploited by adversaries to compromise the security of IoT devices. Additionally, supply chain disruptions, such as natural disasters, geopolitical tensions or trade disputes, can disrupt the availability of critical components or delay the delivery of IoT devices, exposing organisations to operational risks and potential security vulnerabilities. Furthermore, the lack of transparency and oversight in the supply chain poses challenges for organisations to verify the security practices and compliance of suppliers and manufacturers with industry standards and regulations. Subcontractors or third-party vendors involved in the manufacturing process may have inadequate security measures or fail to adhere to established security guidelines, increasing the risk of supply chain attacks or data breaches. To mitigate the vulnerabilities introduced by the global supply chain in manufacturing IoT devices for 6G networks, organisations must implement robust supply chain risk management practices and security controls throughout the entire lifecycle of IoT devices. Several key strategies can be adopted to address these challenges:

- ↣ *Secure supply chain management*: Organisations should implement supply chain risk management practices to assess, monitor and mitigate risks across the supply chain. This includes conducting thorough supplier assessments and due diligence to evaluate the security posture and reliability of suppliers and manufacturers. By prioritising trusted suppliers with robust security measures and compliance with industry standards, organisations can reduce the risk of supply chain vulnerabilities.
- ↣ *Supplier audits and certifications*: Organisations should conduct regular audits and assessments of suppliers to verify compliance with security standards and regulations. Suppliers should be required to demonstrate adherence to recognised security standards, such as ISO 27001, NIST Cybersecurity Framework, or industry-specific security certifications.

Additionally, organisations can establish supplier certification programs or trusted supplier networks to ensure the integrity and reliability of components sourced from suppliers.

- *Supply chain visibility and transparency*: Implementing supply chain visibility and transparency mechanisms is crucial for tracking and monitoring the movement of components and materials throughout the supply chain. By establishing traceability and accountability mechanisms, organisations can identify and mitigate potential security risks or vulnerabilities introduced at various stages of the manufacturing process. This includes leveraging technologies such as blockchain, RFID tags or supply chain management software to enhance visibility and transparency across the supply chain.
- *Supplier contractual obligations*: Organisations should include security requirements and obligations in supplier contracts and agreements to ensure that suppliers adhere to established security standards and practices. This may include requirements for secure handling of materials, adherence to data protection regulations and notification of security incidents or breaches. Contracts should also specify consequences for non-compliance with security requirements, such as termination of contracts or financial penalties.
- *Integrity verification mechanisms*: Implementing integrity verification mechanisms is essential for ensuring the authenticity and integrity of components and materials used in manufacturing processes. This includes implementing cryptographic protections, such as digital signatures or hash functions, to verify the integrity of software, firmware or configuration files. Additionally, organisations can implement hardware-based security features, such as secure boot mechanisms or tamper-resistant seals, to detect and prevent tampering or unauthorised modifications to components during the manufacturing process.
- *Continuous monitoring and response*: Organisations should implement continuous monitoring and response mechanisms to detect and respond to security incidents or anomalies in real time. This includes deploying security monitoring tools, intrusion detection systems and anomaly detection algorithms to monitor for suspicious activities or deviations from expected behaviour. In the event of a security incident or breach, organisations should have incident response plans and procedures in place to contain the incident, mitigate the impact and restore normal operations.

Open-source software (OSS) presents another avenue for potential vulnerabilities. While open-source development harnesses collective developer expertise to enhance software quality, it frequently compromises security. Recent findings indicate that open-source code features in 90% of today's leading applications, with at least 11% harbouring identified vulnerabilities. Such vulnerabilities were notably implicated in the Equifax breach of 2017, resulting in substantial financial losses exceeding $2 billion for the company.

OSS offers numerous benefits, such as cost-effectiveness, flexibility and community-driven innovation. However, it also presents certain risks and challenges that organisations must carefully consider. One of the primary dangers of open-source software lies in its susceptibility to security vulnerabilities. Unlike proprietary software, which is developed and maintained by a single vendor with dedicated resources, open-source projects rely on community contributions. While this collaborative approach fosters rapid development and innovation, it also means that the code is accessible to a wide range of individuals, including potential attackers. As a result, vulnerabilities in open-source software can be more easily discovered and exploited, leading to security breaches, data leaks and other cyber threats. Moreover, the decentralised nature of open-source development can sometimes result in lax security practices. Developers may prioritise functionality and speed of development over rigorous security testing, leading to the inadvertent inclusion of vulnerabilities in the codebase. Additionally, since open-source projects often rely on volunteer contributions, there may be limited resources available for conducting comprehensive security audits and addressing identified vulnerabilities promptly. Another danger of open-source software is the risk of dependency issues. Many modern software applications are built using a multitude of open-source components and libraries, known as dependencies. While leveraging existing open-source code can expedite development and reduce costs, it also means that organisations become reliant on the security and maintenance practices of third-party developers. If a critical vulnerability is discovered in a widely used open-source component, it can have cascading effects, impacting numerous applications and systems across different organisations. Furthermore, the legal and compliance risks associated with open-source software cannot be overlooked. Many open-source licences come with specific requirements and obligations that organisations must adhere to, such as providing attribution to the original authors or making the source code of derivative works publicly available. Failure to comply with these licence terms can result in legal disputes, fines and reputational damage.

To mitigate the dangers of open-source software (OSS), organisations must adopt robust security measures and best practices. This includes regularly monitoring for security updates and patches released by open-source projects, conducting thorough security assessments of all dependencies and implementing strict access controls and authentication mechanisms to prevent unauthorised access to sensitive data. Additionally, organisations should invest in employee training and awareness programs to educate developers and other stakeholders about the risks associated with open-source software and the importance of adhering to security best practices. By taking a proactive approach to managing open-source risks, organisations can harness the benefits of OSS while minimising potential vulnerabilities and threats.

In summary, examining the vulnerabilities introduced by the global supply chain in manufacturing IoT devices for 6G networks highlights the importance of implementing robust supply chain risk management practices and security controls. By prioritising supply chain security, transparency and resilience, organisations can mitigate the risks posed by supply chain vulnerabilities and ensure the integrity and security of IoT deployments in an interconnected and digitised world.

2.4.4 Interconnected infrastructure risks

Investigating the security challenges arising from the interconnection of critical infrastructure with IoT devices reveals a complex landscape of risks that pose significant threats to the integrity, availability and security of essential services and systems. One of the primary challenges is the increased attack surface introduced by the integration of IoT devices into critical infrastructure networks. These devices, ranging from sensors and actuators to industrial control systems and smart metres, provide new entry points for malicious actors to infiltrate and compromise interconnected infrastructure systems. Furthermore, the heterogeneous nature of IoT devices and the diverse range of communication protocols used in critical infrastructure networks make them susceptible to various cyber threats, including malware infections, denial-of-service attacks and unauthorised access. Vulnerabilities in IoT devices, such as insecure default configurations, lack of software updates or inadequate authentication mechanisms, can be exploited by adversaries to gain unauthorised access to critical systems or disrupt essential services. Moreover, the interconnection of critical infrastructure systems with IoT devices introduces complex dependencies and interdependencies between different systems and sectors. A compromise of one IoT device or system can have cascading effects across interconnected infrastructure networks. The potential cascading effects of security breaches in interconnected systems underscore the critical importance of resilience in safeguarding essential services and infrastructure. A security breach in one component or system within interconnected infrastructure networks can trigger a chain reaction of disruptions and failures, leading to widespread service outages, financial losses and even threats to public safety. For instance, a cyberattack targeting IoT devices in a smart grid system could disrupt power distribution, causing cascading outages that impact critical services reliant on electricity, such as healthcare facilities, transportation networks and communication systems. Furthermore, interconnected systems often exhibit complex dependencies and interdependencies, amplifying the ripple effects of security breaches across multiple sectors and domains. Resilience plays a pivotal role in mitigating the impact of security breaches and ensuring the continuity of operations in the face of adversity. Resilient systems are characterised by their ability to withstand, adapt to and recover from disruptions or disturbances while maintaining essential functions and services. This entails implementing redundancy, failover mechanisms and contingency plans to minimise the impact of security incidents and enable rapid recovery. For example, organisations can deploy backup power systems, redundant communication channels and distributed data storage to mitigate the effects of power outages, communication failures or data breaches. Moreover, resilience encompasses proactive measures to identify and mitigate potential risks before they escalate into a full-blown crisis. This includes conducting risk assessments, vulnerability scans and scenario-based exercises to anticipate and prepare for potential security threats and disruptions. By proactively identifying vulnerabilities, strengthening security controls and implementing robust incident response plans, organisations can enhance their resilience and minimise the likelihood and severity of security breaches. Additionally, fostering a culture of resilience within organisations involves promoting collaboration, communication and knowledge sharing among stakeholders. Cross-functional teams, comprising representatives from IT, security, operations and management, can collaborate to develop and implement resilience strategies tailored to the organisation's unique needs and challenges. Furthermore, engaging with external partners, industry peers and regulatory authorities can facilitate information exchange, best practice sharing and collective response efforts to address common security threats and challenges. Furthermore, the reliance on third-party vendors, service providers and cloud-based platforms for IoT deployments in critical infrastructure introduces supply chain risks and dependency issues. Organisations may have limited visibility and control over the security practices and compliance of third-party vendors, making it challenging to ensure the integrity and security of IoT devices and services. Moreover, the outsourcing of critical functions or data to cloud-based platforms introduces additional security considerations, such as data privacy, data sovereignty and compliance with regulatory requirements. To mitigate the security challenges arising from the interconnection of critical infrastructure with IoT devices, organisations must adopt a multi-layered approach to security that encompasses technical, operational and organisational measures. This includes implementing robust security controls, such as network segmentation, access controls, encryption and intrusion detection systems, to protect critical infrastructure networks from unauthorised access and cyber threats. Furthermore, organisations should conduct thorough risk assessments and vulnerability assessments to identify and prioritise security risks and weaknesses in interconnected infrastructure systems. By proactively addressing known vulnerabilities and implementing security patches and updates, organisations can reduce the likelihood of successful cyberattacks and mitigate the impact of security incidents. Moreover, organisations should implement incident response plans and procedures to detect, respond to and recover from security incidents or breaches in critical infrastructure networks. This includes establishing communication protocols, escalation procedures and coordination mechanisms with relevant stakeholders, such as government agencies, law enforcement and regulatory authorities, to facilitate a timely and effective response to cyber threats. Additionally, organisations should prioritise security awareness and training programs for employees, contractors and stakeholders involved in the operation and management of critical infrastructure systems. By raising awareness about cybersecurity best practices, policies and procedures, organisations can empower individuals to identify and report security threats, minimise human error and enhance the overall security posture of interconnected infrastructure networks. Thus, investigating the security challenges arising from the interconnection of critical infrastructure with IoT devices underscores the importance of adopting a proactive and holistic approach to security. By implementing robust security controls, conducting risk assessments and fostering collaboration among stakeholders, organisations can strengthen the resilience of interconnected infrastructure networks and mitigate the risks posed by cyber threats in an increasingly interconnected and digitised world.

2.4.5 Regulatory compliance and standards

Regulations and industry standards play a crucial role in ensuring the security of IoT devices by establishing guidelines, requirements and best practices that manufacturers, vendors and users must adhere to. These regulatory frameworks and standards serve as a cornerstone for promoting cybersecurity, protecting consumer privacy and mitigating risks associated with IoT deployments. One of the primary functions of regulations is to set minimum security requirements for IoT devices, including specifications for authentication, encryption, access control and vulnerability management. Regulatory compliance ensures that manufacturers incorporate essential security features into their products, reducing the risk of vulnerabilities and exploitation by malicious actors. For example, regulations such as the California IoT Security Law and the European Union's Cybersecurity Act mandate security-by-design principles and require manufacturers to implement reasonable security measures to protect IoT devices from unauthorised access, alteration or disclosure. Furthermore, regulations often address data privacy concerns associated with IoT devices by imposing requirements for data protection, transparency and user consent. Regulations such as the General Data Protection Regulation (GDPR) in the European Union and the California Consumer Privacy Act (CCPA) in the United States govern the collection, processing and storage of personal data by IoT devices, ensuring that user privacy rights are respected and upheld. Compliance with these regulations entails implementing measures such as data encryption, anonymisation and user consent mechanisms to protect sensitive information and mitigate privacy risks. In addition to regulations, industry standards play a vital role in driving cybersecurity best practices and promoting interoperability among IoT devices and systems. Standards bodies such as the International Organization for Standardization (ISO), the Institute of Electrical and Electronics Engineers (IEEE) and the Internet Engineering Task Force (IETF) develop technical standards and guidelines for IoT security, covering aspects such as network protocols, device authentication and secure communication. Adherence to industry standards facilitates the adoption of uniform security measures across different IoT devices and ecosystems, enhancing compatibility, reliability and trustworthiness. For example, standards such as ISO/IEC 27001 for information security management systems and NIST Special Publication 800-53 for cybersecurity controls provide comprehensive frameworks for organisations to assess, implement and manage security controls effectively. Moreover, certifications and compliance programs based on regulatory requirements and industry standards enable organisations to demonstrate their commitment to cybersecurity and compliance with legal obligations. Certifications such as the Common Criteria for Information Technology Security Evaluation and the UL 2900 series for cybersecurity assurance offer independent validation of the security posture and resilience of IoT devices and systems, instilling confidence among consumers, regulators and business partners. Thus, regulations and industry standards play a pivotal role in ensuring the security of IoT devices by establishing minimum security requirements, addressing data privacy concerns and promoting cybersecurity best practices. Compliance with regulations and adherence to industry standards help mitigate security risks, protect user privacy and foster trust and confidence in IoT deployments, ultimately contributing to a more secure and resilient IoT ecosystem.

Exploring challenges in enforcing compliance with IoT security regulations and the need for international cooperation to establish effective security standards reveals a complex landscape shaped by technological advancements, diverse regulatory frameworks and global supply chains. One of the primary challenges in enforcing compliance with IoT security regulations is the lack of uniformity and consistency among regulatory frameworks across different jurisdictions. The fragmented regulatory landscape creates compliance burdens for organisations operating in multiple regions, as they must navigate and adhere to a patchwork of conflicting or overlapping requirements. The rapid pace of technological innovation and the evolving nature of cyber threats pose challenges for regulators to keep pace with emerging security risks and vulnerabilities associated with IoT devices. Traditional regulatory approaches may struggle to adapt to the dynamic and heterogeneous nature of IoT ecosystems, leading to delays in updating regulations or gaps in coverage for emerging technologies and use cases. Enforcing compliance with IoT security regulations is complicated by the global nature of supply chains and the diverse ecosystem of stakeholders involved in the design, manufacturing, distribution and deployment of IoT devices. Supply chain complexity introduces challenges for regulators to trace and verify the origin, authenticity and compliance of components and materials used in IoT devices, particularly as components may be sourced from multiple vendors across different regions. Additionally, enforcement mechanisms and penalties for non-compliance with IoT security regulations vary widely among jurisdictions, leading to inconsistencies in enforcement actions and deterrence measures. The lack of harmonised enforcement mechanisms undermines the effectiveness of regulatory efforts and may incentivise non-compliance or circumvention of regulations in regions with weaker enforcement regimes. Addressing these challenges requires international cooperation and collaboration among governments, regulatory agencies, industry stakeholders and standards bodies to establish harmonised security standards and enforcement mechanisms for IoT devices. By fostering dialogue and information sharing among stakeholders, international cooperation can facilitate the development of consensus-based standards and guidelines that reflect global best practices and accommodate diverse regulatory requirements. International cooperation can also promote interoperability and compatibility among IoT devices and systems, enabling seamless integration and communication across different networks and ecosystems. By aligning security standards and certification programs, international cooperation can streamline compliance efforts for organisations operating in multiple jurisdictions and enhance the effectiveness of regulatory oversight and enforcement. Moreover, international cooperation can facilitate capacity-building initiatives and technical assistance programs to support developing countries in enhancing their cybersecurity capabilities and regulatory frameworks for IoT security. By promoting knowledge sharing, capacity building and technology transfer, international cooperation can contribute to the establishment of a more secure and resilient global IoT ecosystem. In conclusion, exploring challenges in enforcing compliance with IoT security regulations highlights the need for international cooperation to establish effective security standards and enforcement mechanisms. By fostering collaboration among governments, regulatory agencies, industry stakeholders and standards bodies, international cooperation can address regulatory fragmentation, supply chain complexities and enforcement challenges, ultimately enhancing the security and trustworthiness of IoT deployments worldwide.

2.4.6 The human factor

In the realm of IoT security, understanding the human element is paramount, as it unveils the intricate dynamics of human behaviour and its significant impact on the integrity of IoT devices and networks. This section delves into the multifaceted aspects of the human factor, including the role of human error, insider threats and social engineering techniques, shedding light on how these elements contribute to the vulnerability of IoT ecosystems.

- ↣ *Human error*: Human error stands out as a prevalent and often underestimated factor in IoT security breaches. These errors, typically unintentional, encompass a wide range of actions or oversights that inadvertently compromise the security of IoT devices and networks. Misconfigurations, for instance, occur when individuals inadvertently configure IoT devices or networks in a manner that exposes vulnerabilities to potential exploitation. Such misconfigurations may arise due to lack of awareness about security best practices, inadequate training or oversight during deployment and configuration processes. Additionally, failure to update firmware or software in a timely manner can leave IoT devices susceptible to known vulnerabilities that threat actors can exploit. Even seemingly innocuous actions, such as sharing credentials or leaving devices unattended, can inadvertently expose sensitive information or grant unauthorised access, highlighting the pervasive nature of human error in IoT security incidents.

- *Insider threats*: Beyond inadvertent errors, insider threats pose a formidable risk to the security of IoT environments. Insider threats involve individuals within an organisation who misuse their access privileges or insider knowledge to intentionally compromise IoT systems for personal gain, sabotage or other malicious purposes. These individuals may include disgruntled employees, contractors or partners with legitimate access to IoT devices or networks. Unlike external threats, insider threats often possess insider knowledge of the organisation's systems and security protocols, making them particularly challenging to detect and mitigate. Insider threats can manifest in various forms, ranging from malicious actions such as tampering with device configurations or stealing sensitive data to unintentional lapses in judgement that inadvertently expose vulnerabilities or weaken security defences.
- *Social engineering techniques*: In addition to human error and insider threats, social engineering techniques represent a potent tool in the arsenal of cybercriminals seeking to exploit human vulnerabilities for malicious purposes. Social engineering tactics leverage psychological manipulation to deceive individuals into divulging sensitive information, granting unauthorised access or taking actions that compromise the security of IoT devices and networks. Phishing attacks, for example, involve the use of fraudulent emails, messages or phone calls to trick recipients into disclosing login credentials, financial information or other sensitive data. Similarly, pretexting techniques involve the use of fabricated scenarios or false pretences to gain the trust of individuals and coax them into providing access to restricted areas or confidential information. Social engineering attacks exploit human psychology and trust relationships, making them difficult to detect through technical

means alone and underscoring the importance of raising awareness and providing ongoing training to educate users about common tactics and red flags.

↣ *Mitigating the human factor*: Addressing the human factor in IoT security requires a multifaceted approach that combines technical controls with comprehensive training and awareness initiatives. Organisations must prioritise cybersecurity education and training to equip employees with the knowledge and skills needed to recognise and respond to potential threats effectively. Regular security awareness programs, simulated phishing exercises and role-based training can help reinforce security best practices and foster a culture of vigilance and accountability across the organisation. Moreover, implementing robust access controls, monitoring mechanisms and behavioural analytics can aid in detecting and mitigating insider threats, while the adoption of multi-factor authentication and stringent security protocols can help thwart the risks posed by social engineering attacks. By empowering individuals to become active participants in safeguarding IoT devices and networks against evolving threats, organisations can strengthen the overall security posture of their IoT environments and mitigate the risks associated with the human factor.

References

[1] Shor, P.W. (1994). "Algorithms for quantum computation: Discrete logarithms and factorin". Proceedings 35th Annual Symposium on Foundations of Computer Science. IEEE Comput. Soc. Press. pp. 124–134. doi:10.1109/sfcs.1994.365700. ISBN 0818665807. S2CID 15291489

[2] M. A. Nielsen and I. L. Chuang, Quantum Computation and Quantum Information: 10th Anniversary Edition. Cambridge: Cambridge University Press, 2010. doi:10.1017/CBO9780511976667

[3] Grover, Lov K. (1996-07-01). "A fast quantum mechanical algorithm for database search". Proceedings of the twenty-eighth annual ACM symposium on Theory of computing - STOC '96. Philadelphia, Pennsylvania, USA: Association for Computing Machinery. pp. 212–219. arXiv:quant-ph/9605043. Bibcode: 1996 quant.ph.5043G. doi:10.1145/237814.237866. ISBN 978-0-89791-785-8. S2CID 207198067.

[4] Bernstein, D.J. (2009). Introduction to post-quantum cryptography. In: Bernstein, D.J., Buchmann, J., Dahmen, E. (eds) Post-Quantum Cryptography. Springer, Berlin, Heidelberg. doi:10.1007/978-3-540-88702-7_1

[5] Marco Barreno, Blaine Nelson, Russell Sears, Anthony D. Joseph, and J. D. Tygar. 2006. Can machine learning be secure? In Proceedings of the 2006 ACM Symposium on Information, computer and communications security (ASIACCS '06). Association for Computing Machinery, New York, NY, USA, pp. 16–25. doi:10.1145/1128817.1128824

[6] Goodfellow, I.J., Shlens, J., & Szegedy, C. (2014). Explaining and Harnessing Adversarial Examples. CoRR, abs/1412.6572.

[7] Battista Biggio, Fabio Roli, "Wild patterns: Ten years after the rise of adversarial machine learning", Elsevier Pattern Recognition, Volume 84, 2018, pp. 317-331, ISSN 0031-3203, DOI:10.1016/j.patcog.2018.07.023.

[8] V. Mathur, Y. Stavrakas, and S. Singh, "Intelligence analysis of tay twitter bot," in 2016 2nd International Conference on Contemporary Computing and Informatics (IC3I). IEEE, 2016, pp. 231–236.

[9] A. Ohlheiser, "Trolls turned tay, microsoft's fun millennial AI bot, into a genocidal maniac," The Washington Post, vol. 25, 2016.

[10] J. R. Correia-Silva, R. F. Berriel, C. Badue, A. F. de Souza, andT. Oliveira-Santos, "Copycat cnn: Stealing knowledge by persuading confession with random non-labelled data," in 2018 International JointConference on Neural Networks (IJCNN). Ieee, 2018, pp. 1–8.

[11] T. Orekondy, B. Schiele, and M. Fritz, "Knockoff nets: Stealing functionality of black-box models," in Proceedings of the IEEE/CVFConference on Computer Vision and Pattern Recognition, 2019, pp. 4954–4963.

[12] A. Madry, A. Makelov, L. Schmidt, D. Tsipras, and A. Vladu, "Towardsdeep learning models resistant to adversarial attacks," in International Conference on Learning Representations, 2018.

[13] R. Storn and K. Price, "Differential evolution–a simple and ef?cientheuristic for global optimization over continuous spaces," Journal of global optimization, vol. 11, no. 4, pp. 341–359, 1997.

[14] N. Hansen, S. D. Müller, and P. Koumoutsakos, "Reducing the time complexity of the derandomised evolution strategy with covariance matrix adaptation (cma-es)," Evolutionary computation, vol. 11, no. 1, pp. 1–18, 2003.

[15] J. Su, D. V. Vargas, and K. Sakurai, "One pixel attack for fooling deep neural networks," IEEE Transactions on Evolutionary Computation, vol. 23, no. 5, pp. 828–841, 2019.

[16] Kotyan S, Vargas DV. Adversarial robustness assessment: Why in evaluation both L0 and L∞ attacks are necessary. PLoS One. 2022 Apr 14;17(4):e0265723. doi:10.1371/journal.pone.0265723. PMID: 35421125; PMCID: PMC9009601.

[17] Kotyan, Shashank. (2023). "A reading survey on adversarial machine learning: Adversarial attacks and their understanding".

[18] John X. Morris, Eli Lifland, Jin Yong Yoo, Jake Grigsby, Di Jin, Yanjun Qi, "TextAttack: A Framework for Adversarial Attacks, Data Augmentation, and Adversarial Training in NLP", Oct 2020, arXiv: 2005.05909, doi:10.48550/arXiv.2005.05909

[19] Papernot, Nicolas & McDaniel, Patrick & Goodfellow, Ian. (2016). Transferability in Machine Learning: from Phenomena to Black-Box Attacks using Adversarial Samples.

[20] Eykholt, Kevin & Evtimov, Ivan & Fernandes, Earlence & Li, Bo & Rahmati, Amir & Xiao, Chaowei & Prakash, Atul & Kohno, Tadayoshi & Song, Dawn. (2018). Robust Physical-World Attacks on Deep Learning Visual Classification. 1625-1634. 10.1109/CVPR.2018.00175.

[21] Finlayson SG, Bowers JD, Ito J, Zittrain JL, Beam AL, Kohane IS. Adversarial attacks on medical machine learning. Science. 2019 Mar 22;363(6433):1287-1289. doi:10.1126/science.aaw4399. PMID: 30898923; PMCID: PMC7657648.

[22] What is the Mirai Botnet?, DDoSpedia, Cyberpedia, Radware, https://www.radware.com/security/ddos-knowledge-center/ddospedia/mirai/

[23] WHAT IS WANNACRY/WANACRYPT0R?, National Cybersecurity and Communications Integration Center, Cybersecurity and Infrastructure Security Agency, 2017.

[24] REvil / Sodinokibi: The Crown Prince of Ransomware, CyberReason, https://www.cybereason.com/blog/research/the-sodinokibi-ransomware-attack

[25] Brundage, Miles & Avin, Shahar & Clark, Jack & Toner, Helen & Eckersley, Peter & Garfinkel, Ben & Dafoe, Allan & Scharre, Paul & Zeitzoff, Thomas & Filar, Bobby & Anderson, Hyrum & Roff, Heather & Allen, Gregory & Steinhardt, Jacob & Flynn, Carrick & hÉigeartaigh, Seán & Beard, Sj & Belfield, Haydn & Farquhar, Sebastian & Amodei, Dario. (2018). The Malicious Use of Artificial Intelligence: Forecasting, Prevention, and Mitigation.

3

Security-preserving Techniques in 6G

In the dynamic landscape of telecommunications, the evolution towards 6G networks represents a significant leap forward in secure and efficient communication. In the context of 6G networks, where the demand for secure and efficient communication is paramount, the implications of quantum threats are profound. The vulnerabilities introduced by quantum computing can potentially render current cryptographic mechanisms obsolete, compromising the confidentiality and integrity of transmitted data. Quantum computing's unparalleled capabilities have the potential to render traditional cryptographic mechanisms obsolete, jeopardising data confidentiality and integrity. As we stand on the brink of the quantum era, collaborative efforts between the scientific community and industry become imperative to integrate quantum-safe solutions. This chapter focuses on security-preserving techniques in 6G networks, exploring proactive measures to safeguard data integrity and resilience in the face of evolving threats. Through a systematic examination of quantum-safe cryptography and other innovative security solutions, we aim to pave the way for a robust communication infrastructure capable of withstanding the challenges of the quantum age.

The concept of the quantum internet, as referenced in [1] and Figure 3.1, represents an advanced paradigm in communication technology that leverages principles from quantum mechanics to enable unprecedented levels of security and efficiency in data transmission. Unlike traditional internet protocols that rely on classical bits to encode and transmit information, the quantum internet utilises quantum bits, or qubits, which can exist in multiple states simultaneously. This property, known as superposition, allows qubits to encode and process information in a highly parallel manner, enabling faster and more efficient communication. Furthermore, the quantum internet has the potential to enable secure communication over long distances through the phenomenon of quantum entanglement. Entangled qubits, when separated by vast distances, exhibit a correlation that transcends classical boundaries,

Figure 3.1 A schematic depiction of the quantum internet.

allowing for instantaneous communication between distant parties. This could revolutionise fields such as telecommunications, cryptography and even quantum computing, by enabling the creation of interconnected networks that are inherently secure and resilient to external threats.

While the quantum internet is still in its early stages of development, ongoing research and advancements in quantum technology are steadily bringing this vision closer to reality. As the field continues to mature, the quantum internet holds the promise of ushering in a new era of secure, efficient and interconnected communication networks that will transform the way we exchange information in the digital age.

3.1 Quantum Key Distribution (QKD)

QKD leverages the principles of quantum mechanics to enable secure key exchange between parties, offering a quantum-safe alternative to classical key distribution protocols. QKD operates on the premise that the fundamental principles of quantum mechanics provide an inherently secure means of key exchange. Unlike classical key distribution methods, which rely on computational complexity, QKD offers information-theoretic security, meaning the security of the exchanged keys is based on the principles of physics rather than the computational limitations of an eavesdropper. A typical QKD system, as referenced in [1], is shown in Figure 3.2. Quantum key distribution facilitates secure communication by utilising principles from quantum mechanics to exchange secret keys over a public channel with unparalleled security.

Designing quantum networks that efficiently connect multiple nodes, while maintaining quantum coherence presents a complex challenge. Research on optimised quantum network topologies and protocols, such as the development of quantum network simulators, aids in designing practical and scalable quantum communication networks. Quantum hacking attempts, including attacks on measurement devices and attempts to exploit vulnerabilities in the quantum channel, demand robust security measures. Ongoing research in quantum-safe cryptographic protocols and continuous monitoring techniques bolster the security of QKD implementations against evolving threats.

QKD leverages the principle of quantum superposition, allowing quantum particles like photons to exist in multiple states simultaneously. Exploiting quantum entanglement, where particles become interconnected regardless of distance, forms the foundation of QKD. QKD often relies on manipulating

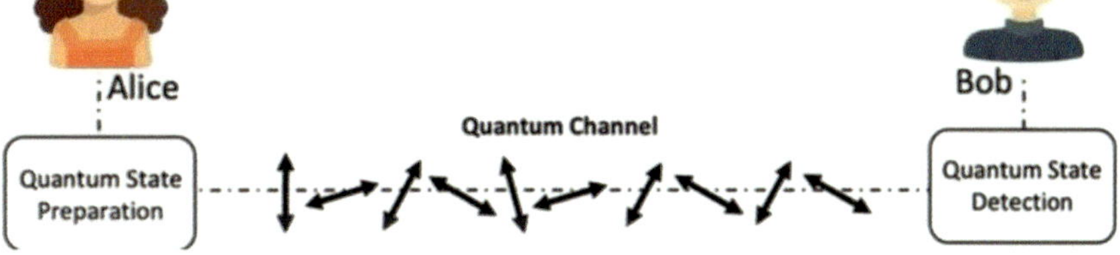

Figure 3.2 Schematic of general quantum key distribution.

the polarisation states of individual photons, encoding quantum information in their properties. Quantum uncertainty ensures that any attempt to measure quantum states inherently disturbs the system, providing a means to detect eavesdropping attempts. QKD often relies on manipulating the polarisation states of individual photons, encoding quantum information in their properties. Quantum uncertainty ensures that any attempt to measure quantum states inherently disturbs the system, providing a means to detect eavesdropping attempts. QKD enables the generation of cryptographic keys through the exchange of quantum particles, ensuring that any eavesdropping attempts would disrupt the delicate quantum states, alerting parties to potential security breaches.

QKD addresses vulnerabilities inherent in classical key distribution methods, particularly those exposed to computational threats posed by quantum computers. QKD achieves a level of perfect secrecy, as the quantum nature of the key exchange process inherently detects any attempt to intercept or measure quantum states. Quantum information carried by photons is susceptible to environmental factors, leading to decoherence and photon loss. Quantum error correction techniques and advancements in photon sources enhance the resilience of QKD systems, mitigating the impact of decoherence and loss.

Various quantum key distribution (QKD) protocols have been developed to facilitate secure key exchange under different conditions, each with its unique approach and advantages:

- The BB84 protocol, proposed by Charles H. Bennett and Gilles Brassard in 1984 [2]. It relies on the encoding of information using the polarisation states of photons and is widely recognised for its robustness and efficiency in establishing secure communication channels. In the BB84 protocol, the sender (often referred to as Alice) prepares a series of photons with randomly chosen polarisation states, such as horizontal or vertical polarisation. These photons are then transmitted to the receiver (often referred to as Bob) through a communication channel. However, due to the principles of quantum mechanics, an eavesdropper (referred to as Eve) may intercept these photons without detection. Upon receiving the photons, Bob randomly selects a measurement basis (either horizontal/vertical or diagonal) to measure the polarisation of each photon. After completing the measurements, Alice and Bob publicly announce which measurement bases were used for each photon transmission, allowing them to compare a subset of their measurement results over a public channel. By comparing their measurement bases and discarding any measurements where Bob's chosen basis does not match Alice's transmission basis, Alice and Bob can establish a shared secret key. If there is no indication of interference or discrepancy in their measurement results, they can be confident that their communication channel is secure. The BB84 protocol's security stems from the fundamental principles of quantum mechanics, including the uncertainty principle and the no-cloning theorem, which ensure that any attempt by Eve to intercept or measure the transmitted photons would disturb their quantum state, thereby revealing her presence. The BB84 protocol is one of the pioneering QKD protocols.

- E91 protocol was developed by Artur Ekert in 1991 [3]. The E91 protocol is based on the concept of entanglement, where pairs of particles are generated in an entangled state and distributed between the communicating parties. By performing measurements on these entangled particles, the parties can establish a secure key without the risk of interception. At its core, the E91 protocol relies on the generation and distribution of entangled particle pairs between the communicating entities. These entangled particles, often photons, are intricately linked in such a way that the properties of one particle instantly correlate with the properties of its entangled counterpart, regardless of the distance separating them. Through a series of measurements performed on the entangled particles, the parties involved in the communication process can derive a shared cryptographic key. Crucially, due to the nature of quantum entanglement, any attempt by an eavesdropper to intercept or tamper with the entangled particles would inevitably disturb their delicate quantum state, thus revealing the presence of unauthorised surveillance.
- BBM92 protocol was named after its inventors Charles H. Bennett, Gilles Brassard and N. David Mermin in 1992 [4]. The BBM92 protocol utilises the principles of quantum mechanics to establish a shared secret key between two parties, ensuring unconditional security against eavesdropping. Utilising pairs of entangled particles, the BBM92 protocol allows two communicating parties to exchange cryptographic keys in a manner that is inherently secure. The BBM92 protocol operates on the principle of quantum measurement, where the properties of entangled particles are observed in such a way that any attempt to intercept or measure the particles without authorisation would disrupt their delicate quantum state, thus revealing the presence of an eavesdropper. This phenomenon, known as quantum indeterminacy, guarantees the security of the key exchange process.

- The MSZ96 protocol, also known as the Mayers-Simon-Smith 1996 protocol, is a pioneering quantum key distribution (QKD) protocol proposed by Mu Yi, Jennifer Siberian Yuliang Zheng in 1996 [5]. MSZ96 is a quantum key distribution protocol which allows a cryptographic key bit to be encoded using four non-orthogonal quantum states described by non-commuting quadrature phase amplitudes of a weak optical field, without photon polarisation (BB84 protocol) or entangled photons (E91 protocol). The protocol consists of an optical coupler and four nonorthogonal coherent states which are analysed by means of quadrature phase amplitudes of a quantised light field.
- The six-state protocol is an extension of the BBM92 protocol QKD [6]. Unlike the BB84 protocol, which uses two non-orthogonal quantum states for encoding bits, the six-state protocol utilises six different non-orthogonal quantum states. This increased number of states enhances the efficiency and security of QKD systems, as it provides more options for encoding information and increases resistance to potential eavesdropping attacks. The six-state protocol is a discrete-variable protocol for quantum key distribution, offering the advantage of tolerating a more noisy channel compared to the BB84 protocol, The six-state protocol builds upon the principles of quantum mechanics to ensure secure communication channels, making it a significant advancement in the field of quantum cryptography.
- In the realm of quantum cryptography, the Decoy state quantum key distribution (QKD) protocol stands out as one of the most widely utilised schemes. Unlike the conventional BB84 protocol, practical QKD systems often employ multi-photon sources, which are vulnerable to photon number splitting (PNS) attacks. These attacks can severely restrict the secure transmission rate or the maximum channel length achievable in practical QKD setups. To counteract this inherent vulnerability, the decoy state technique employs a strategy of utilising multiple intensity levels at the transmitter's source. This involves Alice, the sender, transmitting qubits at randomly selected intensity levels, including one signal state and several decoy states, resulting in varying photon number statistics across the communication channel. Following the transmission, Alice publicly discloses which intensity level was used for each qubit transmission. A successful PNS attack relies on maintaining a consistent bit error rate (BER) at the receiver's end, which becomes challenging when dealing with multiple photon number statistics. By

monitoring the BERs associated with each intensity level, the legitimate parties involved can effectively detect a PNS attack, thereby significantly enhancing the secure transmission rates or maximum channel lengths achievable. This enhancement renders QKD systems more suitable for practical applications in real-world scenarios. The decoy-state protocol was initially introduced by Won-Young Hwang [7]. Its security was subsequently established through the development of a photon number channel model, assuming an infinite number of decoy states. In practical implementations, a commonly employed method involves using two decoy states: the vacuum decoy and the weak decoy. The vacuum+weak decoy state approach was originally suggested by Hoi-Kwong Lo [8]. Studies have demonstrated that employing solely the vacuum and weak decoy states yields a key rate that closely approaches that of the infinite decoy state scenario.

- The SARG04 protocol is a quantum key distribution (QKD) protocol developed as a more robust alternative to the BB84 protocol, particularly against photon-number-splitting attacks [9]. It is designed to be utilised in scenarios where attenuated laser pulses are used, and the information originates from a Poissonian source generating weak pulses, which are then received by an imperfect detector. This protocol addresses vulnerabilities present in such situations, ensuring secure communication through QKD even in environments with less-than-ideal conditions and potential vulnerabilities like photon-number-splitting attacks.
- The three-stage quantum cryptography protocol, also known as Kak's three-stage protocol, is a data encryption method proposed by Subhash Kak [10]. Unlike traditional quantum key distribution (QKD) methods, this protocol allows for direct encryption of data in addition to key exchange. It relies on random polarisation rotations by both authenticated parties, Alice and Bob, to ensure secure communication. In essence, the protocol operates on the principle of sending secrets through an unreliable courier, employing a technique known as double-lock cryptography. Initially, Alice locks the box containing the secret and sends it to Bob. Upon receiving the box, Bob adds his own lock before sending it back to Alice. Alice then removes her lock, verifies the integrity of the box and sends it back to Bob. Finally, Bob unlocks the box, retrieving the secret. This process ensures secure communication between Alice and Bob, with the protocol's braided form requiring only a single pass, provided that Alice and Bob share an initial key.

Unlike QKD methods that utilise classical algorithms for cryptographic transformations, Kak's three-stage protocol is entirely quantum-based, offering a unique approach to secure communication.

- The KMB09 protocol, named after Muhammad Mubashir Khan, Michael Murphy and Almut Beige, presents an alternative approach to quantum key distribution (QKD) [11]. In this protocol, Alice and Bob utilise two mutually unbiased bases, with one base encoding a '0' and the other encoding a '1'. The security of the scheme relies on maintaining a minimum index transmission error rate (ITER) and quantum bit error rate (QBER) introduced by potential eavesdroppers. One notable feature of the KMB09 protocol is its resilience to noise in the transmission line. The ITER increases significantly when higher-dimensional photon states are employed, allowing for greater tolerance to noise. As a result, the protocol enables communication over longer distances between Alice and Bob without the need for intermediate nodes, enhancing its practical applicability in real-world scenarios.
- High-dimensional quantum key distribution (HDQKD) stands as a cutting-edge technology facilitating secure communication between two parties [12]. Unlike traditional binary quantum key distribution (QKD) protocols, which are limited to 1 bit/photon, HDQKD offers higher information efficiency. Additionally, it exhibits greater resilience to noise, allowing for lower signal-to-noise ratios and extended transmission distances. One viable method for implementing HDQKD involves leveraging space division multiplexing technology, where quantum information is encoded in the spatial dimension. Optical angular momentum (OAM) modes serve as a prime example of this approach. While OAM modes have demonstrated success in HDQKD over free-space links, achieving the same over long-distance fibre links poses challenges due to intermodal crosstalk. Alternatively, multicore fibres (MCFs) present a promising solution with their multitude of separate cores and minimal crosstalk between them. Nevertheless, implementing HDQKD with MCFs introduces its own set of challenges. Manipulating high-dimensional quantum states within MCFs necessitates precise phase stability, which can prove challenging to attain. Furthermore, transmitting quantum states through fibre optics introduces noise and loss, leading to diminished fidelity and heightened quantum bit error rates (QBER).

In the realm of secure communication, quantum key distribution (QKD) protocols serve as indispensable tools, addressing a myriad of requirements and conditions across diverse scenarios. These protocols each offer unique features and capabilities suited to specific needs. For instance, BB84 excels in providing security against intercept-resend attacks, while E91 leverages quantum entanglement to achieve unbreakable encryption. Similarly, BBM92 introduces enhanced security against eavesdropping through its utilisation of quantum principles. Furthermore, emerging protocols like the KMB09 protocol and the three-stage quantum cryptography protocol continue to push the boundaries of secure communication, offering innovative approaches to address evolving threats. In practical applications, the choice of QKD protocol depends on factors such as desired security level, environmental conditions and available resources. For instance, in scenarios where resilience to noise and long-distance transmission are paramount, protocols like the KMB09 protocol and HDQKD shine with their ability to tolerate higher levels of interference and achieve extended transmission distances. On the other hand, in environments where simplicity and efficiency are key, established protocols like BB84 and E91 may be preferred for their proven track record and ease of implementation. Overall, these QKD protocols collectively contribute to the advancement of secure communication technologies, enabling organisations and individuals to safeguard sensitive information against unauthorised access and interception. By offering a diverse array of solutions tailored to specific needs and conditions, these protocols empower users to secure their communications effectively in an ever-evolving threat landscape. As research and development in quantum cryptography continue to progress, it is likely that new and improved protocols will emerge, further enhancing the security and resilience of communication systems in the future.

3.1.1 Real-world implementation

The practical implementation of quantum key distribution (QKD) faces several challenges, despite its promising potential to secure communication channels in 6G networks. One significant challenge is the integration of QKD into existing communication infrastructures, which often requires substantial modifications and investments. Traditional fibre-optic networks, for example, may not be compatible with the delicate quantum states transmitted in QKD, necessitating the development of specialised quantum communication channels. Moreover, achieving long-distance transmission with QKD presents a formidable obstacle due to the inherent fragility of quantum states. Quantum signals are susceptible to noise and loss as they travel through optical fibres, leading to increased error rates and reduced key generation rates over extended distances. Overcoming these limitations requires innovations in quantum repeater technology and the development of efficient error-correction techniques to mitigate the effects of noise and loss. Furthermore, ensuring the practical security of QKD implementations against potential attacks is paramount. While QKD protocols offer theoretical security guarantees based on the principles of quantum mechanics, practical implementations may be vulnerable to various types of attacks, including side-channel attacks and Trojan horse attacks on QKD hardware. Addressing these security concerns requires rigorous testing, verification and the implementation of robust cryptographic protocols to complement QKD. Despite these challenges, significant advancements have been made in the practical implementation of QKD, paving the way for its integration into future communication networks such as 6G. Researchers have developed novel QKD protocols, such as high-dimensional QKD and measurement-device-independent QKD, which offer enhanced security and efficiency compared to traditional protocols. Additionally, advancements in quantum memory technologies and quantum repeater architectures hold promise for extending the reach of QKD over long distances. In the context of 6G networks, where secure and efficient communication is paramount, QKD has the potential to play a crucial role in safeguarding data transmission against eavesdropping and interception. By leveraging the inherent properties of quantum mechanics, QKD can provide provably secure key distribution even in the presence of powerful adversaries. As 6G networks continue to evolve, integrating QKD technologies will be essential for realising their full potential in enabling secure and resilient communication infrastructures.

Quantum key distribution (QKD) offers a promising solution for securing communication within the Internet of Things (IoT) devices, mitigating risks associated with traditional key distribution methods. In the IoT ecosystem, where billions of interconnected devices exchange sensitive data, ensuring the confidentiality and integrity of communication is paramount to prevent unauthorised access and cyberattacks. Traditional key distribution methods, such as pre-shared keys or public-key cryptography, are susceptible to various security vulnerabilities, including key compromise and interception by adversaries. QKD, on the other hand, leverages the principles of quantum mechanics to establish secure keys between communicating parties, offering provable security guarantees even in the presence of powerful adversaries.

One of the primary advantages of QKD in securing IoT communication is its resistance to eavesdropping attacks. Unlike classical cryptographic protocols, which rely on the computational complexity of mathematical problems for security, QKD relies on the fundamental properties of quantum mechanics, such as the Heisenberg uncertainty principle and the no-cloning theorem. This makes it inherently immune to attacks based on computational advances, such as quantum computers. Furthermore, QKD provides forward secrecy, ensuring that past communications remain secure even if the long-term secret key is compromised in the future. This is particularly important in IoT environments where devices may have long operational lifetimes and frequently exchange sensitive data.

In practical implementations, QKD can be integrated into IoT devices to establish secure communication channels between them. Quantum-enabled sensors and actuators can utilise QKD protocols to exchange cryptographic keys securely, preventing unauthorised access and tampering of data. Additionally, QKD can be combined with other security mechanisms, such as authentication and access control, to provide comprehensive security solutions for IoT deployments. Moreover, QKD offers the potential for secure communication over long distances, making it suitable for IoT applications deployed in remote or geographically dispersed locations. Advanced QKD technologies, such as satellite-based QKD and free-space QKD, can extend secure communication capabilities to IoT devices in challenging environments where traditional communication infrastructures may be unavailable or unreliable. Overall, by leveraging the unique properties of quantum mechanics, QKD holds great promise for enhancing the security of communication within the Internet of Things. By adopting QKD-based solutions, IoT stakeholders can mitigate the risks associated with traditional key distribution methods and ensure the confidentiality, integrity and authenticity of data exchanged between interconnected devices.

One of the key advantages of QKD is its ability to ensure the secrecy of cryptographic keys even when transmitted over long distances. Unlike classical encryption methods, which rely on the computational complexity of algorithms for security, QKD exploits the fundamental properties of quantum mechanics, such as the uncertainty principle and the no-cloning theorem. By encoding information in quantum states, QKD enables the generation of cryptographic keys that are immune to interception or duplication. Moreover, advancements in QKD technology have led to the development of protocols specifically designed to overcome distance limitations. Techniques such as decoy state methods, entanglement-based QKD and high-dimensional quantum key distribution offer innovative approaches to extend the reach of secure communication channels. These protocols leverage sophisticated quantum phenomena to maintain security even over fibre optic networks spanning hundreds of kilometres. In the context of 6G networks, where the demand for secure and reliable communication is paramount, QKD holds tremendous potential to enhance the resilience of data transmission over vast distances. By integrating QKD into the infrastructure of IoT devices, telecommunications networks and critical infrastructure systems, organisations can establish secure communication channels that protect against cyber threats and ensure data privacy. However, challenges remain in the practical implementation of QKD for long-distance communication. Issues such as signal attenuation, noise and the scalability of quantum systems pose significant obstacles to realising the full potential of QKD in real-world applications. Addressing these challenges requires ongoing research and development efforts to improve the efficiency, reliability and scalability of QKD systems.

- *System integration*: Integrating QKD systems into existing communication infrastructure can be complex and requires compatibility with various network components. Achieving seamless integration with conventional cryptographic protocols and network protocols is essential to ensure interoperability and ease of deployment. Additionally, QKD systems must be compatible with different communication mediums, such as fibre optic cables, free-space links and satellite communication, further complicating integration efforts.
- *Performance*: The performance of QKD systems is influenced by factors such as signal loss, noise and environmental conditions. Signal attenuation in optical fibres can limit the transmission distance of QKD systems, necessitating the use of signal amplification techniques or alternative transmission mediums. Noise, including background noise and detector noise, can degrade the quality of quantum signals and increase the error rate, impacting the security and reliability of the communication channel. Addressing performance challenges requires advancements in hardware technology, signal processing algorithms and error correction techniques to improve the efficiency and resilience of QKD systems.
- *Cost*: The cost of deploying and operating QKD systems is a significant barrier to widespread adoption, particularly for large-scale deployment in telecommunications networks or critical infrastructure. QKD systems involve specialised hardware components, including single-photon sources, detectors and quantum memories, which can be expensive to

manufacture and maintain. Moreover, the complexity of QKD protocols and the need for dedicated infrastructure further contribute to the overall cost of implementation. Reducing the cost of QKD systems through advancements in technology, economies of scale and standardised manufacturing processes is essential to make QKD more accessible to organisations and industries.

↣ *Practical limitations*: Real-world deployment of QKD systems faces practical limitations, such as limited transmission distance, channel loss and susceptibility to environmental factors. Overcoming these limitations requires innovations in system design, protocol optimisation and adaptive strategies to adapt to changing conditions in the operational environment.

By overcoming the barriers to real-world deployment, improving system performance and reducing the cost of implementation, QKD can emerge as a viable and scalable technology for securing communication networks in various applications, including telecommunications, finance, healthcare and government sectors. Ongoing research and development initiatives are focused on overcoming current challenges and advancing the practical applications of quantum key distribution (QKD). These initiatives encompass a wide range of areas, including hardware development, protocol optimisation, system integration and standardisation efforts.

↣ *Hardware development*: Research efforts are underway to develop more efficient and reliable QKD hardware components, such as single-photon sources, detectors and quantum memories. Innovations in semiconductor technology, nanofabrication techniques and materials science are driving the development of next-generation QKD devices with improved performance, reduced noise and enhanced scalability. Additionally, efforts are being made to commercialise QKD hardware and make it more accessible to end-users through partnerships with industry stakeholders. Some examples of hardware development in quantum key distribution (QKD) include:

→ *Single-photon sources*: Researchers are exploring various techniques for creating reliable and efficient sources of single photons, which are essential for generating quantum states in QKD systems. Examples include semiconductor quantum dots, spontaneous parametric down-conversion (SPDC) sources and trapped ions. Innovations in photon generation technologies aim to improve photon purity, emission efficiency and spectral properties to enhance the performance of QKD systems. For example, Toshiba developed semiconductor-based devices capable of generating single photons [13, 14]. This breakthrough has broad implications for quantum communication systems, enabling applications such as quantum key distribution (QKD) and nanoscale logic operations. By leveraging semiconductor quantum dots, which are nanoscale structures, they have achieved precise control over photon generation, ensuring the emission of single photons with high efficiency and reliability. This development opens up new possibilities for secure communication and computing technologies based on quantum principles.

→ *Detectors*: Advancements in detector technology are crucial for improving the detection efficiency, timing resolution and noise characteristics of QKD systems. Avalanche photodiodes (APDs), superconducting nanowire single-photon detectors (SNSPDs) and transition-edge sensors (TESs) are some examples of detector technologies used in QKD. Research efforts focus on increasing detector sensitivity, reducing dark counts and extending the operating temperature range to enable QKD deployment in diverse environments. For example, ID Quantique, a leading manufacturer of quantum-safe security solutions, offers a range of high-performance single-photon detectors for QKD applications [15]. Their ID100 series of detectors feature low noise, high detection efficiency and fast timing resolution, enabling reliable photon detection in challenging environments.

→ *Quantum memories*: Quantum memories play a vital role in storing and manipulating quantum states for various quantum information processing tasks, including QKD. Solid-state quantum memories based on atomic ensembles, rare-earth ions or defects in diamond crystals are under development to provide long-lived storage of quantum information. These memories are essential for implementing quantum repeaters and extending the range of QKD over long distances. Researchers at the University of Oxford have developed a solid-state quantum memory based on rare-earth ions embedded in a crystal lattice [16]. This memory device demonstrates long coherence times and high fidelity for storing quantum information, promising advances in quantum repeater technology for long-distance QKD.

→ *Integrated photonics*: Integrated photonics technologies enable the miniaturisation and integration of optical components on a chip-scale platform, offering advantages in terms of size, power consumption and scalability. Integrated photonics devices, such as waveguides, beam splitters and phase modulators, are essential for building compact and robust QKD systems. Research in integrated photonics focuses on improving device performance, reducing fabrication costs and enhancing compatibility with existing telecommunication infrastructure. PsiQuantum, a startup specialising in quantum computing and communication technologies, is developing integrated photonic devices for QKD applications [17]. Their photonic chips integrate multiple optical components on a silicon substrate, enabling compact and scalable QKD systems for deployment in data centres and network infrastructure.

→ *Commercialisation efforts*: Industry collaborations and startup ventures aim to commercialise QKD hardware and bring quantum-secure communication technology to market. These efforts involve translating research breakthroughs into practical products and solutions suitable for deployment in real-world applications. By partnering with industry stakeholders, academic institutions and government agencies, researchers seek to accelerate the development and adoption of QKD technology and make it accessible to a broader range of users. QuantumCTek, a Chinese company specialising in quantum communication products, offers a range of QKD systems and components for secure communication applications. Their QKD systems are designed for deployment in telecommunications networks, financial institutions and government agencies, providing quantum-secure encryption for sensitive data.

↣ *Protocol optimisation*: Researchers are continuously refining QKD protocols to improve their security, efficiency and practicality. This includes developing new cryptographic primitives, error correction codes and authentication mechanisms to enhance the resilience of QKD systems against various types of attacks and noise sources. Additionally, protocol optimisation efforts aim to increase the key generation rate, extend the transmission distance and minimise the overhead associated with key distribution processes.

  - → For example, researchers have developed efficient error correction codes tailored for QKD systems by proposing a novel error correction scheme for fully correlated noise optimised for quantum communication channels [18]. Their approach significantly improves the reliability and security of QKD protocols by efficiently detecting and correcting errors introduced during qubit transmission.
  - → Furthermore, researchers have made significant contributions to protocol optimisation in QKD, particularly in the development of advanced authentication mechanisms by introducing a novel authentication method based on quantum principles [19]. Their approach leverages quantum signatures to verify the identity of communicating parties in QKD systems, enhancing security while minimising overhead.

- ↣ *System integration*: Integrating QKD systems into existing communication networks requires seamless interoperability with conventional cryptographic protocols, network infrastructure and management systems. Research initiatives are focused on developing standards and interfaces for QKD integration, as well as designing modular and scalable architectures that can adapt to diverse deployment scenarios. Interdisciplinary collaboration between quantum scientists, network engineers and cybersecurity experts is essential to ensure the successful integration of QKD into real-world applications, such as:

  - → Integration of QKD technology into existing optical fibre networks by integration of QKD components onto a silicon photonics chip, enabling compatibility with conventional optical communication infrastructure [20]. By leveraging silicon photonics technology, the researchers aim to create compact and scalable QKD systems that can seamlessly interface with standard optical network equipment.

- ↣ *Standardisation efforts*: Standardisation bodies and industry consortia are actively engaged in developing technical standards and best practices for QKD deployment and operation. These standards cover various aspects of QKD, including system requirements, performance metrics, interoperability protocols and security guidelines. Standardisation efforts play a crucial role in promoting interoperability, facilitating technology adoption and ensuring compliance with regulatory requirements across different industries and regions.

→ One prominent example of standardisation efforts in the field of quantum key distribution (QKD) is the work carried out by the International Telecommunication Union (ITU), a specialised agency of the United Nations responsible for setting global telecommunications standards. The ITU has established a dedicated focus group known as 'FG QIT' (Focus Group on Quantum Information Technology) to address the standardisation needs for QKD deployment. The FG QKD group brings together experts from industry, academia and government to develop technical specifications, guidelines and recommendations for QKD implementation. Through its meetings and publications, the ITU FG QKD group has contributed to the development of standards covering various aspects of QKD technology, including system architecture, key exchange protocols, security requirements and performance evaluation metrics [21, 22].

→ The Industry Specification Group (ISG) on quantum key distribution (QKD) within the European Telecommunications Standards Institute (ETSI) is another key player in standardisation efforts for QKD technology. This group is focused on addressing standardisation issues related to quantum cryptography and associated quantum technologies, with the aim of facilitating the deployment of QKD solutions in next-generation telecommunications networks. The ISG on QKD brings together experts from science, industry and commerce to develop specifications for QKD system interfaces, implementation security requirements and optical characterisation of QKD systems and their components. By establishing standardised interfaces and security protocols, the ISG aims to ensure interoperability and compatibility among QKD solutions from different vendors, thereby promoting the widespread adoption of quantum-safe cryptographic techniques. The work of the ISG on QKD is instrumental in enabling the private sharing of digital keys without relying on computational complexity, thus providing security that is resistant to future advances in algorithms, computational power or the emergence of quantum computers. By addressing standardisation challenges and developing robust deployable solutions, the ISG on QKD plays a crucial role in safeguarding the integrity and confidentiality of communications in next-generation telecommunications networks.

→ Additionally, industry consortia such as the Quantum-Safe Security Working Group (QSSWG) within the Cloud Security Alliance (CSA) have also contributed to standardisation efforts for QKD. The QSSWG focuses on developing best practices, frameworks and guidelines for quantum-safe cryptography, including QKD, to address the emerging threats posed by quantum computers to cryptographic systems.

These organisations play a vital role in shaping the standardisation landscape for QKD and quantum technologies, ensuring interoperability, security and reliability in quantum communication systems.

↣ *Field trials and demonstrations*: Field trials and demonstrations are essential for validating the performance and feasibility of QKD in real-world environments. Research organisations, government agencies and private companies are conducting field trials to assess the practicality of QKD for securing communication networks, critical infrastructure and sensitive data transmission. These trials provide valuable insights into the challenges and opportunities associated with deploying QKD at scale and help guide further research and development efforts.

Overall, ongoing research and development initiatives are driving the advancement of QKD technology and paving the way for its widespread adoption in various applications, including telecommunications, cybersecurity and secure data exchange. By addressing current challenges and pushing the boundaries of quantum communication capabilities, these initiatives are shaping the future of secure communication in the digital age.

3.1.2 Satellite-based QKD

Traditional QKD systems face limitations in transmitting quantum keys over long distances due to fibre attenuation and other factors. Satellite-based QKD and the development of quantum repeaters aim to extend the transmission range, addressing the challenge of distance limitations. Integrating QKD into existing communication infrastructures poses challenges, particularly when adapting to diverse network architectures and equipment. Research focuses on developing practical interfaces that seamlessly integrate QKD with classical communication systems, enabling a smooth transition to quantum-safe communication in 6G networks. Building QKD systems with multiple components, including single-photon sources, detectors and quantum memories, requires intricate system integration. Advances in modular QKD architectures and standardisation efforts simplify system integration, making QKD more accessible and scalable for deployment in 6G networks. Achieving high quantum key rates and transmission speeds is crucial for practical applications in fast-paced communication networks. Continuous improvements in hardware components, such as efficient single-photon sources and high-speed detectors, contribute to boosting quantum key rates and transmission speeds. QKD implementations have historically faced cost barriers and scalability challenges, hindering widespread adoption. Technological innovations, cost-effective manufacturing processes and collaborative efforts to standardise QKD components contribute to reducing costs and enhancing scalability. Emerging technologies, such as satellite-based quantum key distribution (QKD), hold significant promise for enabling secure communication on a global scale. Satellite-based QKD leverages the unique properties of quantum mechanics to establish secure cryptographic keys between distant locations, overcoming the limitations of traditional key distribution methods. This approach offers several advantages, including:

- ↣ *Global coverage*: Satellite-based QKD enables secure communication between any two points on Earth, regardless of geographic distance or terrestrial infrastructure. This global coverage is particularly valuable for applications requiring secure communication in remote or inaccessible locations.
- ↣ *Unconditional security*: Quantum key distribution provides unconditional security, meaning that the secrecy of the cryptographic keys is guaranteed by the laws of quantum mechanics. This ensures that encrypted data remains secure even against the most advanced cryptographic attacks, including those based on quantum computing.
- ↣ *Resilience to eavesdropping*: Satellite-based QKD is inherently resistant to eavesdropping and interception attempts. Quantum mechanics dictates that any attempt to measure or intercept the quantum states used for key distribution will inevitably disturb them, alerting the communicating parties to the presence of an eavesdropper.
- ↣ *Long-distance communication*: Satellites facilitate long-distance communication without the need for intermediate infrastructure, making them ideal for establishing secure links between geographically distant locations. This capability is particularly valuable for applications requiring secure communication over vast distances, such as global financial transactions or secure government communications.

↣ *Rapid deployment*: Satellite-based QKD systems can be rapidly deployed and scaled to meet evolving security requirements. Unlike terrestrial infrastructure, which may require extensive planning and construction, satellite deployments can be launched relatively quickly, providing rapid access to secure communication capabilities.

Several research and development initiatives are currently underway to advance satellite-based QKD technology and demonstrate its practical feasibility. For example, space agencies have conducted experiments to demonstrate the feasibility of QKD using satellites, such as the Quantum Experiments at Space Scale (QUESS) mission by China's Micius satellite (Figure 3.3). The Eagle-1 satellite will be the first space-based quantum key distribution system to be developed under a partnership between ESA, the European Commission and space companies in Europe. The project is led by SES, a satellite company based in Luxembourg, in collaboration with over 20 European companies. Initially, it will utilise an upgraded optical ground terminal from the German Aerospace Centre (DLR), along with a newly developed optical ground terminal by a team from the Netherlands. The satellite platform, Eagle-1, manufactured by Italian company Sitael, will carry a quantum-key payload constructed by Tesat Spacecom of Germany and operated by SES. Several other ESA member states, including Austria, Belgium, the Czech Republic, Italy and Switzerland, are also participating in

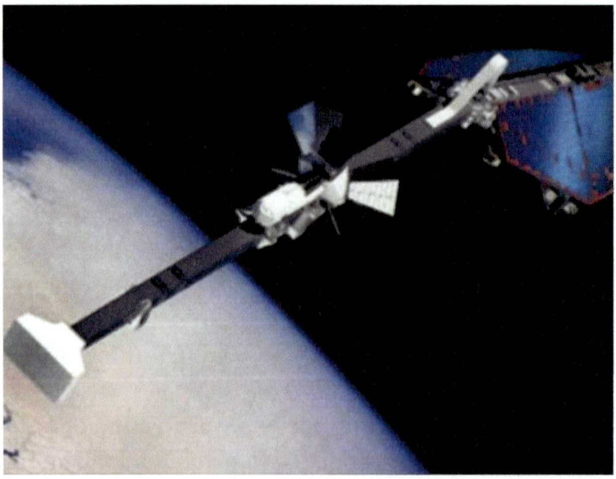

Figure 3.3 Micius is the world's first quantum communication satellite (Credit: Chinese Academy of Sciences, licensed under the Creative Commons Attribution 4.0 International Licence).

the project. The launch of the Eagle-1 satellite is scheduled for 2024, followed by three years of in-orbit validation supported by the European Commission.

QKD promises ultra-secure communication by offering information-theoretic security, ensuring that any attempt to eavesdrop on quantum key distribution is detectable. QKD can play a pivotal role in securing communication channels for Internet of Things (IoT) devices within the intricate fabric of 6G networks, addressing the unique security challenges associated with hyper-connected devices. With advancements like satellite-based QKD, the potential for global secure communication in 6G networks becomes more feasible, offering secure links between distant locations. Thus, navigating the implementation challenges of QKD, advancements across various fronts contribute to establishing QKD as a formidable candidate for securing communication channels in 6G networks. The ongoing synergy of research, technological innovation and practical integration efforts underscores the potential of QKD to provide quantum-safe communication, shaping the security landscape of the next generation of communication networks. In essence, quantum key distribution stands as a paradigm shift in secure key exchange, utilising the intricate principles of quantum mechanics to offer a quantum-safe alternative to classical key distribution protocols. QKD provides a robust framework for secure key distribution in the hyperconnected landscape of 6G networks. Its conceptual framework provides a glimpse into the future of secure communication, especially in the context of the advanced and interconnected networks envisioned in 6G technology.

3.2 Quantum Random Number Generators (QRNGs)

Random number generation lies at the core of information security, serving as the foundation for cryptographic protocols and a myriad of other applications. While conventional methods like pseudo-random number generators (PRNGs) have long been prevalent, they come with inherent limitations due to their deterministic nature, leaving them vulnerable to predictability risks. In response to this challenge, quantum random number generation (QRNG) has emerged as a promising alternative, leveraging the principles of quantum mechanics to produce genuinely random outcomes. This subchapter embarks on a thorough exploration of QRNG, examining its principles, technologies, security features, applications and regulatory considerations. We begin by clarifying the concept of randomness and the constraints of classical methods, setting the stage for a detailed analysis of QRNG's underlying principles and the diverse technological approaches utilised. Additionally, we explore the security attributes of QRNG, including entropy generation rate, bias and resistance to tampering, illustrating how they bolster the security of cryptographic systems. Furthermore, we explore the wide-ranging applications of QRNG across various domains, spanning from cryptography to gaming and scientific research, highlighting its pivotal role in securing communication networks and sensitive data. Regulatory frameworks and standardisation initiatives governing QRNG deployment are also examined, alongside practical considerations and implementation challenges. By offering insights into QRNG's multifaceted dimensions and future prospects, this subchapter underscores its significance in enhancing information security landscapes, particularly in anticipation of the forthcoming era of 6G and beyond.

3.2.1 Introduction to randomness

Randomness serves as the fundamental building block of security in various domains, particularly in cryptography and information security. At its core, randomness refers to the absence of pattern or predictability, a quality that is indispensable for safeguarding sensitive information and ensuring the integrity of cryptographic systems. In the realm of cryptography, randomness plays a pivotal role in generating secure cryptographic keys, which form the bedrock of encryption algorithms used to protect data transmission and storage. Without true randomness, cryptographic keys become susceptible to exploitation by adversaries, compromising the confidentiality and integrity of encrypted communications.

The significance of randomness extends beyond cryptography, permeating diverse applications across industries. From secure communication protocols to financial transactions and scientific simulations, the unpredictable nature of random data underpins the reliability and trustworthiness of numerous systems and processes. In cryptographic protocols, such as digital signatures and key exchange mechanisms, the unpredictability of random numbers is essential for thwarting adversaries' attempts to guess or reverse-engineer cryptographic secrets.

However, generating truly random numbers poses significant challenges when relying solely on classical methods. Traditional pseudo-random number generators (PRNGs) utilise deterministic algorithms to produce sequences of seemingly random numbers. While adequate for many applications, PRNGs are inherently predictable and vulnerable to exploitation if their internal state is compromised. The deterministic nature of classical algorithms introduces patterns and correlations that may be exploited by attackers to compromise cryptographic systems.

In contrast, true randomness, or entropy, derived from natural physical processes offers a higher degree of unpredictability and security. Quantum random number generation (QRNG) leverages the principles of quantum mechanics to generate truly random numbers, harnessing quantum uncertainty, superposition and measurement to produce outcomes that are inherently unpredictable. Unlike classical methods, which rely on deterministic algorithms, QRNG technologies exploit the inherent randomness of quantum phenomena, such as photon detection, vacuum fluctuations or nuclear decay, to generate random numbers with unparalleled unpredictability and security.

Despite the promise of QRNG, integrating quantum-based randomness into practical cryptographic systems presents its own set of challenges, including technological constraints, scalability issues and cost considerations. However, ongoing research and advancements in quantum technologies offer promising avenues for overcoming these challenges and harnessing the full potential of randomness in bolstering the security of cryptographic systems and ensuring the resilience of digital infrastructure in the face of evolving threats.

3.2.2 Classical random number generation

Classical methods for generating random numbers, such as pseudo-random number generators (PRNGs), have long been employed in various applications across industries. PRNGs operate by utilising deterministic algorithms to produce sequences of numbers that exhibit statistical properties similar to those of random numbers. While PRNGs offer a convenient and efficient means of generating seemingly random data, they possess inherent limitations that impact their suitability for cryptographic applications and other security-sensitive scenarios.

One of the primary limitations of classical PRNGs lies in their predictability. Despite appearing random, the sequences generated by PRNGs are entirely deterministic and predictable given knowledge of their initial state. This predictability introduces vulnerabilities that can be exploited by adversaries seeking to compromise cryptographic systems or undermine the security of applications relying on random data. Through reverse-engineering or analysing the PRNG's algorithm and seed value, attackers may gain insight into future outputs and potentially mount successful attacks, such as cryptographic key guessing or replay attacks.

Moreover, classical PRNGs are susceptible to cryptographic attacks that exploit weaknesses in their design or implementation. Vulnerabilities such as insufficient entropy sources, inadequate seeding mechanisms or flawed algorithmic choices can undermine the randomness and security of PRNG outputs. For instance, certain PRNG algorithms may exhibit periodicity or patterns in their output sequences, compromising their unpredictability and making them vulnerable to cryptanalysis techniques aimed at identifying and exploiting such weaknesses.

Furthermore, the security of classical PRNGs relies heavily on the secrecy of their internal state, particularly the seed value used to initialise the generator. If an attacker gains access to the PRNG's seed value through observation, inference or exploitation of system vulnerabilities, they can predict future outputs and undermine the confidentiality and integrity of cryptographic operations relying on those outputs.

In summary, while classical PRNGs offer a convenient means of generating random-like sequences for non-cryptographic applications, their deterministic nature and susceptibility to attacks make them unsuitable for cryptographic purposes. As the demand for robust and secure random number generation continues to grow, there is an increasing recognition of the need for alternative approaches, such as quantum-based randomness, to address the shortcomings of classical methods and enhance the security of cryptographic systems and applications.

3.2.3 Principles of quantum random number generation

Quantum random number generation (QRNG) harnesses the inherent unpredictability of quantum mechanics to produce truly random numbers, offering an innovative solution to the limitations of classical methods. At the heart of quantum randomness lie fundamental principles such as quantum uncertainty, superposition and measurement, which underpin the generation of unpredictable outcomes essential for cryptographic applications and other security-sensitive tasks.

Quantum uncertainty, a cornerstone of quantum mechanics, asserts that certain pairs of physical properties, such as position and momentum, cannot be precisely determined simultaneously. This principle implies inherent unpredictability at the quantum level, where the behaviour of particles and systems is governed by probabilistic distributions rather than deterministic rules. By exploiting quantum uncertainty, QRNG devices can generate random numbers with unparalleled unpredictability, providing a robust foundation for cryptographic key generation, secure communications and other applications requiring high levels of randomness.

Superposition, another fundamental concept in quantum mechanics, describes the ability of quantum systems to exist in multiple states simultaneously until measured or observed. In the context of QRNG, superposition enables the simultaneous representation of multiple possible outcomes, each with a certain probability of occurrence. By leveraging superposition, QRNG devices can generate random numbers by encoding quantum states that encompass all potential outcomes, ensuring that the final result is truly random and unpredictable.

Measurement, the process by which a quantum system's state is determined through observation, plays a crucial role in QRNG. When a quantum system in a superposition state is measured, it collapses into a single definite state, yielding a random outcome based on the probabilities associated with each possible state. QRNG devices exploit this phenomenon by performing measurements on quantum systems, such as photons or electron spins, to extract random numbers with properties rooted in the inherent uncertainty of quantum mechanics.

In addition to understanding the fundamental concepts of quantum mechanics, it is crucial to explore the diverse physical processes employed in QRNG implementations. These processes leverage the unique properties of quantum systems to generate randomness and ensure the integrity of cryptographic operations and other security-sensitive tasks.

- ↣ *Photon detection* stands out as one of the most widely used techniques in QRNG devices. Photons, as fundamental particles of light, exhibit quantum properties such as superposition and polarisation, making them ideal candidates for generating random numbers. QRNG devices based on photon detection typically utilise specialised detectors, such as single-photon avalanche diodes (SPADs) or photomultiplier tubes (PMTs), to measure the arrival times or polarisation states of individual photons. By exploiting the inherently random nature of quantum phenomena at the photon level, these devices can generate unpredictable sequences of bits essential for cryptographic applications.
- ↣ Another intriguing avenue for QRNG involves tapping into the *fluctuations of the vacuum*, the state devoid of matter and electromagnetic fields. Vacuum fluctuations, governed by the principles of quantum field theory, give rise to spontaneous fluctuations in the electromagnetic field's energy density. QRNG devices based on vacuum fluctuations capitalise on this inherent randomness by measuring subtle fluctuations in electromagnetic fields using sensitive detectors. While challenging

to implement in practice due to technical constraints, vacuum-based QRNG holds promise for generating truly random numbers with minimal reliance on external sources.

- *Quantum tunnelling*, a phenomenon rooted in quantum mechanics, offers yet another pathway for generating randomness in QRNG systems. Quantum tunnelling occurs when particles, such as electrons, overcome potential energy barriers by tunnelling through them, defying classical notions of particle behaviour. QRNG devices leveraging quantum tunnelling exploit the probabilistic nature of this phenomenon to produce random numbers. By monitoring the tunnelling events of individual particles across nanoscale barriers, these devices can extract random bits with high entropy, ensuring cryptographic security and unpredictability.

Understanding the principles behind quantum uncertainty is essential for grasping the underlying mechanisms of randomness generation in QRNG. Quantum uncertainty arises from the probabilistic nature of quantum mechanics, which dictates that certain physical properties, such as particle position or momentum, cannot be precisely determined simultaneously. This inherent uncertainty forms the bedrock of quantum randomness, enabling QRNG devices to produce random numbers with properties rooted in the probabilistic nature of quantum phenomena. By embracing the principles of quantum uncertainty, QRNG technologies pave the way for enhanced security, privacy and reliability in cryptographic systems and beyond.

3.2.4 QRNG technologies

Quantum random number generation (QRNG) technologies encompass a diverse array of approaches, each leveraging unique physical phenomena rooted in quantum mechanics to produce truly random numbers. Exploring these technologies offers insights into their advantages, limitations and suitability for various applications across different domains.

Photonic-based QRNG (Table 3.1) relies on the principles of quantum optics to generate randomness by measuring properties of individual photons, such as their arrival times, polarisation states or phase shifts. One of the most common implementations of photonic QRNG involves using optical components like beam splitters, polarisers and single-photon detectors to manipulate and measure the quantum properties of photons.

Non-optical trusted device QRNGs include random number generators based on radioactive decays and other atomic systems and the systems based on electronic noise present in circuits. *Nuclear decay-based QRNG* (Table 3.2) exploits the inherently random nature of radioactive decay processes to generate unpredictable bit sequences. These devices typically involve detecting and timestamping radioactive decay events to extract random numbers. Certain contemporary random number generators that rely on radioactive decay employ semiconductor components instead of traditional GM tubes because they demand lower voltage for operation and offer enhanced convenience. Despite yielding weaker output signals, these semiconductor devices can be amplified more effectively, thereby streamlining the design process for the generators [23].

Electronic noise (Table 3.3), originating from the inherent fluctuations within electronic circuits, serves as a potential source of entropy for extracting randomness. Random number generators utilising electronic noise typically employ circuit elements such as resistors or diodes to generate this noise. The randomness arises due to the quantum nature of charge carriers within the circuit, governed by the uncertainty principle of quantum mechanics.

In addition to the methods discussed earlier, there are proposals to use *atomic systems* for random number generation. Trapped ions and spin noise of alkali metal vapour are examples. While these methods require complex setups and result in lower generation rates, they exploit quantum uncertainty to produce randomness. The spin noise of Rubidium vapour, probed optically,

Table 3.1 Advantages and limitations of photonic-based quantum random number generators (QRNGs).

Advantages	Limitations
High entropy generation rate: Photonic QRNG devices can achieve high bit rates due to the inherently random nature of photon emissions and detections.	Complexity and cost: Building and maintaining photonic QRNG systems can be complex and expensive due to the need for specialised optical components and precise alignment.
Strong security guarantees: Quantum properties of photons, such as superposition and entanglement, provide robust security against various attacks, including eavesdropping.	Susceptibility to environmental factors: External factors such as temperature fluctuations and optical noise can introduce biases or interfere with photon measurements, affecting the randomness of generated numbers.
Compatibility with fibre-optic networks: Photonic QRNG devices can be integrated seamlessly into existing fibre-optic communication infrastructures, making them suitable for secure communication applications.	Limited scalability: Scaling photonic QRNG systems to support high-throughput applications may pose challenges in terms of cost and complexity.

Table 3.2 Advantages and limitations of nuclear decay-based quantum random number generators (QRNGs).

Advantages	Limitations
High entropy per bit: Nuclear decay processes exhibit inherently random and unpredictable behaviour, resulting in high-quality random numbers with minimal bias.	Safety concerns: Handling radioactive materials for QRNG purposes requires adherence to strict safety protocols and regulations to mitigate potential health and environmental risks.
Independence from external factors: Unlike photonic and semiconductor-based QRNG, nuclear decay-based QRNG devices are less susceptible to environmental influences or technological limitations, ensuring robust randomness generation.	Efficiency over time: The presence of radioactivity can also have adverse effects on the detectors, leading to a decline in their efficiency over time.
	Limited scalability: Due to safety considerations and logistical constraints, scaling nuclear decay-based QRNG systems for widespread deployment may be impractical or cost-prohibitive.
Long-term stability: Radioactive decay processes have well-characterised decay rates and lifetimes, providing a stable and reliable source of randomness over extended periods.	Recovery period necessary: Additionally, the accumulation of ions inside the detector can result in detector dead-time, which presents a constraint. This dead-time necessitates a recovery period for GM tubes and semiconductor tubes to regain their full detection capabilities following a successful detection event.
	Complexity of implementation: Nuclear decay-based QRNG systems involve complex detection and measurement setups, which may pose challenges in terms of deployment and maintenance.

can be separated from background noise to generate random numbers. Solid-state systems have also shown promise in increasing bit generation rates.

The methods discussed thus far for generating random numbers rely heavily on trusting the devices involved. However, this trust may not hold in practical scenarios. Trusted QRNGs, which rely solely on the Q1 axiom for generating randomness, are susceptible to device defects or potential manipulation by adversaries, rendering the generated random numbers vulnerable. Therefore, it is essential to implement some form of testing system to verify the integrity of the random number generator's output sequence. These testing systems can monitor the internal state of the generator and alert the user to sudden failures or biases in the output. However, relying on such testing systems introduces another layer of trust, as the user must trust the checking device. Moreover, the implementations discussed so far cannot eliminate the

Table 3.3 Advantages and limitations of using electronic noise for quantum random number generators (QRNGs).

Advantages	Limitations
Quantum nature: The noise generated from electronic circuits, particularly shot noise, is inherently probabilistic due to the quantum behaviour of charge carriers. This intrinsic randomness can be harnessed for generating truly unpredictable random numbers.	Difficulty in isolating quantum effects: While shot noise theoretically offers pure quantum randomness, isolating these effects from other noise sources, such as thermal noise, presents a challenge. This difficulty compromises the extraction of randomness from shot noise in practical implementations.
Amplification potential: Once generated, electronic noise can be amplified, enhancing its suitability for random number generation applications.	Memory effects: Electronic noise, particularly shot noise, can exhibit memory effects wherein voltage spikes are influenced by previous charge flow in the diode. This dependency on past events can impact the quality and unpredictability of the randomness extracted from the noise.
Simplified implementation: The use of electronic noise as a source of entropy simplifies the design and implementation of random number generators, as it leverages readily available circuit components.	Practical constraints: Despite the potential advantages, electronic noise-based random number generators may face practical limitations, including issues related to circuit complexity, calibration and stability over time.

risk of malicious vendors supplying the checking devices. Without adequate testing systems, trusted device QRNGs cannot discern classical noise from genuine randomness, posing a security risk to the generated random numbers. Therefore, incorporating self-testing systems for security purposes is preferable. To address this, self-testing protocols have been proposed to verify the integrity of the random number generator's output sequence: Self-testing randomness amplification and self-testing random number expansion. These protocols monitor the internal state of the generator and detect any sudden failures or biases in the output.

In practical scenarios, certain components of a random number generation device may be thoroughly characterised while others are not. In such cases, it is possible to trust some parts of the device while disregarding details about others. This approach is particularly useful when focusing on device imperfections and noisy channels rather than potential adversarial threats. The security level of such a device falls between that of fully trusted devices and fully self-testing ones, representing a trade-off between performance, cost and credibility. Various devices of this nature can be considered depending on which part of the system is characterised.

- *Source device independent QRNGs* utilise uncharacterised randomness sources, with a trusted measurement device monitoring the source. Measurement bases are randomly chosen from a complementary pair to detect noise, exploiting uncertainty relations where Q1 alone suffices. An initial random seed is needed to select different measurement settings.
- *Measurement-device-independent QRNGs* generate randomness even when the input source is well characterised but the measurement device is untrusted. Randomly chosen states are used to validate the measurement device, acting as a complement to source-independent QRNGs.
- *Self-testing QRNGs with bounded dimensions* do not rely on trust in either the source or the measurement device. Instead, they assume a bound on the dimension of the system used and employ a witness to certify the randomness generation process. For instance, the preparation and measurement devices could operate within a two-dimensional quantum subspace. Any dimension witness value greater than 0 certifies randomness. However, these protocols typically have low generation rates, around 23 bps. The generator assumes no classical randomness is shared between the preparation and measurement devices.

3.2.5 Security properties

In an ideal scenario, quantum random number generators (QRNGs) feature high entropy generation rates, exhibit minimal bias, demonstrate robust resistance to tampering and offer unpredictable outputs, all of which are paramount for fortifying the security of cryptographic systems.

- *Entropy generation rate*: Entropy refers to the measure of randomness or unpredictability in a system. In the context of QRNGs, the entropy generation rate represents how quickly truly random numbers can be produced. Higher entropy generation rates mean that more random numbers can be generated in a given time frame, enhancing the security of cryptographic systems that rely on random inputs. Essentially, a high entropy generation rate ensures that cryptographic keys and other sensitive data are generated with sufficient randomness, making them harder to predict or crack by potential attackers.
- *Bias*: Bias refers to the deviation of the generated random numbers from a uniform distribution. In an ideal scenario, random numbers should be evenly distributed across all possible outcomes. Any deviation from this

uniform distribution introduces bias, which can be exploited by attackers to predict or manipulate the random numbers. QRNGs aim to minimise bias to ensure that the generated random numbers are truly unpredictable and unbiased, thus enhancing the security of cryptographic algorithms that rely on randomness.

- *Resistance to tampering*: QRNGs should be designed to resist tampering or manipulation attempts by adversaries. This involves ensuring the integrity and authenticity of the generated random numbers throughout the generation process. Any tampering with the QRNG could compromise the randomness of the output, making it susceptible to attacks. Therefore, QRNGs employ various techniques such as physical security measures, error detection and correction mechanisms to prevent or detect tampering attempts and maintain the integrity of the generated random numbers.

Overall, the security properties of QRNGs play a vital role in ensuring the robustness and resilience of cryptographic systems. By providing provably secure random numbers with high entropy generation rates, minimal bias, resistance to tampering and unpredictability, QRNGs serve as a cornerstone for enhancing the security of various cryptographic applications, including encryption, authentication and digital signatures.

3.2.6 Applications of QRNGs

Quantum random number generators (QRNGs) find applications across a wide array of domains, ranging from cryptography to scientific research. In cryptography, QRNGs play a pivotal role in generating truly random cryptographic keys, enhancing the security of communication networks, financial transactions and sensitive data storage. With the emergence of advanced communication technologies like 6G, as well as the widespread adoption of Internet of Things (IoT) devices and blockchain systems, the demand for secure random number generation has become increasingly critical. QRNGs provide a robust solution for ensuring the integrity and confidentiality of data exchanged over these networks by generating unpredictable random numbers that are resistant to cryptographic attacks. Beyond cryptography, QRNGs are utilised in gaming, gambling and simulations to introduce randomness, enhancing the realism and unpredictability of virtual environments. In scientific research, QRNGs are employed in various experiments and simulations where true randomness is essential, such as quantum physics, Monte Carlo simulations and random sampling techniques. Overall,

QRNGs serve as fundamental components in modern technology, safeguarding critical systems and enabling innovative applications across diverse fields.

3.2.7 Regulatory and standardisation considerations

Standardisation plays a crucial role in ensuring compliance with industry regulations and international standards when it comes to the use of quantum random number generators (QRNGs). These standards provide guidelines and benchmarks that help establish best practices, promote consistency and ensure the reliability and security of QRNG implementations across various industries and applications.

In different sectors such as finance, healthcare, telecommunications and defence, regulatory frameworks are in place to govern the use of QRNGs. These regulations often require adherence to specific standards to ensure the integrity and confidentiality of sensitive data. For example, in financial transactions, compliance with standards such as Payment Card Industry Data Security Standard (PCI DSS) and ISO 27001 is essential to protect against fraud and unauthorised access.

Furthermore, international standards bodies like the International Organization for Standardization (ISO) and the National Institute of Standards and Technology (NIST) develop and maintain standards related to random number generation and cryptographic algorithms. These standards define requirements for randomness, entropy generation and cryptographic protocols, providing a benchmark for evaluating the security and reliability of QRNGs.

Standardisation also plays a vital role in ensuring interoperability and trustworthiness of QRNG implementations. By adhering to established standards, QRNG manufacturers and developers can ensure that their products are compatible with existing systems and technologies. This interoperability fosters seamless integration and enables the exchange of random numbers across different platforms and devices.

Moreover, adherence to recognised standards enhances the trustworthiness of QRNGs in the eyes of users and regulators. Compliance with industry standards demonstrates a commitment to quality, security and reliability, instilling confidence in the integrity of QRNG solutions.

In summary, standardisation is essential for ensuring compliance with regulations, promoting interoperability and enhancing the trustworthiness of QRNG implementations. By following established standards and regulatory frameworks, organisations can mitigate risks, protect sensitive data and achieve greater confidence in the security of their systems and applications.

3.2.8 Practical considerations and implementation

When selecting and implementing quantum random number generator (QRNG) devices, several factors must be considered to ensure optimal performance and compatibility with specific use cases. These factors include speed, size, power consumption and integration requirements.

- *Speed*: The speed of a QRNG device determines how quickly it can generate random numbers. Depending on the application, high-speed QRNGs may be necessary for real-time encryption, while slower devices may suffice for applications with lower data throughput requirements.
- *Size*: The physical size of QRNG devices is crucial, especially for applications where space is limited, such as mobile devices or embedded systems. Compact QRNG modules are preferred for seamless integration into existing hardware platforms.
- *Power consumption*: QRNG devices should consume minimal power to extend battery life in portable devices and reduce energy costs in larger systems. Low-power QRNG solutions are essential for energy-efficient operation, especially in IoT devices and remote sensors.
- *Integration requirements*: Compatibility with existing systems and protocols is vital for seamless integration of QRNG devices into various applications. QRNGs should support standard interfaces and communication protocols to facilitate interoperability with other components and platforms.
- *Challenges and limitations*: Despite their advantages, QRNG technology faces challenges such as scalability, integration complexity and cost constraints. Ongoing research efforts focus on overcoming these limitations by developing scalable architectures, streamlining integration processes and reducing manufacturing costs.

Example of implementation: The IDQ Quantis QRNG platform is a commercially available QRNG device that utilises photon detection and interference to generate random numbers [24]. It is widely used in secure communication systems, cryptographic applications and research laboratories. Its use cases include Samsung Galaxy Quantum 4 smartphone, DocuSign Quantum Secured Electronic Signature, Thales TCT Luna T-Series HSM with embedded QRNG chip, EzQuant Security Key powered with

QRNG, Hitachi Energy Quantum-enhanced encryption cards, VoIP phone with Quantum-Enhanced Crypto module, NS&I Banking and Lottery QRNG, IDQ-Certes QRNG Solution Brief and Swiss Lottery QRNG. Quantis QRNG Chip received NIST Entropy Source Validation (ESV) Certification on IID Track in September 2023 [25]. These are the first quantum-based RNGs to receive NIST Entropy Source Validation (ESV) certification on IID Track.

3.2.9 Future outlook

The future of quantum random number generator (QRNG) technology is full of potential, driven by emerging trends and anticipated applications that will shape the landscape of security and data integrity in various domains. QRNG promises to overcome limitations of classical RNGs by harnessing quantum phenomena such as entanglement and superposition to generate truly unpredictable random numbers.

Scalability of QRNGs is an interesting question; enabling the creation of interconnected systems of QRNGs that can seamlessly generate random numbers on a large scale. These networks would offer enhanced reliability and redundancy, making them well-suited for applications requiring high levels of security and resilience.

Anticipated applications of QRNGs extend beyond traditional cryptographic protocols, encompassing emerging technologies such as quantum computing and the Internet of Things (IoT). In quantum computing, QRNGs are essential for generating random inputs to quantum algorithms and ensuring the security of quantum communication protocols. In the IoT space, QRNGs provide a foundation for securing interconnected devices and safeguarding data transmissions in smart networks.

Despite the promising outlook, widespread adoption of QRNG technology may face challenges and obstacles. These include technological barriers such as scalability and integration complexities, as well as regulatory and standardisation issues surrounding the certification and validation of QRNG devices. Additionally, concerns about the cost-effectiveness and accessibility of QRNG solutions may need to be addressed to ensure equitable access to secure random number generation technologies.

Looking ahead, QRNGs are poised to play a major role in the era of 6G and beyond, where the demand for secure and reliable data transmission will continue to grow. As quantum technologies mature and become more accessible, QRNGs could play a major role in secure communications infrastructure, providing the essential randomness needed to protect sensitive information in an increasingly interconnected world.

3.3 Post-quantum Cryptography

Post-quantum cryptography encompasses cryptographic algorithms that resist attacks not only from classical computers but also from quantum adversaries, including those armed with Shor's algorithm. The primary objective of post-quantum cryptography is to provide robust security in a quantum-computing landscape, ensuring the continued confidentiality and integrity of communications. Post-quantum cryptography refers to a subset of cryptographic algorithms designed to withstand attacks not only from classical computers but also from quantum adversaries, including those equipped with powerful algorithms like Shor's algorithm. The fundamental goal of post-quantum cryptography is to establish and maintain robust security in a landscape where quantum computing capabilities pose a significant threat to traditional cryptographic systems.

In traditional cryptographic systems, security relies on mathematical problems that are believed to be hard for classical computers to solve efficiently. However, the advent of quantum computers, which leverage quantum mechanics to perform computations at a vastly accelerated rate compared to classical computers, undermines the security assumptions of many classical cryptographic algorithms. Shor's algorithm, developed by mathematician Peter Shor in 1994, is particularly concerning for cryptographic systems as it can efficiently factor large integers and compute discrete logarithms, two problems at the core of widely used cryptographic schemes such as RSA and elliptic curve cryptography (ECC). With a sufficiently powerful quantum computer, Shor's algorithm could break these cryptographic schemes, compromising the confidentiality and integrity of encrypted communications. In response to the looming threat posed by quantum computing, post-quantum cryptography aims to develop alternative cryptographic algorithms that remain secure even in the presence of quantum adversaries. These algorithms are typically based on mathematical problems that are believed to be hard for both classical and quantum computers to solve. Examples include lattice-based cryptography, code-based cryptography, hash-based cryptography and multivariate polynomial cryptography, among others.

- ↣ *Lattice-based cryptography* stands out as one of the most promising avenues in the post-quantum era, providing mathematical frameworks that exhibit resilience against attacks from quantum adversaries. Unlike traditional cryptographic schemes that rely on the hardness of factoring large integers or computing discrete logarithms, lattice-based cryptography leverages the computational complexity of problems related to lattices in high-dimensional spaces. The security of lattice-based cryptography is rooted in the difficulty of solving certain lattice problems, such as the shortest vector problem (SVP) and the learning with errors (LWE) problem, which are believed to be hard even for quantum computers. These problems involve finding the shortest nonzero vector in a lattice or distinguishing random noisy linear equations from truly random ones, respectively. One of the key advantages of lattice-based cryptography is its versatility and flexibility in constructing various cryptographic primitives, including encryption, digital signatures and key exchange protocols. Lattice-based encryption schemes, such as the learning with errors-based encryption (LWE) and ring learning with errors (Ring-LWE), offer robust security guarantees while maintaining efficiency in terms of computational overhead and key sizes. Moreover, lattice-based cryptography exhibits desirable properties such as post-quantum security, provable security based on well-established mathematical assumptions and resistance against side-channel attacks. These attributes make lattice-based schemes suitable candidates for securing sensitive information in a wide range of applications, including secure communication over the internet, secure cloud computing and privacy-preserving data analytics. Research efforts in lattice-based cryptography continue to advance the state-of-the-art, with ongoing work focusing on optimising cryptographic primitives for performance, exploring new mathematical structures and addressing practical considerations for implementation in real-world systems. Standardisation initiatives, such as the NIST Post-Quantum Cryptography Standardisation project, play a crucial role in evaluating and standardising lattice-based cryptographic algorithms to ensure interoperability and adoption across diverse technological ecosystems.

↣ *Multivariate cryptography*, a branch of cryptography rooted in the complexity of solving systems of multivariate polynomial equations over finite fields, offers a promising avenue for achieving cryptographic security. Particularly, when these polynomials are of degree two, they are termed multivariate quadratics. Known to be NP-complete, solving such equations makes multivariate cryptography an attractive candidate for post-quantum cryptographic schemes. Despite its complexity, multivariate cryptography has undergone significant development and analysis, leading to the identification of robust schemes. Notably, multivariate cryptography has found particular success in signature schemes, providing shorter signatures compared to other post-quantum algorithms. Multivariate cryptography typically revolves around systems of multivariate quadratic equations, involving variables and coefficients represented as matrices or vectors. The security of the cryptosystem relies on the computational hardness of solving these equations. Similar to other asymmetric cryptographic systems, multivariate cryptography involves generating public and private keys. The public key, derived from a set of multivariate equations, is used for encryption, while the private key consists of secret parameters needed to solve the equations and is used for decryption. In multivariate cryptography, plaintext is encrypted using the public key, resulting in ciphertext that appears random and unintelligible without knowledge of the private key. Decryption involves solving the system of multivariate equations using the private key to recover the original plaintext. The security of multivariate cryptography relies on the presumed computational hardness of solving systems of multivariate equations. It assumes that solving these equations is computationally infeasible, even for adversaries with significant computational resources. Multivariate cryptography is believed to be resistant to quantum attacks, including those based on Shor's algorithm, which can efficiently break many traditional cryptographic systems. This makes multivariate cryptography an attractive option for post-quantum security. Multivariate cryptography can offer efficient implementations, particularly in hardware-constrained environments. The computational overhead of encryption and decryption operations can be relatively low compared to some other post-quantum cryptographic schemes. One of the challenges of multivariate cryptography is the potentially large key sizes required to achieve adequate security levels. This can impact performance, particularly in bandwidth-constrained scenarios. Furthermore, while multivariate cryptography is resistant to known quantum attacks, it may be susceptible to other types of cryptanalytic attacks. As with any cryptographic system, ongoing analysis and research are necessary to identify and address potential vulnerabilities. Multivariate cryptography is considered a promising candidate for post-quantum cryptographic schemes, offering resistance to quantum attacks while maintaining efficiency and practicality. Moreover, multivariate cryptography can be used for digital signatures, providing a means for authentication and non-repudiation in secure communication protocols. Finally, multivariate cryptography can be applied to secure messaging applications, ensuring the confidentiality and integrity of transmitted data in scenarios where traditional cryptographic systems may be vulnerable to quantum attacks. With ongoing research and development, multivariate cryptography holds promise for securing digital communications in the post-quantum era.

- *Hash-based cryptographic algorithms*, which rely on the security of hash functions, are another avenue of exploration. Hash-based cryptography, pioneered by Leslie Lamport and Ralph Merkle in the late 1970s, revolves around the creation of digital signature algorithms whose security is based on the robustness of a chosen cryptographic hash function. A hash function serves as a unique identifier for any given data, transforming plaintext of any size into a fixed-length ciphertext. Common cryptographic hash functions like SHA2, SHA3 or Blake2 produce digests ranging from 256 to 512 bits. The foundation of a hash-based signature scheme lies in a one-time signature scheme (OTS), where each key pair is used only once to sign a message to prevent signature forgery. Ralph Merkle proposed a method to extend this concept to sign multiple messages, which involves several steps:
    - Generating N separate Lamport key pairs, such as (PK_1, SK_1), ..., (PK_N, SK_N).
    - Assigning each public key to a leaf of a Merkle hash tree and computing the tree's root, which serves as the 'master' public key for the new Merkle signature scheme.
    - Retaining all Lamport public and secret keys for signing purposes.

A Merkle tree, also known as a hash tree, is a data structure where each leaf node represents the cryptographic hash value of a data block and each non-leaf node is labelled with the hash of its child nodes' labels. This structure enables efficient and secure verification of large data structures' contents. Various hash-based signature schemes, including extended Merkle signature scheme (XMSS), Leighton–Micali signature (LMS), SPHINCS and blockchained post-quantum signatures (BPQS), have been developed to improve performance and address specific use cases. These schemes differ in their statefulness, with some requiring the update of secret keys during signing. Notably, SPHINCS is a stateless scheme, while XMSS and LMS are stateful. SPHINCS, known for its larger signatures compared to XMSS and LMS, employs the HORST few-time signature mechanism, designed to enhance security. Looking ahead, NIST has selected three digital signature algorithms based on structured lattices – CRYSTALS-Dilithium, FALCON and SPHINCS+ – for standardisation to ensure quantum-safe digital signatures. Hash-based signatures are favoured due to their quantum-safe properties and established reliability.

- ↣ *Code-based cryptography* is a branch of public-key cryptography that relies on error-correcting codes for its security. Unlike other post-quantum cryptographic approaches that are based on mathematical problems believed to be hard for classical and quantum computers, code-based cryptography derives its security from the difficulty of decoding certain types of linear error-correcting codes. The fundamental idea behind code-based cryptography is to utilise the difficulty of decoding linear error-correcting codes as the basis for constructing cryptographic primitives such as encryption and digital signatures. These codes are used to introduce redundancy into transmitted messages, allowing the receiver to detect and correct errors introduced during transmission. One of the key advantages of code-based cryptography is its resistance to attacks from quantum computers. While many traditional cryptographic schemes, such as RSA and ECC, are vulnerable to attacks using quantum algorithms like Shor's algorithm, code-based cryptography remains secure even in the presence of quantum adversaries. This is because the best-known quantum algorithms for solving the decoding problem for linear codes, such as the Grover's search algorithm, offer only a quadratic speedup over classical algorithms, making them impractical for breaking code-based schemes with large key sizes. Furthermore, code-based cryptography has a long history and is well-studied, providing confidence in its security properties. It offers relatively efficient implementations and has been standardised by organisations such as NIST. However, one drawback of code-based cryptography is the larger key sizes required compared to some other post-quantum cryptographic approaches, which can impact performance and efficiency in certain scenarios.
- ↣ *Isogeny-based cryptography* is a relatively new and promising area of post-quantum cryptography that relies on the mathematical properties of isogenies, which are mappings between elliptic curves with certain algebraic properties. This cryptographic approach is based on the computational hardness of the isogeny problem, which involves finding the isogeny between two given elliptic curves. The core idea behind isogeny-based cryptography is to use the difficulty of computing isogenies as the foundation for cryptographic primitives such

as key exchange, digital signatures and encryption. The security of isogeny-based schemes relies on the assumption that finding the isogeny between two elliptic curves is a computationally hard problem, even for quantum computers. One of the most well-known isogeny-based cryptographic protocols is the Supersingular Isogeny Diffie–Hellman (SIDH) key exchange, proposed by David Jao, Luca De Feo and others. SIDH leverages the properties of supersingular elliptic curves and the difficulty of computing isogenies between them to establish a shared secret between two parties. Isogeny-based cryptography offers several advantages over other post-quantum cryptographic approaches. First, it is believed to be resistant to attacks from both classical and quantum computers, as the best-known quantum algorithms for solving the underlying computational problems offer only a limited speedup compared to classical algorithms. Additionally, isogeny-based schemes often have relatively compact key sizes and efficient implementations, making them suitable for resource-constrained environments. However, there are also challenges associated with isogeny-based cryptography. One notable challenge is the relatively slow key generation and computation times compared to some other post-quantum cryptographic approaches. Additionally, the security of isogeny-based schemes relies on the choice of parameters and the underlying mathematical assumptions, which need to be carefully analysed and standardised.

↣ *Symmetric key quantum resistance* refers to the resilience of symmetric cryptographic algorithms against attacks by quantum computers. Symmetric key cryptography relies on shared secret keys for both encryption and decryption processes and is widely used for securing data transmission and storage in various applications. In the context of symmetric key cryptography, the most significant threat from quantum computers comes from Grover's algorithm. Grover's algorithm is a quantum algorithm that can provide a quadratic speedup for certain types of search problems, including brute-force attacks on symmetric encryption keys. The implications of Grover's algorithm for symmetric key cryptography are twofold:

  → Key length doubling: Grover's algorithm reduces the effective key length of symmetric encryption algorithms by half. For example, a symmetric encryption algorithm with a 128-bit key, which is considered secure against classical brute-force attacks, would only provide 64 bits of security against quantum attacks. To maintain the same level of security against quantum adversaries, the key length needs to be doubled. Therefore, symmetric encryption algorithms with key lengths of 256 bits or more are typically recommended for post-quantum security.

→ Increased security margin: While Grover's algorithm reduces the effective key length, it does not completely break symmetric encryption algorithms. Instead, it halves the security margin provided by the key length. Therefore, even with quantum computers, symmetric encryption algorithms with sufficiently long keys can still offer practical security against brute-force attacks. However, to withstand potential quantum threats, it is advisable to use longer keys than those traditionally recommended for classical security.

Several symmetric encryption algorithms are believed to be quantum-resistant when used with sufficiently long keys. Examples include the Advanced Encryption Standard (AES) with 256-bit keys, the Keccak family of hash functions (including SHA-3) and the HMAC construction for message authentication. Provided one uses sufficiently large key sizes, symmetric key cryptographic systems like AES and SNOW 3G are already resistant to attack by a quantum computer. Further, key management systems and protocols that use symmetric key cryptography instead of public key cryptography, like Kerberos and the 3GPP mobile network authentication structure, are also inherently secure against attack by a quantum computer. Given its widespread deployment in the world already, some researchers recommend expanded use of Kerberos-like symmetric key management as an efficient way to get post-quantum cryptography today. Ongoing research and standardisation efforts continue to explore and develop symmetric key cryptographic techniques that offer robust protection against quantum adversaries.

Table 3.4 offers a comparative analysis of classical and post-quantum cryptographic algorithms, delineating their respective strengths and vulnerabilities. In the classical realm, cryptographic standards like RSA for encryption, Diffie-Hellman for key exchange, ECDSA for digital signatures and SHA-256 for hash functions have long been trusted for their proven security and widespread deployment. They have demonstrated efficient performance across various applications and are well-understood mathematically. However, with the advent of quantum computing, classical cryptographic algorithms face the looming threat of quantum attacks, which can compromise their security. To counter this threat, post-quantum cryptographic algorithms have emerged as quantum-resistant alternatives. These include

Table 3.4 Comparison chart between classical and post-quantum cryptographic algorithms, showcasing their strengths and vulnerabilities.

Cryptographic algorithm	Classical (pre-quantum)	Post-quantum
Encryption	RSA, AES, DES	Lattice-based, code-based, isogeny-based
Key exchange	Diffie-Hellman, ECDH	SIDH, NTRUEncrypt, NewHope
Digital signatures	RSA, ECDSA	Dilithium, Falcon, SPHINCS+
Hash functions	SHA-256, SHA-3	XMSS, Leighton-Micali, SPHINCS
Strengths	Proven security, widely deployed	Quantum-resistant, efficient
	Efficient performance in many applications	Suitable for various platforms
	Mathematically well-understood	Continuous development and research
Vulnerabilities	Vulnerable to quantum attacks	Potential for implementation issues
	Key exchange and digital signatures at risk	Limited deployment in production systems
	Limited scalability for key sizes	Key sizes and signature lengths may be larger

lattice-based encryption, code-based key exchange and isogeny-based digital signatures, among others. While still in the developmental stage, post-quantum algorithms offer the promise of security against quantum adversaries and are continuously evolving through research and innovation. Despite their quantum resilience, post-quantum cryptographic algorithms may present challenges in terms of implementation and efficiency. Key sizes and signature lengths may be larger compared to their classical counterparts, and there could be potential issues with deployment in production systems.

3.3.1 Real-world application

Ongoing efforts in implementing post-quantum cryptographic algorithms are essential for advancing the practical adoption of secure solutions in real-world applications. However, several challenges need to be addressed to ensure the efficiency, scalability and feasibility of these algorithms across diverse use cases.

- *Performance optimisation*: One of the primary challenges in implementing post-quantum cryptography is optimising performance to achieve acceptable levels of efficiency and speed. While post-quantum schemes offer strong security guarantees, they often come with higher computational overhead compared to classical cryptographic algorithms. Researchers are actively working on developing efficient algorithms and optimising parameters to reduce computational complexity and improve performance without compromising security.
- *Key size and bandwidth*: Post-quantum encryption schemes typically require larger key sizes compared to classical algorithms, which can pose challenges in terms of key management, storage and transmission bandwidth. Efforts are underway to explore techniques for reducing key sizes while maintaining security levels or developing alternative approaches to minimise the impact of larger keys on practical deployments.
- *Standardisation and interoperability*: Standardisation efforts are essential for ensuring interoperability and compatibility between different implementations of post-quantum cryptographic algorithms. Initiatives like the NIST Post-Quantum Cryptography Standardisation project play a vital role in evaluating and standardising post-quantum schemes, but ongoing collaboration and consensus-building among stakeholders are necessary to develop robust standards that address the diverse needs of various applications.
- *Hardware and software integration*: Implementing post-quantum cryptography in hardware and software platforms requires specialised expertise and infrastructure. Integration challenges arise from differences in computational capabilities, memory constraints and operating environments across different devices and systems. Research efforts focus on developing optimised software libraries, hardware accelerators and system architectures tailored to efficiently support post-quantum cryptographic operations.
- *Side-channel attacks and security assurance*: Like any cryptographic algorithm, post-quantum schemes are susceptible to side-channel attacks that exploit physical implementation characteristics such as power consumption or electromagnetic emissions. Mitigating side-channel vulnerabilities requires rigorous analysis, secure implementation practices and validation techniques to ensure the resilience of post-quantum systems against practical attack scenarios.

↣ *Education and awareness*: Promoting education and awareness about post-quantum cryptography among developers, system integrators and end-users is essential for fostering trust and confidence in these emerging technologies. Training programs, workshops and educational resources play a vital role in equipping stakeholders with the knowledge and skills needed to effectively implement and deploy post-quantum cryptographic solutions.

The ongoing efforts in implementing post-quantum cryptographic algorithms focus on addressing performance challenges, standardisation issues, integration complexities and security concerns to enable the widespread adoption of secure solutions in the post-quantum era. Collaborative research, industry partnerships and community engagement are essential for overcoming these challenges and realising the full potential of post-quantum cryptography in ensuring the confidentiality, integrity and authenticity of digital communications. Transitioning to post-quantum cryptography is a multifaceted process that requires a concerted effort from stakeholders across various domains. By educating, standardising, diversifying algorithms, ensuring interoperability, conducting pilot implementations, integrating with quantum-safe technologies, fostering collaborative research and aligning with regulatory frameworks, the cryptographic community can navigate this transition strategically, fortifying communication systems against the evolving threats posed by quantum adversaries. Research and development in post-quantum cryptography are ongoing, with the aim of identifying and standardising algorithms that offer strong security guarantees while also being efficient and practical for real-world applications. Standardisation efforts are crucial to ensure interoperability and widespread adoption of post-quantum cryptographic solutions across various domains, including communication networks, data protection and secure digital transactions.

3.3.2 Navigating transition strategies

As the era of quantum computing approaches, the cryptographic landscape is undergoing a significant transformation. Classical cryptographic algorithms, which have long served as the foundation of digital security, are facing an existential threat from quantum adversaries. To navigate this transition effectively and ensure the continued confidentiality and integrity of digital communications, it is imperative to adopt post-quantum cryptographic strategies.

This subchapter outlines key strategies for navigating the transition to post-quantum cryptography, encompassing education, standardisation, algorithmic diversity, interoperability, pilot implementations and integration with quantum key distribution (QKD), collaborative research initiatives and regulatory compliance frameworks. By embracing these strategies, stakeholders can proactively address the challenges posed by quantum computing while laying the groundwork for a secure and resilient cryptographic ecosystem. Now, the specific strategies for navigating this transition will be explored.

- ↣ *Educating stakeholders*: In the realm of educating stakeholders, it is imperative to establish a comprehensive awareness among industry stakeholders, including developers, policymakers and end-users, regarding the looming quantum threat and the indispensable necessity of transitioning to post-quantum cryptography. This entails disseminating information about the potential vulnerabilities posed by quantum computing to existing cryptographic systems and emphasising the urgency of adopting quantum-resistant algorithms as a proactive measure. To achieve this, stakeholders need to be educated about the distinctive characteristics of quantum-resistant algorithms and their pivotal role in future-proofing cryptographic systems against the impending quantum threat. This involves elucidating the fundamental principles underlying these algorithms, such as their resilience to attacks from quantum adversaries and their ability to maintain security in the face of quantum computing advancements. By fostering a deeper understanding of the significance of quantum-resistant algorithms, stakeholders can better appreciate the importance of embracing these innovative cryptographic solutions to safeguard sensitive data and ensure the integrity of communication channels in the quantum era.
- ↣ *Standardisation initiatives*: Within the landscape of standardisation initiatives, a pivotal strategy involves fostering global collaboration and active participation in international efforts aimed at standardising post-quantum cryptographic algorithms. By engaging in collaborative endeavours on a global scale, stakeholders can ensure a unified approach to transitioning away from vulnerable classical algorithms towards more resilient and quantum-safe cryptography solutions. One prominent initiative in this regard is led by the National Institute of Standards and Technology (NIST), which plays a central role in orchestrating the standardisation of post-quantum cryptographic algorithms. NIST's

efforts entail the evaluation, selection and validation of candidate algorithms through a rigorous and transparent process involving input from experts across academia, industry and government sectors. Emphasising the importance of adherence to recognised standards, NIST provides a framework for evaluating the security, efficiency and practicality of post-quantum cryptographic algorithms, thus guiding stakeholders in making informed decisions regarding their adoption and implementation. Through NIST's standardisation efforts, stakeholders gain access to a curated selection of vetted post-quantum cryptographic algorithms that meet stringent criteria for security and performance. By adhering to these established standards, stakeholders can ensure interoperability, compatibility and trustworthiness in the deployment of post-quantum cryptographic solutions, laying the foundation for a robust and resilient cryptographic ecosystem in the quantum era.

↣ *Algorithmic diversity*: As we navigate the transition towards post-quantum cryptography, embracing algorithmic diversity emerges as a pivotal strategy. Rather than relying solely on a single cryptographic approach, stakeholders are encouraged to adopt a diverse portfolio of post-quantum cryptographic algorithms. This multifaceted approach recognises that different algorithms may offer distinct advantages and excel in specific use cases, ensuring resilience and adaptability in the face of evolving threats. The portfolio approach advocates for the exploration and integration of various post-quantum cryptographic primitives, each with its unique properties and strengths. By diversifying cryptographic implementations, organisations can mitigate the risk of vulnerabilities associated with a single algorithm and enhance overall security posture. Moreover, a diverse portfolio enables stakeholders to tailor cryptographic solutions to specific application requirements, optimising performance and efficacy. Alongside the adoption of a diverse cryptographic portfolio, promoting flexibility in implementations is paramount. Recognising the dynamic nature of the cryptographic landscape, stakeholders should have the capability to seamlessly switch between algorithms based on evolving threat landscapes, technological advancements and emerging cryptographic standards. This flexibility empowers organisations to adapt their cryptographic strategies in real-time, proactively addressing emerging threats and vulnerabilities. By embracing algorithmic diversity and fostering flexibility in implementations, stakeholders can establish a robust and adaptive cryptographic framework capable of withstanding the challenges of quantum and classical adversaries. This strategic approach lays the foundation for building resilient cryptographic ecosystems that safeguard sensitive data and ensure long-term security in an ever-changing threat landscape.

↣ *Interoperability considerations*: In navigating the transition to post-quantum cryptography, careful consideration of interoperability emerges as a critical aspect of successful implementation. Interoperability refers to the ability of different cryptographic algorithms and systems to seamlessly communicate and operate together, ensuring smooth transitions and consistent security across diverse environments. A key aspect of interoperability is ensuring compatibility between various post-quantum cryptographic algorithms. Given the diverse landscape of cryptographic primitives available, stakeholders must prioritise interoperability to facilitate the integration and coexistence of different algorithms within cryptographic ecosystems. This entails developing standards, protocols and interfaces that enable effective communication and interaction between disparate cryptographic components. By ensuring compatibility, organisations can leverage the strengths of different post-quantum algorithms while maintaining a cohesive and interoperable security infrastructure. In addition to ensuring compatibility between cryptographic algorithms, stakeholders must also address the challenge of backward compatibility. Many existing systems and protocols rely on classical cryptographic algorithms that may not be quantum-resistant. As organisations transition to post-quantum cryptography, it is essential to develop strategies for maintaining backward compatibility with legacy systems while introducing and implementing new cryptographic measures. One approach to achieving backward compatibility is through the use of hybrid cryptographic schemes, which combine classical and post-quantum algorithms to provide transitional security solutions. By integrating post-quantum cryptographic primitives alongside traditional algorithms, organisations can ensure continued functionality and security in legacy systems while gradually transitioning to quantum-resistant solutions. Furthermore, establishing clear migration paths and transition strategies is crucial for minimising disruption and ensuring seamless integration of post-quantum cryptographic measures. This may involve phased deployments, gradual adoption of new standards and comprehensive testing to validate interoperability and compatibility across different environments. Overall, prioritising interoperability considerations and addressing backward compatibility challenges are essential steps in navigating the transition to post-quantum cryptography. By fostering compatibility and coexistence between diverse cryptographic systems, organisations can effectively future-proof their security infrastructure and mitigate the risks posed by quantum adversaries.

- *Pilot implementations*: As organisations navigate the transition to post-quantum cryptography, they must prioritise pilot implementations as a pivotal step in the process. Real-world testing of post-quantum cryptographic algorithms in practical settings offers invaluable opportunities for organisations to thoroughly assess their performance, uncover potential challenges and iteratively refine implementation strategies. By engaging in pilot programs, organisations can gain first-hand experience and insights into the practical implications of adopting post-quantum cryptographic measures. These insights serve to inform the development of best practices, deepen understanding of the impact on system performance and enable organisations to refine their transition strategies based on real-world experiences. Additionally, pilot implementations provide a platform for collaboration and knowledge sharing among stakeholders, fostering a collective effort towards the successful integration of post-quantum cryptography into existing cryptographic systems.
- *Quantum key distribution (QKD) integration*: In the context of navigating the transition to post-quantum cryptography, it is essential to consider the integration of quantum key distribution (QKD) as a complementary component in building comprehensive quantum-safe communication systems. By exploring the potential synergy between post-quantum cryptographic algorithms and QKD, organisations can leverage the strengths of both approaches to enhance the overall security posture. The integration of post-quantum cryptographic algorithms with QKD offers a promising avenue for bolstering the security of communication networks against both quantum and classical threats. QKD provides a mechanism for secure key distribution based on the principles of quantum mechanics, offering unparalleled levels of security against eavesdropping attacks. By combining QKD with post-quantum cryptographic algorithms, organisations can establish a robust and multifaceted defence strategy that addresses the evolving landscape of cybersecurity threats. In a combined defence strategy, QKD and post-quantum cryptography work in tandem to create a layered security architecture that mitigates vulnerabilities at multiple levels. QKD serves as the foundation for establishing secure communication channels by enabling the distribution of cryptographic keys with provable security guarantees. Post-quantum cryptographic algorithms complement this foundation by

providing additional layers of encryption and authentication, further fortifying the security of transmitted data. By integrating QKD and post-quantum cryptography, organisations can achieve a holistic approach to cybersecurity that ensures resilience against both current and future threats. This combined defence strategy enables organisations to stay ahead of emerging risks posed by quantum computing advancements while maintaining compatibility with existing cryptographic systems. Additionally, the synergy between QKD and post-quantum cryptography fosters innovation and collaboration within the cybersecurity community, driving the development of robust and interoperable solutions for securing communication networks in the quantum era.

↣ *Collaborative research initiatives*: Collaborative research initiatives play a pivotal role in addressing the multifaceted challenges associated with this paradigm shift. By fostering cross-industry collaboration involving academia, industry and government bodies, organisations can leverage collective expertise and resources to accelerate progress towards achieving quantum-safe cryptography solutions. Encouraging collaboration across diverse sectors, including academia, industry and government, is essential for tackling the complex challenges posed by the transition to post-quantum cryptography. By bringing together experts from different domains, organisations can leverage a wide range of perspectives and insights to develop innovative solutions and address critical research gaps. Collaborative research initiatives enable stakeholders to pool resources, share knowledge and coordinate efforts towards common goals, ultimately driving progress in the field of post-quantum cryptography. Furthermore, fostering an innovation ecosystem that supports research and development in post-quantum cryptographic algorithms is essential for ensuring a continuous pipeline of secure solutions. By investing in research infrastructure, funding opportunitics and interdisciplinary collaborations, organisations can create an environment conducive to innovation and discovery. An innovation ecosystem encourages the exploration of new ideas, methodologies and technologies, fuelling advancements in post-quantum cryptography. Moreover, it facilitates the translation of research findings into practical applications, driving the adoption of quantum-safe cryptography solutions across various industries and sectors. By promoting cross-industry collaboration and nurturing an innovation ecosystem, organisations can harness the collective expertise and creativity of diverse stakeholders to navigate the transition to post-quantum cryptography successfully.

These collaborative efforts not only advance the state-of-the-art in cryptographic research but also pave the way for the development of robust and resilient security solutions capable of addressing the challenges of the quantum era.

↣ *Regulatory and compliance frameworks*: Regulatory and compliance frameworks play a crucial role in shaping the adoption and implementation of post-quantum cryptographic measures, ensuring that organisations adhere to legal requirements and industry standards while navigating the transition to quantum-safe security solutions. Emphasising the need for regulatory bodies to adapt and align compliance frameworks with the transition to post-quantum cryptography is essential for fostering a regulatory environment that supports innovation while safeguarding sensitive information. Regulatory bodies must recognise the importance of addressing the emerging threat posed by quantum computing to cryptographic systems and take proactive measures to update existing regulations accordingly. By providing clear guidance and standards for the adoption of post-quantum cryptographic algorithms, regulatory bodies can promote the development and deployment of quantum-safe security solutions across various industries and sectors. Discussing legal implications and compliance considerations associated with the adoption of post-quantum cryptographic measures is critical for ensuring that organisations navigate the transition within legal boundaries and uphold regulatory requirements. As organisations transition to quantum-safe cryptographic algorithms, they must assess the legal implications of implementing new security measures, including data protection laws, intellectual property rights and contractual obligations. Additionally, compliance considerations such as data sovereignty, data residency requirements and industry-specific regulations must be taken into account to ensure compliance with applicable laws and regulations. By addressing regulatory and compliance considerations, organisations can mitigate legal risks, ensure compliance with relevant regulations and build trust with stakeholders. By working closely with regulatory bodies, industry associations and legal experts, organisations can navigate the transition to post-quantum cryptography effectively and lay the foundation for a secure and compliant future in the quantum era.

In conclusion, navigating the transition to post-quantum cryptography requires a multifaceted approach that encompasses various strategies and considerations. From educating stakeholders about the quantum threat and the importance of quantum-resistant algorithms to fostering global collaboration and standardisation efforts, each step plays a vital role in ensuring a smooth and secure transition. The adoption of a diverse portfolio of cryptographic algorithms, coupled with flexibility in implementations and interoperability considerations, is essential for building robust and resilient cryptographic systems capable of withstanding quantum attacks. Pilot implementations provide valuable insights into real-world performance and help refine transition strategies based on practical experiences. Moreover, the integration of quantum key distribution (QKD) with post-quantum cryptographic algorithms offers a combined defence strategy against quantum and classical threats, bolstering the security of communication systems. Collaborative research initiatives and the fostering of an innovation ecosystem further drive advancements in post-quantum cryptography, ensuring a continuous pipeline of secure solutions. Finally, alignment with regulatory and compliance frameworks is crucial for navigating the legal implications of transitioning to post-quantum cryptography and ensuring compliance with relevant regulations. By addressing these strategies comprehensively, organisations can effectively navigate the transition to post-quantum cryptography and lay the groundwork for a secure digital future in the quantum era.

3.3.3 Standardisation initiatives: Fortifying 6G against quantum threats

In anticipation of the advent of 6G networks and the looming quantum threat, standardisation initiatives are emerging as crucial endeavours aimed at fortifying 6G against potential quantum vulnerabilities. As the telecommunications industry prepares to usher in the next generation of wireless technology, the spectre of quantum computing poses unprecedented challenges to conventional cryptographic methods. To mitigate these risks and ensure the security and integrity of 6G networks in the quantum era, concerted efforts are underway to establish standardised frameworks and protocols for quantum-resistant communication technologies. This chapter explores the pivotal role of standardisation initiatives in enhancing the quantum resilience of 6G networks, highlighting key strategies, collaborations and regulatory considerations driving this critical aspect of 6G development.

- *NIST post-quantum cryptography standardisation*: The National Institute of Standards and Technology (NIST) is an agency of the US Department of Commerce aimed at fostering American innovation and enhancing industrial competitiveness [26]. Its work spans various scientific areas, such as nanotechnology, engineering and information technology. Previously known as the National Bureau of Standards from 1901 to 1988, NIST continues to advance research and development across multiple sectors. As the vanguard of cryptographic research and standardisation, the National Institute of Standards and Technology (NIST) holds a pivotal position in the realm of post-quantum cryptography. In response to the looming threat posed by quantum computing to traditional cryptographic algorithms, NIST has embarked on a comprehensive standardisation effort aimed at fortifying the security landscape for future generations of communication networks. At the heart of NIST's standardisation initiative lies a rigorous and multi-round evaluation process designed to scrutinise the security, efficiency and practical feasibility of candidate post-quantum cryptographic algorithms. This process involves soliciting submissions from cryptographic researchers and developers worldwide, followed by successive rounds of evaluation and feedback. Throughout each round, algorithms undergo extensive scrutiny through cryptographic analysis, algorithmic performance assessment and real-world implementation testing. Against the backdrop of the impending rollout of 6G networks, NIST's standardisation efforts take on heightened significance. By providing a standardised framework for evaluating and selecting quantum-resistant cryptographic algorithms, NIST equips stakeholders in the telecommunications industry with essential tools to safeguard the integrity and confidentiality of communication in the 6G landscape. Moreover, NIST's standardised algorithms serve as the cornerstone for the development and deployment of secure communication protocols, ensuring that 6G networks are resilient against the looming quantum threat.

↣ *NIST's post-quantum cryptography (PQC) competition* stands as a landmark initiative, offering a comprehensive platform for evaluating and standardising cryptographic algorithms in the face of quantum threats. This structured competition format, initiated by NIST, serves as a global call to action, inviting submissions of candidate algorithms from researchers and institutions worldwide. The competition facilitates a rigorous assessment process, meticulously scrutinising each algorithm for its security, efficiency and practical implementation considerations. One of the key strengths of the NIST PQC competition lies in its embrace of diverse algorithmic approaches. Researchers are encouraged to explore a spectrum of cryptographic methodologies, ranging from lattice-based and hash-based schemes to code-based and multivariate polynomial cryptography. This diversity fosters innovation and ensures that a wide array of potential solutions is considered in the quest for quantum-resistant algorithms. The significance of the NIST PQC competition extends far beyond the realm of academia and research laboratories. It directly addresses the pressing need for standardised cryptographic algorithms that can withstand the disruptive capabilities of quantum computers. As we look towards the advent of 6G networks, characterised by unprecedented levels of connectivity and data exchange, the security of these networks becomes paramount. The algorithms emerging from the NIST PQC competition are poised to play a pivotal role in fortifying the security posture of 6G networks, safeguarding sensitive information and critical infrastructure against emerging quantum threats. In July 2022, NIST announced the winners of the PQC competition and has chosen to standardise four algorithms: CRYSTALS-Kyber for key encapsulation mechanism (KEM) and CRYSTALS-Dilithium, Falcon and SPHINCS+ for digital signatures [27]. Kyber and Dilithium are the main algorithms slated for widespread application, both being cryptographic techniques rooted in structured lattices. Falcon serves as an alternative in scenarios where Dilithium's signatures might exceed desired lengths, while SPHINCS+ offers diversity by providing a non-lattice-based signature algorithm to complement the others. While the initial selection of standardised algorithms has been made, the NIST PQC competition persists with its fourth round, featuring four key encapsulation mechanism (KEM) algorithms: BIKE, Classic McEliece, HQC and SIKE. Both BIKE and HQC utilise structured codes, making them viable options as general-purpose key encapsulation mechanisms (KEMs) that do not rely on lattices. NIST anticipates selecting at most one of these candidates for standardisation upon the completion of the fourth round. SIKE remains a compelling candidate for standardisation due to its compact key and ciphertext sizes. NIST will continue to evaluate SIKE in the fourth round. Although Classic McEliece was a finalist, NIST has opted not to standardise it at this time. While Classic McEliece is considered secure, its large public key size may limit its widespread adoption. NIST may revisit the possibility of standardising Classic McEliece at the conclusion of the fourth round.

↣ *ISO/IEC quantum-safe cryptography working group*: International Organization for Standardization (ISO) and International Electrotechnical Commission (IEC) are two prominent international standard-setting bodies that play essential roles in developing and promoting standards across various industries [28, 29]. ISO focuses on standardisation in fields such as technology, manufacturing and services, while IEC specialises in standards related to electrical, electronic and related technologies. Both organisations facilitate global collaboration and consensus-building among stakeholders to address common challenges and promote innovation.

The quantum-safe cryptography working group, established jointly by ISO and IEC, represents a collaborative effort to address the growing concern over quantum threats to cryptographic systems. This working group brings together experts from around the world to develop standardised approaches for quantum-safe cryptography. Its primary objective is to create a roadmap for standardisation, providing guidelines and recommendations for the implementation of cryptographic solutions that are resilient against quantum attacks. By establishing global standards through the quantum-safe cryptography working group, ISO and IEC aim to ensure interoperability and compatibility among cryptographic implementations across different industries and regions. The ISO/IEC joint technical committee (JTC) 1 began exploring the challenges and opportunities posed by quantum computing and quantum technologies in 2015, initially focusing on the study of post-quantum cryptography [30]. In 2018, JTC 1 expanded its efforts to evaluate standardisation possibilities in quantum computing. This led to the formation of a dedicated quantum computing working group in 2020, which later transitioned into the quantum information technology working group in 2022. Currently, this group has been assigned two approved projects and three preliminary work items, highlighting its ongoing dedication to advancing standards in quantum information technology. This collaborative effort is crucial for 6G networks, where secure communication is paramount. Standardisation in quantum-safe cryptography will help safeguard these networks against emerging quantum threats, enabling a unified defence strategy and fostering trust in the security of communications infrastructure.

↣ *ETSI cyber quantum safe cryptography (QSC) working group*: The European Telecommunications Standards Institute (ETSI) serves as a pivotal organisation in the telecommunications industry, tasked with developing globally applicable standards for information and communication technologies (ICT). Founded in 1988, ETSI operates as an independent, not-for-profit organisation based in Sophia Antipolis, France. It brings together a diverse array of stakeholders, including manufacturers, network operators, service providers, regulators and academia, to collaborate on the development of technical standards that facilitate interoperability, efficiency and innovation in telecommunications. ETSI's work encompasses a wide range of areas, from network architecture and protocols to cybersecurity, IoT and emerging technologies such as quantum-safe cryptography. Through its consensus-based approach and extensive expertise, ETSI plays a vital role in driving forward the evolution of telecommunications infrastructure and ensuring the seamless integration of new technologies into global networks. ETSI plays a major role in shaping the landscape of telecommunications standards, including those related to quantum-safe cryptography. At the forefront of this effort is ETSI's quantum-safe cryptography (QSC) working group, a dedicated body focused on the development of standards and specifications for quantum-safe cryptographic solutions [31]. This group brings together industry experts, researchers and stakeholders to collaborate on defining robust cryptographic protocols that can withstand quantum attacks. One of the key strengths of ETSI's approach lies in its emphasis on industry integration. By actively involving industry stakeholders in the standardisation process, ETSI ensures that the developed standards are not only technically sound but also practical and relevant to real-world applications. This collaborative approach fosters the exchange of ideas, expertise and best practices, resulting in standards that reflect the diverse needs and perspectives of the telecommunications industry. Moreover, ETSI's initiatives are closely aligned with the evolving security needs of future telecommunications networks, including 6G. As the telecommunications landscape continues to evolve, with increasing reliance on interconnected devices, edge computing and high-speed data transmission, the importance of robust security measures cannot be overstated. ETSI's standards provide a framework for standardised post-quantum cryptographic implementations that are tailored to the specific requirements of 6G networks. By addressing security concerns at the protocol level, ETSI contributes to the development of a secure and resilient telecommunications infrastructure capable of withstanding emerging threats, including those posed by quantum computing. In August 2020, the ETSI quantum-safe cryptography (QSC) working group announced the release of Technical Report TR 103 619 [32], outlining migration strategies and recommendations for quantum-safe schemes, aimed to raise awareness of cryptography across diverse business sectors . The growing threat posed by quantum computing to asymmetric cryptography had been extensively acknowledged, prompting the need for proactive measures within various industries reliant on asymmetric cryptography. ETSI emphasised the necessity for businesses to prepare for migration towards a fully quantum-safe cryptographic state (FQSCS). The technical report underscored the importance of increasing awareness regarding cryptography's role and integration depth within organisations, advocating for encrypted data transmission with foresight into potential future vulnerabilities. Scott Cadzow, the rapporteur of the technical report in the ETSI QSC group, highlighted the significance of bolstering cryptography awareness to mitigate potential harvesting attacks. The migration framework, delineated in the technical report, encompassed three key stages: inventory compilation, preparation of the migration plan and migration execution. The initial stage emphasised the imperative of compiling an inventory of assets susceptible to quantum computing impact, requiring dedicated managerial oversight and resource allocation. Subsequent planning stages focused on meticulous preparation and execution, treating migration as a structured business process. While migration aimed for like-for-like protection of cryptographic assets, the planning phase acknowledged potential asset redesigns or retirements. Lastly, the technical report furnished comprehensive checklists to guide the management and planning of migration efforts effectively.

↣ *Collaboration with academic and industry partners*: In the realm of post-quantum cryptography standardisation, collaboration extends beyond the confines of formal standardisation bodies to encompass a diverse array of stakeholders, including academia, industry experts and cryptographic researchers. This collaborative approach fosters an environment of knowledge exchange, where insights from various domains contribute to the refinement and enhancement of cryptographic solutions. By engaging with academic institutions, industry partners and research communities, standardisation bodies can leverage a wealth of expertise and perspectives to address complex challenges and explore innovative approaches to cryptographic security. Furthermore, collaboration ensures that standardised post-quantum cryptographic algorithms are not only robust but also comprehensive and effective in mitigating emerging threats. In the context of 6G security readiness, this collaborative effort plays a crucial role in ensuring that cryptographic standards are adaptive and resilient, capable of safeguarding communication networks against the evolving landscape of quantum and classical threats.

In navigating the transition to post-quantum cryptography, understanding the anticipated timeline for the finalisation of cryptographic standards is paramount. Organisations such as NIST, ISO/IEC and ETSI are actively engaged in the standardisation process, with ongoing initiatives aimed at evaluating and selecting quantum-resistant algorithms. While the exact timeline may vary depending on the complexity of the evaluation process and the consensus-building efforts within these organisations, there is a shared commitment to expeditiously finalise standards that meet the stringent security requirements of 6G networks.

Moreover, alongside the timeline for standardisation, the development of an implementation roadmap is equally essential. An implementation roadmap provides a structured approach for organisations and industries to transition from classical to post-quantum cryptographic solutions seamlessly. This roadmap encompasses various stages, including assessment of existing cryptographic infrastructure, identification of critical systems requiring migration, selection and integration of post-quantum algorithms and comprehensive testing and validation processes. By adhering to a well-defined implementation roadmap, organisations can effectively navigate the complexities of transitioning to quantum-resistant cryptography, ensuring the security and resilience of their communication networks in the era of 6G.

In conclusion, standardisation initiatives led by organisations such as NIST, ISO/IEC and ETSI represent a concerted global effort to prepare for the quantum threat in the 6G landscape. These initiatives provide a structured and collaborative approach to developing and adopting post-quantum cryptographic standards, ensuring the robustness of communication systems against the evolving challenges posed by quantum adversaries in the next generation of networks.

3.4 AI-driven Threat Detection

The upcoming chapter delves into the multifaceted realm of AI-driven threat detection, offering a comprehensive spectrum of insights that traverse technical intricacies to ethical dilemmas. By looking at different aspects, it seeks to give a complete understanding of how artificial intelligence and cybersecurity are connected.

Advancements in technology and emerging threats continually reshape the landscape of cybersecurity, with artificial intelligence (AI) and machine learning (ML) emerging as pivotal tools to fortify defence systems and identify novel risks. Over recent years, numerous cybersecurity studies have integrated AI and ML methodologies, marking a significant trend in the field. Notably, AI and ML show promise in bolstering intrusion detection and response (IDR) mechanisms, pivotal for identifying and mitigating system breaches. Leveraging decision trees, neural networks and support vector machines, these systems have demonstrated enhanced accuracy and adaptability to evolving attack strategies. Additionally, AI and ML have found application in malware detection, a critical component in safeguarding against malicious software. By employing similar algorithms, researchers have developed systems adept at recognising new threats and adapting to changing malware patterns. Moreover, AI and ML technologies have made significant strides in reinforcing network security measures, offering advanced capabilities to combat threats like distributed denial-of-service (DDoS) attacks and unauthorised network infiltrations. Network security systems infused with AI and ML can effectively monitor network traffic, identify anomalies and swiftly respond to suspicious activities. Beyond these applications, AI and ML also hold promise in automating security processes, enhancing threat intelligence and streamlining security management tasks. However, while AI and ML stand to enhance cybersecurity, they also introduce challenges such as model interpretability, biases and potential errors, underscoring the need for ongoing research and development in the field.

3.4.1 Intrusion detection and response

IDR stands for intrusion detection and response. It is a critical component of cybersecurity strategies aimed at identifying and mitigating threats to computer networks and systems. Intrusion detection refers to the process of monitoring network traffic and system activities for signs of malicious behaviour or security policy violations. This is typically done through the use of specialised software and hardware sensors deployed throughout the network. These sensors analyse network packets, system logs and other data sources to detect anomalies that may indicate a security breach. There are two main types of intrusion detection systems (IDS):

- ↣ *Network-based IDS (NIDS)*: These systems monitor network traffic in real-time, searching for patterns indicative of known attack signatures or unusual behaviour. Some key aspects of NIDS are:
  - → *Passive monitoring*: NIDS passively monitor network traffic by analysing packets as they pass through the network. Unlike firewalls, which actively block or allow traffic based on predefined

rules, NIDS operate in a non-intrusive manner, observing network activity without directly affecting it.

- → *Packet inspection*: NIDS inspect network packets at the protocol level, examining header information and payload content to identify patterns indicative of known attack signatures or suspicious behaviour. This analysis allows NIDS to detect a wide range of threats, including malware infections, denial-of-service (DoS) attacks and unauthorised access attempts.
- → *Signature-based detection*: One of the primary methods used by NIDS is signature-based detection, which involves comparing observed network traffic to a database of known attack signatures. These signatures are predefined patterns or characteristics associated with specific types of attacks or malicious activity. When a match is found between observed traffic and a known signature, the NIDS generates an alert or takes action to block the malicious activity.
- → *Anomaly detection*: In addition to signature-based detection, some NIDS incorporate anomaly detection techniques to identify deviations from normal network behaviour. Anomaly detection algorithms analyse network traffic patterns and statistical metrics to detect unusual activity that may indicate a security breach. This approach can help detect previously unknown or zero-day attacks that do not match any known signatures.
- → *Alerting and reporting*: When suspicious activity is detected, NIDS generate alerts to notify security personnel or administrators of potential security incidents. These alerts typically include details about the detected activity, such as the source and destination IP addresses, the type of attack and the severity level. NIDS may also provide reporting capabilities for analysing historical network traffic and identifying trends or patterns indicative of security risks.
- → *Scalability*: NIDS are designed to scale across large and complex network environments, monitoring traffic across multiple network segments and locations. They can be deployed at strategic points within the network, such as at network boundaries, critical infrastructure points, or in the cloud, to provide comprehensive coverage and visibility.

↣ *Host-based IDS (HIDS)*: A host-based intrusion detection system (HIDS) is a cybersecurity tool designed to monitor and analyse activity on individual computer systems or endpoints. Unlike network-based IDS (NIDS), which operates at the network level, HIDS focuses on the internal activity of a single host, such as a server, desktop or mobile device. Some key aspects of HIDS are:

→ *System-level monitoring*: HIDS monitors various aspects of a host system's activity, including file system changes, log file entries, system calls, registry modifications (in the case of Windows systems), network connections and running processes. By analysing this data, HIDS can detect signs of unauthorised access, malware infections and other security threats.

→ *Agent-based deployment*: HIDS typically operates using software agents installed directly on the host systems being monitored. These agents continuously collect and analyse data related to system activity, comparing it against known attack signatures, behavioural profiles and policy rules to identify potential security incidents.

→ *Signature-based detection*: Similar to NIDS, HIDS often employs signature-based detection techniques to identify known patterns or signatures of malicious activity. These signatures may include specific sequences of system calls, file hashes associated with malware or other indicators of compromise.

→ *Anomaly detection*: In addition to signature-based detection, some HIDS systems utilise anomaly detection techniques to identify deviations from normal system behaviour. By establishing a baseline of typical system activity, HIDS can detect unusual patterns or behaviours that may indicate a security breach or compromise.

→ *Alerting and response*: When suspicious activity is detected, HIDS generates alerts and notifications to alert system administrators or security teams. These alerts typically include details about the detected event, such as the type of activity, affected system or user, severity level and timestamp. Security personnel can then investigate the alert and take appropriate response actions to mitigate the threat.

Intrusion response, on the other hand, refers to the actions taken in response to detected security incidents. This may involve isolating compromised systems, blocking malicious network traffic and implementing corrective measures to prevent further damage. The intrusion detection and response process typically involves the following steps:

- *Monitoring*: Continuous monitoring of network traffic, system logs and other data sources for signs of suspicious activity.
- *Detection*: Analysing monitored data to identify potential security incidents or policy violations. This may involve the use of signature-based detection, anomaly detection or machine learning algorithms to identify known threats or unusual behaviour.
- *Alerting*: Notifying security personnel or administrators when potential security incidents are detected. This allows for timely response and mitigation efforts.
- *Analysis*: Investigating detected incidents to determine the nature and scope of the security breach. This may involve forensic analysis of network traffic, system logs and other digital evidence to understand how the attack occurred and what data may have been compromised.
- *Response*: Taking appropriate actions to contain and mitigate the impact of the security incident. This may involve isolating compromised systems, blocking malicious traffic and implementing security patches or configuration changes to prevent similar incidents in the future.

Overall, IDR plays a crucial role in defending against cyber threats by providing early detection and rapid response to security incidents, helping organisations protect their networks, data and critical assets from unauthorised access and malicious activity. The integration of AI/ML intrusion detection techniques has significantly improved the performance of intrusion detection and response (IDR) systems in identifying and addressing potential security threats. There are various AI and ML intrusion detection techniques which all come along with their advantages and challenges. These techniques underscore the diverse approaches to enhancing intrusion detection within cybersecurity systems.

- *Anomaly detection*, within the realm of intrusion detection, is widely recognised for its effectiveness in identifying previously unseen or unknown threats within a network or system. Unlike traditional signature-based detection methods that rely on known patterns of malicious activity, anomaly detection techniques can uncover suspicious behaviour that deviates from established norms or baseline activities. This capability is particularly valuable in detecting novel threats or sophisticated attacks that may not have been encountered before. However, despite its effectiveness in flagging potential security issues, anomaly detection faces a significant challenge in distinguishing between benign anomalies and truly malicious activities. In any complex system, there may be numerous legitimate reasons for deviations from the norm, such as system upgrades, changes in user behaviour or fluctuations in network traffic due to legitimate activities. As a result, anomaly detection systems must strike a delicate balance between identifying genuine threats and minimising false positives caused by harmless anomalies. Achieving this balance requires sophisticated algorithms and robust modelling techniques that can accurately differentiate between normal variations and abnormal behaviour indicative of a security breach. Furthermore, anomaly detection systems often rely on comprehensive contextual information, such as historical data, user profiles and system configurations, to better understand the underlying context of detected anomalies. Incorporating such contextual information enables the system to make more informed decisions about the severity and potential threat posed by each anomaly. Advances in machine learning and artificial intelligence continue to drive innovation in anomaly detection, improving its accuracy, efficiency and ability to adapt to evolving cybersecurity threats.

↣ *Supervised learning* is a powerful machine learning technique that excels in detecting known threats within intrusion detection systems. In supervised learning, the algorithm is trained on a labelled dataset, where each data point is associated with a corresponding label indicating its class or category. For instance, in the context of intrusion detection, the labelled dataset may consist of network traffic data, where each data instance is labelled as either normal or malicious activity. The key advantage of supervised learning lies in its ability to achieve high accuracy in classifying data instances based on the patterns and features learned during the training phase. By learning from labelled examples of known threats, the supervised learning algorithm can effectively discern between normal network behaviour and malicious activities that match known attack signatures or patterns. This enables the intrusion detection system to accurately identify and classify incoming data instances, thereby providing a reliable means of detecting known threats. However, the effectiveness of supervised learning in intrusion detection is contingent upon the availability of high-quality labelled training data. Building a robust labelled dataset often requires significant human effort and domain expertise to accurately annotate data instances with the appropriate labels. Moreover, maintaining the relevance and representativeness of the labelled dataset over time can be challenging, particularly in dynamic and evolving cybersecurity landscapes where new threats constantly emerge. Additionally, supervised learning models may struggle to generalise well to unseen or unknown threats that deviate significantly from the patterns observed in the training data. This limitation underscores the importance of regularly updating and diversifying the labelled dataset to encompass a wide range of potential threats and attack scenarios. Without sufficient diversity in the training data, supervised learning algorithms may fail to effectively detect novel or previously unseen threats, leaving the system vulnerable to emerging cybersecurity risks. Despite these challenges, supervised learning remains a valuable tool in the arsenal of intrusion detection systems, offering high accuracy and reliability in detecting known threats when coupled with comprehensive and up-to-date labelled training data. Continued advancements in data labelling techniques, dataset curation and algorithmic approaches hold the potential to further enhance the effectiveness of supervised learning in cybersecurity applications.

↣ *Unsupervised learning* represents a valuable approach in the realm of intrusion detection, offering the capability to detect new and previously unseen threats without relying on labelled training data. Unlike supervised learning, which requires labelled examples of known threats for training, unsupervised learning algorithms operate on unlabelled data, allowing them to uncover hidden patterns and anomalies inherent in the data without prior knowledge of attack signatures or patterns. One of the key advantages of unsupervised learning is its ability to autonomously identify novel threats and anomalies within network traffic or system logs, making it particularly well-suited for detecting previously unseen attack patterns or emerging cybersecurity threats. By analysing the inherent structure and distribution of the data, unsupervised learning algorithms can detect deviations from normal behaviour that may indicate the presence of malicious activity, even in the absence of explicit labels. However, despite its efficacy in detecting unknown threats, unsupervised learning approaches face inherent challenges in interpretability and explainability. Unlike supervised learning models, which learn to classify data based on labelled examples with clear class distinctions, unsupervised learning algorithms often produce results that are more difficult to interpret and explain. This lack of interpretability stems from the fact that unsupervised learning algorithms operate solely based on the intrinsic structure of the data, without explicit guidance on the nature or significance of the detected anomalies. As a result, while unsupervised learning algorithms may successfully identify anomalous behaviour indicative of potential threats, understanding the underlying reasons behind these detections and providing meaningful explanations for the observed anomalies can be challenging. This limitation poses obstacles to the adoption and deployment of unsupervised learning-based intrusion detection systems, particularly in contexts where interpretability, transparency and accountability are essential considerations. Despite these challenges, ongoing research efforts are focused on addressing the interpretability and explainability issues associated with unsupervised learning approaches, aiming to develop more transparent and understandable intrusion detection systems. By leveraging techniques such as anomaly visualisation, feature importance analysis and model introspection, researchers seek to enhance the interpretability of unsupervised learning models and provide actionable insights into the detected threats, thereby facilitating their adoption and integration into real-world cybersecurity environments.

The adoption of AI/ML intrusion detection techniques has significantly improved the effectiveness of intrusion detection and response (IDR) systems in identifying and mitigating potential threats. However, several challenges must be overcome to fully leverage the potential of AI and ML in cybersecurity. Addressing issues such as enhancing the interpretability of AI/ML models, managing imbalanced datasets and reducing false alarms are critical for the development of robust AI/ML-based IDR systems in the future.

Protecting computer networks and systems from unauthorised access, misuse and disruption is imperative in maintaining network security. Traditional security methods may fall short in addressing evolving threats, prompting the integration of artificial intelligence (AI) and machine learning (ML) techniques. These advanced approaches are designed to detect unknown threats and adapt to changing attack patterns. In the realm of network security and protection tools, the integration of artificial intelligence (AI) and machine learning (ML) techniques offers a promising avenue for enhancing threat detection and response capabilities.

- ↣ *Behaviour-based intrusion*: In the realm of network security and protection tools, behaviour-based intrusion detection systems play a pivotal role in safeguarding computer networks against potential cyber threats. These systems utilise advanced AI algorithms to meticulously analyse and understand normal network behaviour, establishing a baseline against which anomalies are identified and classified. By discerning deviations from established behavioural norms, these intrusion detection systems can effectively flag potential cyberattacks, enabling timely response and mitigation efforts. However, despite their efficacy, these systems encounter challenges when confronted with new or previously unknown threats. Their reliance on established behavioural patterns may render them less accurate in detecting emerging threats that deviate significantly from existing norms. Consequently, while behaviour-based intrusion detection systems serve as valuable tools in network security, their effectiveness in addressing novel threats may be somewhat limited.

- *Unsupervised learning*: In the context of network security and protection tools, unsupervised learning techniques offer a distinct advantage in identifying irregular patterns within network traffic, which could signify the presence of previously unidentified cyber threats. By autonomously analysing vast volumes of network data, unsupervised learning algorithms can discern deviations from established behavioural norms, thus flagging suspicious activities that may indicate a cyberattack. This capability to detect novel threats without relying on predefined labels or training data makes unsupervised learning particularly valuable in environments where emerging threats are prevalent. However, a notable challenge associated with unsupervised learning techniques is their limited interpretability and explainability. Unlike supervised learning methods, which rely on labelled data to train models with explicit knowledge of desired outcomes, unsupervised learning algorithms operate without clear guidance, often resulting in difficulty in understanding and interpreting the rationale behind their decisions. Consequently, while unsupervised learning holds promise for enhancing network security by identifying unknown threats, efforts to improve interpretability and explainability are essential to fully leverage its potential in real-world applications.
- *Reinforcement learning*: In the realm of network security and protection tools, reinforcement learning offers a valuable approach to optimising the behaviour and decision-making processes of security systems. By employing reinforcement learning techniques, these systems can continuously adapt and refine their strategies in response to evolving cyber threats and dynamic network conditions. Reinforcement learning algorithms operate based on a feedback loop mechanism, wherein the security system receives feedback from its environment (i.e., the network) regarding the consequences of its actions. Through this iterative process of trial and error, the system learns to make decisions that lead to favourable outcomes, such as detecting and mitigating security breaches

while minimising false alarms and resource consumption. One of the key advantages of reinforcement learning in network security is its ability to dynamically adjust security policies and response mechanisms based on real-time feedback. For example, a network intrusion detection system (NIDS) employing reinforcement learning may learn to prioritise certain types of alerts or allocate resources more efficiently based on the current threat landscape and network conditions. This adaptability allows the security system to effectively address both known and emerging threats without requiring manual intervention or reconfiguration. However, the adoption of reinforcement learning in network security tools comes with its challenges, particularly in the context of the trial-and-error learning approach. Since reinforcement learning algorithms rely on experimentation to discover optimal strategies, there is a potential risk of introducing vulnerabilities or disruptions during the learning process. Moreover, the time and computational resources required for reinforcement learning training can be substantial, especially in complex network environments with diverse threat scenarios. Despite these challenges, the potential benefits of reinforcement learning in enhancing the agility and efficacy of network security systems justify further research and development efforts in this area.

↣ *Ensemble learning*: In the context of network security and protection tools, ensemble learning methods offer a compelling approach to enhancing detection system performance by leveraging the collective insights of multiple models. By combining diverse detection algorithms or classifiers, ensemble learning techniques aim to mitigate individual model weaknesses and improve overall detection accuracy and robustness. For instance, an ensemble model may integrate different types of intrusion detection algorithms, such as anomaly-based and signature-based detection systems, each of which excels in capturing distinct aspects of network behaviour and identifying different types of threats. By aggregating the outputs of these diverse detectors, the ensemble model can achieve a more comprehensive and nuanced understanding of network activity, thereby enhancing its ability to detect both known and novel threats. However, the implementation of ensemble learning in network security tools is not without its challenges, particularly in terms of computational resources. Since ensemble models typically involve the simultaneous operation of multiple constituent models, they may impose significant computational overhead, requiring ample processing power and memory resources to execute efficiently. Additionally, the training and optimisation of ensemble models can be computationally intensive, as it involves not only training each individual model but also determining the optimal combination or weighting of their outputs. Despite these challenges, the potential benefits of ensemble learning in network security – such as improved detection accuracy, resilience to evasion tactics and adaptability to evolving threat landscapes – justify the investment in computational resources and the development of sophisticated ensemble learning frameworks tailored to the specific requirements of network security applications. Moreover, advancements in hardware acceleration technologies and distributed computing architectures may help alleviate some of the computational burdens associated with ensemble learning, making it a viable and promising approach for enhancing network security and protection capabilities.

↣ *Deep learning*: In the realm of network security and protection tools, deep learning techniques, particularly convolutional neural networks (CNNs) and recurrent neural networks (RNNs), offer notable advantages for malware detection and analysis. CNNs excel in extracting hierarchical representations of data, making them well-suited for tasks involving image recognition and pattern detection. In the context of malware detection, CNNs can analyse various file attributes and network traffic patterns to identify suspicious behaviour indicative of malicious software. For example, they can analyse packet headers, payload content and traffic flow characteristics to discern potential threats. On the other hand, RNNs are specialised for processing sequential data and are particularly effective in capturing temporal dependencies and patterns in time-series data. In the context of network security, RNNs can analyse sequences of network events and identify anomalous patterns or sequences of activities that may signify malicious behaviour. For instance, they can detect patterns of network communication associated with malware propagation, command and control (C2) communication or data exfiltration attempts. While CNNs and RNNs offer promising capabilities for malware detection, they also present certain challenges in the context of network security tools. One significant challenge is the requirement for large amounts of labelled training data to train these deep learning models effectively. Acquiring and annotating such datasets can be time-consuming and resource-intensive, particularly for rare or novel malware variants. Additionally, deep learning models like CNNs and RNNs are often characterised by their black-box nature, meaning that the internal mechanisms governing their decision-making processes may be opaque and difficult to interpret. This lack of interpretability can pose challenges in understanding how these models arrive at their conclusions and may hinder the development of trust in their outputs. Despite these challenges, the potential benefits of leveraging CNNs and RNNs for malware detection in network security applications are substantial. Their ability to automatically learn complex patterns and features from raw data can enhance the efficacy and efficiency of malware detection systems, enabling organisations to better protect their networks against evolving threats. Moreover, ongoing research efforts aimed at addressing the challenges associated with deep learning models, such as techniques for interpretability and explainability, hold promise for further advancing the state-of-the-art in network security using CNNs and RNNs.

↣ *Generative models*, such as generative adversarial networks (GANs) and variational autoencoders (VAEs), present a novel approach to augmenting the capabilities of network security and protection tools. GANs are composed of two neural networks: a generator and a discriminator, which are trained simultaneously in a competitive manner. The generator generates synthetic data samples, while the discriminator attempts to distinguish between real and synthetic data. Through this adversarial training process, GANs can produce realistic synthetic data that closely resemble real-world examples. In the context of network security, GANs can generate synthetic network traffic data that encapsulates various patterns and characteristics of malicious activities, enabling more robust training of detection systems. Similarly, VAEs are a type of autoencoder neural network architecture that is trained to learn a compressed representation of input data. Unlike traditional autoencoders, VAEs are probabilistic models that learn the underlying distribution of the input data. This enables VAEs to generate new data samples by sampling from the learned distribution. In the context of network security, VAEs can be trained on a dataset of benign network traffic to learn a probabilistic model of normal network behaviour. By sampling from this learned distribution, VAEs can generate synthetic network traffic data that resembles legitimate network activities, providing additional training data for detection systems. While generative models like GANs and VAEs offer the potential to enhance the training and detection capabilities of network security tools, they also pose challenges in terms of interpretability and explainability. The inner workings of these models can be complex and difficult to interpret, making it challenging to understand how they generate synthetic data or make decisions. Additionally, the generated synthetic data may not always accurately capture the full diversity of real-world network traffic patterns, leading to potential biases or inaccuracies in the training process. Despite these challenges, the use of generative models in network security holds promise for improving the resilience and effectiveness of intrusion detection and prevention systems. Continued research efforts aimed at addressing the interpretability and robustness of generative models, as well as exploring innovative applications of these techniques in network security, are essential for realising their full potential in enhancing cybersecurity defences.

In conclusion, network security is a critical aspect of cybersecurity and the integration of AI and ML into network security systems has shown promising results in improving performance

Transitioning to malware detection, AI-based approaches have emerged as promising solutions for identifying and mitigating malicious software threats. Malware, a portmanteau of 'malicious software', represents a ubiquitous and pernicious threat in the digital landscape, embodying a diverse array of software specifically designed to disrupt, damage or gain unauthorised access to computer systems. This nefarious class of software encompasses a spectrum of malicious entities, ranging from relatively innocuous adware and spyware to more insidious forms such as ransomware, trojans, worms and viruses, each engineered with distinct malevolent intents. The advent of malware has catalysed a paradigm shift in the cybersecurity landscape, amplifying the complexity and severity of cyber threats encountered by individuals, organisations and even governments worldwide. These malicious entities operate stealthily, exploiting vulnerabilities in software, networks or human behaviour to infiltrate systems and execute their deleterious agendas. Such incursions often result in dire consequences, ranging from financial losses, data breaches and identity theft to the disruption of critical infrastructure, intellectual property theft and even espionage.

One infamous example illustrating the profound impact of malware is the NotPetya ransomware attack in 2017, which wreaked havoc on numerous multinational corporations, including Maersk, Merck and FedEx. Leveraging a sophisticated propagation mechanism, NotPetya propagated rapidly across networks, encrypting data and rendering systems inoperable. The attack inflicted staggering financial losses, with some estimates surpassing $10 billion, underscoring the profound economic ramifications of malware-induced disruptions.

In response to the escalating threat posed by malware, cybersecurity practitioners and researchers have pioneered innovative approaches leveraging artificial intelligence (AI) and machine learning (ML) to fortify defensive strategies. These AI-driven malware detection systems harness the power of advanced algorithms to analyse vast datasets, discerning subtle patterns indicative of malicious activity and pre-emptively identifying emerging threats before they wreak havoc. By discerning anomalous behaviours, scrutinising code signatures and detecting previously unseen malware variants, AI-based malware detection systems offer a potent line of defence against the ever-evolving threat landscape. These techniques underscore the diverse approaches to enhancing malware detection within cybersecurity systems.

↣ *Deep learning*, a subset of machine learning, holds remarkable promise in the realm of malware detection due to its inherent capability to identify intricate patterns and features within data. This makes it particularly adept at uncovering sophisticated and previously unseen malware variants that may evade traditional detection methods. By analysing vast amounts of data, deep learning models can discern subtle nuances and correlations that may signify malicious behaviour, enabling them to effectively identify emerging threats. However, the effectiveness of deep learning models in malware detection is heavily reliant on the availability of large volumes of high-quality training data. These datasets need to encompass diverse and representative samples of both benign and malicious software to ensure the model's robustness and generalisation ability. Acquiring such extensive datasets can be challenging, especially in resource-constrained environments where access to labelled malware samples may be limited or restricted. Moreover, the training process for deep learning models can be computationally intensive and time-consuming, requiring substantial computational resources and infrastructure. This poses a significant barrier for organisations with limited computing capabilities or budgets, hindering their ability to leverage deep learning effectively for malware detection. Despite these challenges, advancements in data collection techniques, such as crowdsourcing and data augmentation, along with the proliferation of cloud computing services, have mitigated some of the obstacles associated with training deep learning models for malware detection. Additionally, ongoing research efforts focus on developing more efficient and scalable deep learning architectures tailored specifically for cybersecurity applications, aiming to overcome the challenges posed by limited data availability and computational resources.

- *Ensemble learning*, an influential technique in the realm of malware detection, capitalises on the synergy of multiple individual models to bolster detection accuracy and fortify resilience against evasion strategies employed by malware authors. By integrating diverse models, each with its own unique strengths and capabilities, ensemble learning aggregates their collective intelligence, thereby enhancing the overall effectiveness of the detection system. One of the key advantages of ensemble learning is its ability to mitigate the limitations of individual models by leveraging the diversity of the ensemble. Each constituent model may excel in detecting specific types of malware or capturing distinct patterns within the data. By combining their outputs through techniques such as voting or averaging, ensemble learning can produce more robust and reliable predictions, even in the presence of noisy or ambiguous data. However, the adoption of ensemble learning in malware detection comes with its own set of challenges, chief among them being the significant computational overhead associated with training and deploying multiple models simultaneously. The computational demands of ensemble methods scale with the size of the ensemble and the complexity of the constituent models, necessitating robust infrastructure and ample computational resources to support their operation effectively. Moreover, the complexity of ensemble learning algorithms and the increased computational burden may pose challenges in terms of scalability and deployment in resource-constrained environments. Organisations must invest in robust computing infrastructure and optimisation strategies to accommodate the computational demands of ensemble learning, which may not always be feasible for smaller or budget-constrained organisations. Despite these challenges, ensemble learning remains a valuable and widely adopted approach in malware detection, particularly in scenarios where detection accuracy and resilience are paramount. Ongoing research efforts focus on developing more efficient ensemble learning techniques and optimisation strategies to alleviate the computational burden while preserving the efficacy of ensemble-based detection systems.
- *Behaviour-based analysis* revolutionises malware detection by shifting the focus from static signatures to dynamic behavioural attributes,

enabling the identification of previously unknown malware variants based on their actions and interactions with the system. Unlike traditional signature-based approaches that rely on predefined patterns or characteristics, behaviour-based analysis observes how programs behave during execution, allowing for the detection of anomalous or suspicious activities indicative of malware presence. The strength of behaviour-based analysis lies in its ability to detect emerging threats and zero-day attacks that evade traditional detection methods, as it does not rely on specific signatures or patterns that may not yet be known or documented. By monitoring activities such as file modifications, network communications, system calls and process behaviour, behaviour-based analysis can uncover malicious behaviour patterns that deviate from normal operation, enabling timely detection and mitigation of potential threats. However, the effectiveness of behaviour-based analysis hinges on its ability to accurately distinguish between benign and malicious behaviour, a task that can be challenging due to the inherent complexity and variability of system behaviour. Malicious actors often employ sophisticated techniques to camouflage their activities and mimic legitimate behaviour, making it difficult for traditional behaviour-based analysis methods to differentiate between genuine and malicious actions. Mitigating the risk of false positives and false negatives is a critical challenge in behaviour-based analysis, as erroneously flagging legitimate activities as malicious or failing to detect actual threats can undermine the reliability and usability of the detection system. To address this challenge, advanced techniques such as machine learning and anomaly detection algorithms are employed to analyse and classify behaviour patterns, enabling more accurate and adaptive detection of malware while minimising the risk of false alarms. Despite these challenges, behaviour-based analysis remains a cornerstone of modern malware detection strategies, offering unparalleled capabilities for identifying and mitigating emerging threats in dynamic and evolving computing environments. Ongoing research and development efforts focus on refining and enhancing behaviour-based analysis techniques to improve detection accuracy, scalability and resilience against sophisticated malware attacks.

↣ *Natural language processing (NLP)* holds significant promise in the realm of malware detection by leveraging its ability to decipher obfuscated code and linguistic constructs commonly found in malicious software. By analysing the textual components of malware samples, such as comments, variable names and function calls, NLP techniques can uncover subtle patterns and linguistic anomalies indicative of malicious intent. For example, malware authors often use obfuscation techniques to conceal their code's true purpose, such as encoding strings or using unconventional variable names. NLP algorithms can detect and decode these obfuscated elements, providing insights into the underlying functionality of the malware. Furthermore, NLP techniques can analyse the linguistic characteristics of malware samples, such as grammar, syntax and semantics, to identify patterns consistent with known malicious behaviour. For instance, malware often contains linguistic artefacts that betray its origins or intentions, such as grammatical errors, unnatural language usage or domain-specific jargon associated with hacking and cybercrime. By recognising these linguistic cues, NLP models can flag suspicious code snippets or files for further investigation, enabling the early detection and mitigation of potential threats. Despite its potential, the applicability of NLP in malware detection may be limited in certain contexts, particularly for malware variants that do not exhibit clear linguistic characteristics amenable to NLP analysis. For example, some malware may be predominantly composed of binary code or machine instructions, with minimal textual components for NLP algorithms to analyse. In such cases, the effectiveness of NLP-based detection methods may be diminished, requiring alternative approaches or supplementary techniques to achieve robust detection capabilities. Additionally, the performance of NLP models in malware detection can be influenced by factors such as the diversity and complexity of the linguistic features present in the malware samples, the availability of labelled training data for model training and the adaptability of the models to evolving linguistic patterns used by malware authors. Addressing these challenges requires ongoing research and development efforts to enhance the accuracy, scalability and applicability of NLP techniques in the context of cybersecurity. Overall, while NLP presents a promising avenue for malware detection, particularly in cases where linguistic analysis can provide valuable insights into the nature of the threats, its effectiveness may be constrained by the inherent limitations and complexities of analysing linguistic artefacts in malware samples. As researchers continue to innovate and refine NLP-based detection methods, the role of NLP in cybersecurity is expected to evolve, offering new opportunities for enhancing the detection and mitigation of malicious software threats. Antivirus software plays a critical role in cybersecurity, serving to identify and thwart malware attacks targeting computer systems. Traditional antivirus tools have traditionally relied on signature-based detection methods, which are limited to recognising known threats and often fall short against new or evolving malware variants. However, the incorporation of artificial intelligence (AI) and machine learning (ML) algorithms has notably boosted the precision and efficacy of antivirus solutions in identifying and preventing malware infections. Today, numerous antivirus programs leverage AI and ML technologies, including Norton Antivirus, Kaspersky Antivirus, McAfee Antivirus, Avast Antivirus and Bitdefender Antivirus. These applications harness diverse AI and ML approaches such as machine learning, deep learning and predictive modelling to analyse extensive datasets, uncover patterns and detect potential threats more effectively.

↣ *Machine learning algorithms* play a crucial role in modern antivirus programs by enabling them to analyse extensive datasets, identifying patterns indicative of potential threats with enhanced accuracy. These algorithms can sift through vast amounts of data, including known malware signatures, system behaviours, network traffic patterns and file attributes, to detect emerging threats and evolving attack techniques. By continuously learning from this data, machine learning models become more adept at recognising both known and previously unseen malware variants. However, the effectiveness of machine learning algorithms in antivirus programs heavily relies on the quality and quantity of data available for training. To achieve optimal performance, these algorithms require access to diverse and representative datasets containing examples of various types of malware and legitimate software. Additionally, the datasets need to be regularly updated to account for new threats and changes in attack trends. Without access to sufficient and up-to-date training data, machine learning models may struggle to accurately identify and classify threats, leading to false positives or false negatives. Furthermore, ensuring the privacy and security of the data used for training machine learning models is paramount to prevent potential misuse or exploitation. Antivirus vendors must adhere to strict data protection regulations and implement robust security measures to safeguard sensitive information. Norton Antivirus, McAfee Antivirus and Avast Antivirus leverage machine learning algorithms to detect and block various online threats, including malware, phishing scams and ransomware, by analysing extensive datasets to identify patterns and predict potential threats.

↣ *Deep learning algorithms*, a subset of artificial intelligence, revolutionise antivirus capabilities by enabling them to identify and combat previously unknown threats, a vital aspect in the ever-evolving landscape of cyber threats. Unlike traditional signature-based detection methods, which rely on recognising known malware patterns, deep learning models can autonomously learn from vast amounts of data, detecting new and emerging threats based on their underlying characteristics rather than specific signatures. This adaptability allows antivirus programs to stay ahead of cybercriminals who constantly devise new attack strategies to bypass conventional defences. However, the implementation of deep learning in antivirus solutions poses significant computational challenges. Training deep learning models requires immense computational resources, including high-performance hardware such as graphics processing units (GPUs) and specialised infrastructure. Additionally, the process demands extensive time and expertise to fine-tune and optimise the models for optimal performance. Despite these challenges, the benefits of deep learning in antivirus programs are profound, offering a proactive approach to cybersecurity that can effectively counter the ever-changing threat landscape. Kaspersky Antivirus utilises a diverse array of AI and ML techniques, including deep learning algorithms, to enhance its malware detection and prevention capabilities. Similarly, Avast Antivirus leverages machine learning algorithms to combat malware infections, phishing attacks and other online threats, harnessing the power of deep learning models to analyse extensive datasets and detect emerging threats effectively.

↣ *Behavioural detection* technology represents a significant advancement in antivirus systems, allowing for the continuous monitoring of system activity to promptly identify any suspicious behaviour that may indicate the presence of malware. This proactive approach enhances the overall security posture by enabling the detection of threats in real-time, potentially preventing significant damage to the system or network. However, the effectiveness of behavioural detection methods can be hindered by the possibility of false positives or false negatives. False positives occur when legitimate activities are incorrectly flagged as malicious, leading to unnecessary alerts and potentially causing user frustration. On the other hand, false negatives occur when actual threats go undetected, leaving the system vulnerable to exploitation. Striking a balance between minimising false alarms and ensuring comprehensive threat detection is crucial for maximising the reliability and effectiveness of behavioural detection technology in antivirus systems. Kaspersky Antivirus utilises behavioural detection technology to monitor system activity for potential threats in real-time.

↣ *Predictive threat modelling* within antivirus software is a sophisticated application of artificial intelligence (AI) that revolutionises how potential security risks are identified and pre-emptively addressed. This technique involves the deployment of AI algorithms to meticulously analyse massive volumes of data collected from various sources, such as network traffic, file metadata and historical security incidents. By scrutinising this extensive dataset, the AI-powered predictive models can discern subtle patterns, correlations and anomalies indicative of emerging threats and potential attack vectors. One of the key strengths of predictive threat modelling lies in its ability to forecast potential security risks before they materialise into full-fledged cyberattacks. By analysing historical data and identifying trends, the AI models can anticipate evolving tactics, techniques and procedures (TTPs) employed by threat actors. This proactive approach enables security teams to stay one step ahead of cybercriminals, allowing them to fortify their defences and pre-emptively mitigate vulnerabilities before they are exploited. However, the effectiveness of predictive threat modelling hinges on several critical factors. Firstly, ensuring the accuracy and quality of data inputs is paramount. The predictive models rely heavily on the integrity and relevance of the data they analyse. Therefore, meticulous data collection, validation and normalisation processes are essential to minimise inaccuracies and biases that could compromise the reliability of the predictions. Additionally, the dynamic nature of the cybersecurity landscape necessitates regular updates and recalibration of the predictive models. Threat actors continually evolve their tactics, and new vulnerabilities emerge with alarming frequency. As such, the predictive models must be continuously trained on the latest data to remain effective in identifying emerging threats and adapting to shifting attack vectors. Moreover, the complexity and diversity of modern cyber threats pose challenges in accurately modelling and predicting their behaviour. Cybercriminals employ sophisticated techniques, including polymorphic malware, fileless attacks and social engineering tactics, to evade detection and infiltrate networks. Predictive threat modelling must contend with this complexity by incorporating advanced AI algorithms capable of discerning nuanced patterns and anomalies amidst the noise of everyday network activity. By harnessing the power of AI and sophisticated data analysis techniques, predictive threat modelling enables security teams to anticipate, identify and mitigate potential security risks with unprecedented speed and accuracy. However, to fully realise its potential, organisations must prioritise data accuracy, continuous model refinement and the integration of cutting-edge AI capabilities into their cybersecurity infrastructure. McAfee Antivirus employs predictive threat modelling technology, which has the capability to analyse extensive datasets to detect emerging threats and possible attack routes.

- *Zero-day attack detection* represents a pivotal AI-driven feature in antivirus software, geared towards identifying and pre-emptively blocking previously unknown threats. By leveraging advanced machine learning algorithms, these systems can analyse behavioural patterns and anomalous activities to flag potentially malicious behaviour indicative of zero-day attacks. This proactive approach to threat detection enables antivirus programs to stay ahead of emerging threats, safeguarding systems and networks against exploitation of vulnerabilities that have yet to be discovered or patched. However, the effectiveness of zero-day attack detection may encounter challenges when faced with highly sophisticated or targeted attacks, which employ stealthy tactics to evade detection. Despite these potential limitations, integrating zero-day attack detection capabilities into antivirus solutions significantly enhance their ability to mitigate the risks posed by emerging cyber threats. Bitdefender Antivirus boasts sophisticated threat detection methods which enable the identification and prevention of zero-day attacks.
- *Personalised machine learning models* in antivirus software provide a customised security approach, adapting to individual user behaviours and preferences. This tailored protection enhances security efficacy by focusing on specific user patterns, such as browsing habits or file usage, to detect and prevent potential threats. However, the implementation of personalised models can strain system resources due to the need for continuous monitoring and analysis of user activities, potentially impacting system performance.
- On the other hand, *real-time monitoring and analysis* capabilities enable antivirus programs to swiftly detect and respond to emerging threats as they occur. This proactive approach enhances the antivirus software's ability to mitigate risks and protect against evolving attack vectors in real time. Nevertheless, the requirement for continuous monitoring and analysis demands significant computational resources and may lead to

a high volume of alerts, which can overwhelm security teams and pose operational challenges in managing and prioritising responses. Balancing the need for real-time threat detection with resource constraints and alert management remains a critical consideration in optimising antivirus efficacy and operational efficiency.

Detecting malware is crucial for cybersecurity, as it aims to prevent the spread of harmful software. However, attackers can easily bypass traditional methods that rely on predefined rules and signatures. To enhance malware detection, artificial intelligence (AI) and machine learning (ML) techniques have been employed, with deep learning being a popular approach to AI. Advanced deep learning algorithms like convolutional neural networks (CNNs) and recurrent neural networks (RNNs) are trained on vast datasets, substantially improving their ability to identify and categorise malware with nuanced precision. To further enhance training capabilities, generative models such as generative adversarial networks (GANs) and variational autoencoders (VAEs) are employed to create high-quality synthetic data that mimics real-world patterns. In addition, ensemble learning techniques, which amalgamate the insights of multiple machine learning models, have emerged as a particularly effective strategy for boosting the overall performance and reliability of detection systems. The integration of AI and ML has shown promising results in enhancing malware detection. However, while AI and ML techniques offer significant potential for advancing malware detection capabilities, addressing the associated challenges is imperative to realise their full efficacy in combating the evolving threat landscape posed by malware. Despite the strides made in AI-driven malware detection, the cat-and-mouse game between cyber adversaries and defenders persists, with threat actors continuously refining their tactics, techniques and procedures to evade detection. As such, the battle against malware remains an ongoing endeavour, demanding continual innovation, collaboration and vigilance from the cybersecurity community to safeguard digital ecosystems against these insidious threats.

3.4.2 Security automation and management

Building upon the advancements in AI and ML techniques for network security and protection tools, the integration of security automation emerges as a natural progression in enhancing cybersecurity defences. Security automation leverages AI and ML algorithms to automate various security processes, such as threat detection, incident response and vulnerability management, thereby enabling organisations to rapidly detect, mitigate and adapt to evolving cyber threats. By seamlessly integrating with existing security infrastructure and workflows, security automation empowers cybersecurity teams to streamline their operations, reduce response times and enhance overall resilience against cyberattacks. This synergy between AI/ML techniques and security automation represents a paradigm shift in cybersecurity, offering organisations the ability to proactively defend against sophisticated threats in today's dynamic threat landscape.

Security automation optimises cybersecurity workflows by automating repetitive and time-consuming tasks, such as incident response, vulnerability management and compliance monitoring. AI and ML techniques play a crucial role in enhancing automation systems, boosting their precision and decision-making capabilities. Rule-based systems, a prevalent AI approach in security automation, employ pre-established rules and algorithms to handle specific events like intrusions or failed login attempts. The distribution of ML/AI adoption across different security operations illustrates its widespread use [33]. Identity management and vulnerability management each account for 20% of ML/AI usage, indicating their application in bolstering user identity management, access control and vulnerability scanning and prioritisation. Intrusion prevention constitutes 25% of ML/AI usage, showcasing its role in detecting and thwarting intrusions and network-based attacks through the analysis of network traffic patterns. Anomaly detection, representing the largest share at 35%, signifies ML/AI's utility in identifying and addressing unusual or malicious activities, whether by employing unsupervised learning algorithms to spot abnormal behaviour or supervised learning algorithms to recognise known attack patterns.

AI and ML techniques play a pivotal role in advancing security automation (Figure 3.4), offering a spectrum of advantages and challenges.

- *Rule-based systems* are foundational components of security automation, providing a structured approach to handling security events and incidents. These systems excel in automating routine and repetitive tasks within cybersecurity workflows, such as incident response and access control management. By employing predefined rules and algorithms, they enable swift and consistent responses to specific security events, such as intrusions or unauthorised access attempts. However, the effectiveness of rule-based systems may be limited when it comes to detecting emerging or evolving threats. Since these systems rely on predefined rules, they may struggle to adapt to new attack vectors or sophisticated

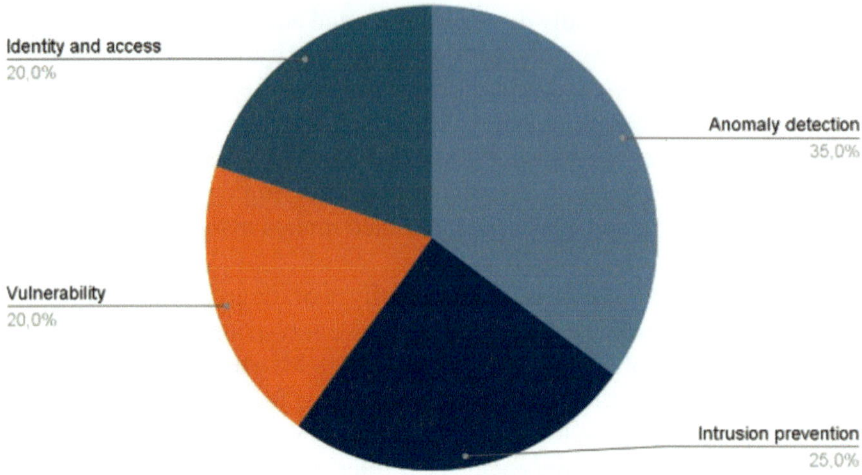

Figure 3.4 AI/ML in security automation.

cyberattack techniques that deviate from established patterns. As a result, rule-based systems may generate a high rate of false positives, triggering alerts for benign activities that resemble known threat indicators. Moreover, the lack of adaptability and context-awareness inherent in rule-based systems can hinder their interpretability and explainability. Understanding the rationale behind security decisions made by these systems may prove challenging, especially when faced with complex or ambiguous scenarios. This limitation can impede effective collaboration between security teams and hinder efforts to fine-tune automated responses based on evolving threat landscapes. In summary, while rule-based systems offer valuable automation capabilities in security operations, their reliance on predefined rules may limit their ability to effectively detect and respond to emerging threats. As organisations strive to enhance their security automation strategies, it is essential to complement rule-based approaches with more adaptive and intelligent solutions to address the dynamic nature of cybersecurity threats.

↣ *Expert systems* play a crucial role in security automation by emulating the decision-making abilities of human experts, thereby automating complex security tasks and augmenting the capabilities of security teams. These systems leverage a combination of predefined rules, heuristics and domain-specific knowledge to analyse and respond to security incidents in a manner akin to human experts. One of the key advantages of expert systems is their ability to handle intricate security tasks that require nuanced judgement and expertise. By codifying expert knowledge into automated decision-making processes, these systems can perform tasks such as threat assessment, incident triage and remediation actions with consistency and accuracy. This capability significantly enhances the efficiency of security operations, allowing organisations to respond rapidly to security incidents and mitigate potential threats. However, the effectiveness of expert systems may be limited by the availability of human expertise. Building and maintaining expert systems requires access to subject matter experts who can provide the necessary domain knowledge and insights. In some cases, organisations may face challenges in recruiting or retaining qualified experts, leading to gaps in the expertise available to inform the development of these systems. Additionally, the scalability of expert systems may be constrained by the complexity of the security tasks they are designed to automate. As security environments evolve and grow in complexity, expert systems may struggle to adapt and scale to meet increasing demands, potentially resulting in performance bottlenecks or limitations in coverage. Furthermore, while expert systems excel in automating specific security tasks within well-defined domains, they may lack the flexibility and adaptability needed to address novel or unforeseen threats. Since these systems rely on predefined rules and heuristics, they may struggle to effectively respond to emerging threats or evolving attack techniques that fall outside their established parameters. As a result, organisations may need to supplement expert systems with more agile and adaptive automation solutions to address the dynamic nature of cybersecurity challenges. In summary, while expert systems offer valuable capabilities for automating complex security tasks, organisations must carefully consider the availability of human expertise, scalability concerns and the need for adaptability when incorporating these systems into their security automation strategies. By striking the right balance between human expertise and automated decision-making, organisations can maximise the effectiveness of expert systems in enhancing their security posture and mitigating cyber threats.

- *Decision trees* play a significant role in security automation by providing a structured framework for decision-making within security systems. These decision trees organise and classify security events or data points based on a series of predefined rules or conditions, enabling automated analysis and response to security incidents. One of the primary advantages of decision trees is their ability to streamline the decision-making process within security automation systems. By breaking down complex security scenarios into a series of binary decisions, decision trees can efficiently navigate through various possible outcomes and determine appropriate actions or responses. This streamlined approach enhances the efficiency of security operations by automating routine decision-making tasks and reducing the cognitive burden on security analysts. Furthermore, decision trees contribute to system accuracy by providing a transparent and interpretable model for analysing security data. Unlike some black-box machine learning algorithms, decision trees offer a clear and intuitive representation of the decision-making logic used by the system. This transparency enables security analysts to understand how decisions are made and to interpret the rationale behind automated actions, enhancing trust and confidence in the system's outputs. However, decision trees may encounter challenges in the context of security automation, particularly when it comes to detecting new or evolving threats. Since decision trees rely on predefined rules or conditions, they may struggle to adapt to novel attack techniques or previously unseen patterns of malicious behaviour. As a result, decision trees may be less effective in scenarios where the threat landscape is constantly evolving, requiring frequent updates and revisions to maintain relevance and accuracy. Interpretability challenges can also arise with decision trees, particularly as the complexity of the decision-making logic increases. While decision trees offer a transparent representation of individual decisions, complex or deeply nested trees may become difficult to interpret or understand, especially for security analysts who are not familiar with the underlying model. This lack of interpretability can hinder the effectiveness of decision trees in security automation, as it may obscure the reasoning behind automated decisions and make it challenging to troubleshoot or debug the system. In summary, decision trees play a valuable role in security automation by streamlining decision-making processes and enhancing system accuracy. However, organisations must be mindful of the challenges associated with new threat detection and interpretability when incorporating decision trees into their security automation strategies. By carefully balancing the benefits and limitations of decision trees, organisations can leverage their strengths to improve the efficiency and effectiveness of their security operations.

These techniques underscore the evolving landscape of security automation, presenting both opportunities and hurdles in the quest for robust cybersecurity measures. Transitioning from the discussion on AI/ML techniques in security automation, where systems are empowered to automate various security tasks, we delve into the realm of security management. This pivotal aspect involves identifying, assessing and prioritising risks to an organisation's information assets, necessitating robust measures for mitigation and control. Leveraging AI and ML capabilities, security management systems automate these processes, enabling seamless risk assessment and proactive security measures implementation.

- *Security automation*, a cornerstone in modern security frameworks, streamlines repetitive tasks such as incident response, vulnerability management and compliance monitoring. By improving accuracy and decision-making capabilities and reducing manual intervention, it significantly enhances overall security posture. However, challenges arise concerning data quality, accuracy and integrity, necessitating effective data governance and management strategies.
- Within this context, *security analytics* emerges as a vital component, utilising AI/ML techniques to analyse diverse data sources for identifying potential threats. In the domain of security management, the utilisation of security analytics empowered by AI and ML technologies represents a significant advancement. These analytics tools are designed to comb through extensive datasets sourced from diverse channels, including network traffic logs, system logs and threat intelligence feeds. By applying AI and ML algorithms, these tools can identify patterns, anomalies and correlations within the data, enabling organisations to swiftly detect and respond to potential security threats. However, despite the advantages offered by security analytics, challenges related to data quality and governance persist. The effectiveness of security analytics heavily relies on the quality and integrity of the data being analysed. Inaccurate, incomplete or inconsistent data can lead to erroneous conclusions and false positives, undermining the reliability of threat detection and incident response processes. Additionally, ensuring proper data governance practices is essential to maintain data privacy, compliance with regulations and protection against unauthorised access or manipulation of sensitive information. Therefore, while security analytics powered by AI/ML holds promise in bolstering security management efforts, addressing issues surrounding data quality and governance is

imperative to maximise its effectiveness and reliability in safeguarding organisational assets and mitigating security risks.

↣ *AI/ML-driven security incident response platforms* automate the detection and resolution of security incidents, ensuring rapid and effective responses to emerging threats. In the realm of security management, the adoption of AI and ML technologies has revolutionised the process of incident response, offering automated solutions to identify and mitigate security threats swiftly and accurately. These AI/ML-driven security incident response mechanisms are designed to collect and analyse data from various sources, including security devices, network logs and threat intelligence feeds, in real time. By leveraging sophisticated algorithms, these systems can detect anomalies, patterns of malicious behaviour and potential security breaches, enabling organisations to respond proactively to emerging threats. However, despite their significant advantages, AI/ML-driven security incident response mechanisms encounter challenges related to data quality and governance. The effectiveness of these systems heavily relies on the quality, accuracy and integrity of the data being processed. Inaccurate or incomplete data can lead to false positives or false negatives, compromising the reliability of incident detection and response. Moreover, ensuring proper data governance practices, including data classification, access controls and encryption, is crucial to protect sensitive information and maintain compliance with regulatory requirements. Therefore, while AI/ML-driven security incident response mechanisms offer valuable capabilities in enhancing response time and accuracy, addressing issues pertaining to data quality and governance is essential to maximise their effectiveness and reliability in safeguarding organisational assets and maintaining robust security posture.

Integrating AI and ML methods into security management systems has shown encouraging results in enhancing security automation, analytics and incident response. However, challenges related to data quality, accuracy and integrity persist, highlighting the need for effective data governance and management practices. Overcoming these challenges is essential to fully leverage the benefits of AI and ML in security management.

3.4.3 Threat intelligence and cyberattack prediction

Threat intelligence encompasses the process of gathering, analysing and disseminating information about potential or current cyber threats. It plays a critical role in providing organisations with the knowledge they need to protect themselves against cyberattacks. AI and ML techniques have been utilised to enhance the capabilities of threat intelligence systems, enabling them to automatically collect, analyse and disseminate large amounts of data.

- ↣ One of the most popular applications of AI and ML in threat intelligence is in the field of *threat hunting*. Threat hunting entails a proactive approach to identifying signs of compromise and adversarial activities within an organisation's network infrastructure. Systems based on artificial intelligence and machine learning significantly amplify these efforts by leveraging an array of sophisticated techniques. These include natural language processing (NLP) for textual data analysis, deep learning algorithms for pattern recognition in complex data structures and graph analysis for mapping intricate relationships among various network entities. Utilising these methods, AI and ML-powered threat hunting platforms can autonomously sift through immense volumes of data, discern intricate patterns and flag potential threats with a level of efficiency and accuracy that would be challenging to achieve manually. However, challenges such as maintaining data quality, accuracy and integrity persist.
- ↣ Another notable application of AI and ML in threat intelligence is in the domain of *threat prediction*. Threat prediction systems leverage AI and ML techniques to analyse historical data and recognise patterns that may indicate future threats. This allows organisations to take proactive measures to safeguard themselves before an attack occurs. Yet, effective data governance and management remain essential to overcome associated challenges.
- ↣ Additionally, AI and ML can automate the process of *threat intelligence sharing*. Threat intelligence sharing platforms employ AI and ML techniques to automatically gather and analyse threat intelligence data from multiple sources, facilitating its dissemination to other organisations. Nevertheless, ensuring the security and privacy of shared data, alongside concerns regarding data quality and accuracy, pose ongoing challenges in this domain.

Cyberattack prediction stands out as a highly promising application of AI and machine learning in cybersecurity. The ability to forecast and pre-emptively address attacks has immense potential for enhancing the security of networks and systems. Recent advancements in machine learning, particularly in deep learning and reinforcement learning, have enabled the development of predictive models capable of recognising patterns and anomalies in network behaviour and traffic. This empowers the timely detection and alerting of cyber threats, offering the possibility of thwarting attacks before they are executed.

- *Deep neural networks* (DNNs) represent a powerful tool in the realm of cyberattack prediction due to their ability to scrutinise network traffic and identify anomalies suggestive of impending attacks. By analysing patterns within network data, DNNs can discern irregularities such as atypical data transmission behaviours or unauthorised attempts to access restricted resources. This capability holds significant promise in fortifying cybersecurity measures by pre-emptively detecting potential threats before they materialise into full-fledged attacks. However, the effectiveness of DNNs in this regard heavily relies on the availability of extensive datasets for training purposes. Without access to sufficiently large and diverse datasets, DNNs may struggle to accurately learn and recognise the multitude of subtle cues indicative of various cyber threats. Consequently, the successful deployment of DNNs for cyberattack prediction necessitates robust data collection and curation efforts to ensure the model's efficacy in identifying emerging threats.
- *Reinforcement learning* (RL) offers a dynamic approach to cyberattack prediction by leveraging adaptability and efficiency in responding to novel and unidentified threats. By learning from past experiences and adapting its decision-making processes to the current context, RL models can swiftly detect and mitigate emerging cyber threats. This adaptability allows RL-based systems to continually evolve and improve their predictive capabilities, thereby enhancing overall cybersecurity resilience. However, the implementation of RL in cyberattack prediction requires substantial computational resources and specialised expertise. RL algorithms often involve complex training processes and sophisticated optimisation techniques, demanding robust computational infrastructure to support their execution. Additionally, expertise in RL methodologies and algorithms is essential for effectively designing, training and deploying RL models tailored to the specific challenges of cyberattack prediction. Consequently, while RL holds immense potential in bolstering cybersecurity defences, its successful integration into cyberattack prediction frameworks necessitates careful consideration of resource allocation and expertise requirements.
- *Unsupervised machine learning techniques* play a crucial role in cyberattack prediction by autonomously identifying patterns or behaviours

that deviate from the expected norms within a system. This capability enables the detection of anomalies indicative of potential cyber threats without relying on labelled data for training. By analysing large volumes of network traffic and system behaviour, unsupervised learning models can uncover subtle deviations or irregularities that may signify the presence of malicious activities. However, despite their effectiveness, unsupervised learning techniques confront challenges related to false positives and false negatives. False positives occur when the model incorrectly identifies normal behaviour as anomalous, leading to unnecessary alerts or alarms. Conversely, false negatives occur when the model fails to detect genuine cyber threats, allowing malicious activities to go unnoticed. The risk of false positives and false negatives underscores the importance of fine-tuning unsupervised learning models to achieve an optimal balance between sensitivity and specificity. Moreover, the performance of unsupervised learning techniques may vary depending on the complexity and heterogeneity of the datasets being analysed. Highly complex or heterogeneous datasets may pose challenges in accurately identifying anomalies or distinguishing between benign and malicious behaviour. As a result, practitioners must carefully evaluate the suitability of unsupervised learning approaches for the specific characteristics of the data and the objectives of cyberattack prediction tasks. Despite these challenges, unsupervised machine learning techniques remain valuable tools in the arsenal of cyber defence strategies, offering automated and data-driven insights into potential security threats. Continued research and development efforts aimed at improving the robustness and scalability of unsupervised learning algorithms will further enhance their efficacy in cyberattack prediction applications.

- *Visualisation and feature extraction methods* play a crucial role in cyberattack prediction by improving the interpretability of anomaly detection systems. These techniques enable security analysts to visually explore and understand complex data patterns, facilitating the identification of potential threats more effectively. By representing data in intuitive visual formats, such as charts, graphs or heatmaps, visualisation techniques provide insights into the underlying structure of network traffic and system behaviour. Moreover, feature extraction methods extract relevant information or characteristics from raw data, enabling anomaly detection systems to focus on the most informative aspects of the data. By selecting and transforming features that are most indicative of cyber threats, feature extraction enhances the accuracy and efficiency of predictive models. For example, features related to network packet attributes, user behaviours or system activities can be extracted and analysed to identify anomalous patterns associated with potential cyberattacks. However, the effectiveness of visualisation and feature extraction methods relies heavily on the quality and relevance of the underlying data. Effective data governance practices are essential to ensure that the data used for visualisation and feature extraction is accurate, comprehensive and representative of the actual cyber threat landscape. Data governance encompasses processes for data collection, storage, processing and validation, as well as mechanisms for ensuring data privacy and security. Additionally, dimensionality reduction and density estimation techniques play a critical role in cyberattack prediction by identifying anomalies within complex datasets.

↣ *Dimensionality reduction methods* reduce the number of features or dimensions in the data while preserving important information, thereby simplifying the analysis process and improving computational efficiency. Density estimation techniques estimate the underlying probability distribution of the data, enabling the identification of rare or unusual events that may signify cyber threats. Despite their benefits, dimensionality reduction and density estimation techniques may encounter challenges when applied to highly complex or heterogeneous datasets. Complex datasets with diverse types of data and varying degrees of variability may pose difficulties in accurately estimating the underlying probability distribution or identifying meaningful patterns. As a result, practitioners must carefully select and tailor dimensionality reduction and density estimation techniques to suit the characteristics of the data and the requirements of the cyberattack prediction task. In summary, visualisation and feature extraction methods, along with dimensionality reduction and density estimation techniques, play integral roles in cyberattack prediction by enhancing the interpretability and effectiveness of anomaly detection systems. However, ensuring the accuracy, relevance and quality of the underlying data is essential to maximise the efficacy of these methods in identifying and mitigating cyber threats.

Cyberattack prediction holds tremendous potential for bolstering cybersecurity defences by leveraging AI and machine learning techniques to anticipate and pre-emptively address threats. AI/ML approaches offer automated and data-driven insights into potential security threats, underscoring the importance of continued research and development to enhance their efficacy in cyberattack prediction. However, even though AI and ML methods offer considerable potential for enhancing cyberattack prediction within cybersecurity, they confront notable hurdles. These obstacles encompass the demand for extensive datasets to train deep learning algorithms, the necessity of substantial computational capabilities for implementing reinforcement learning and the risk of erroneous outcomes with unsupervised machine learning. Although visualisation and feature extraction can augment the clarity and comprehensibility of predictive models, ensuring precise and pertinent data usage necessitates robust data governance and management.

3.4.4 Vulnerability management and security education and awareness

AI and machine learning find applications in cybersecurity for the purpose of vulnerability management. Vulnerability management entails the process of identifying, assessing and mitigating security weaknesses or vulnerabilities within a system or network. It involves activities such as vulnerability scanning, risk assessment and remediation to safeguard against potential cyber threats. This practice is crucial in maintaining the security and integrity of systems and data, as vulnerabilities serve as entry points for attackers to exploit and compromise sensitive information or disrupt operations. Automating vulnerability management using AI and machine learning technologies offers several advantages. Firstly, it enhances efficiency by automating repetitive tasks involved in vulnerability scanning and assessment, allowing security teams to focus on more strategic and high-priority activities. Secondly, machine learning algorithms can analyse vast amounts of data to identify potential vulnerabilities and prioritise them based on their severity and potential impact on the organisation's security posture. This helps security teams in efficiently allocating resources and addressing critical vulnerabilities in a timely manner, reducing the risk of exploitation and compromise. AI and ML techniques play a crucial role in vulnerability management, offering various advantages but also presenting notable challenges.

- *Natural language processing (NLP)* plays a crucial role in vulnerability management by automating the analysis of security advisories and identifying vulnerabilities that are relevant to the specific needs of an organisation. NLP techniques enable systems to parse through large volumes of textual data, such as security bulletins and advisories, and extract pertinent information regarding potential vulnerabilities. This allows security teams to quickly assess the severity and relevance of each vulnerability and prioritise their remediation efforts accordingly. However, NLP also presents challenges that need to be addressed. One such challenge is accuracy, as NLP algorithms may sometimes misinterpret or incorrectly extract information from unstructured text, leading to inaccurate vulnerability assessments. Ensuring the accuracy of NLP models requires rigorous testing and validation against known datasets to verify their effectiveness in correctly identifying and categorising vulnerabilities. Scalability is another challenge associated with NLP in vulnerability management. As the volume of security advisories and data sources increases, NLP systems may struggle to efficiently process and analyse large amounts of text in real time. Scaling NLP systems to handle growing volumes of data requires robust infrastructure and optimisation techniques to ensure timely and accurate vulnerability identification. Addressing these challenges is essential to fully leverage the benefits of NLP in vulnerability management. By improving the accuracy and scalability of NLP algorithms, organisations can enhance their ability to identify and mitigate vulnerabilities effectively, thereby strengthening their overall security posture.

↣ *Reinforcement learning* (RL) offers a promising approach to vulnerability management by facilitating the efficient patching of vulnerabilities while minimising potential impacts on system performance and stability. RL algorithms learn from past experiences and interactions with the system environment to make decisions regarding vulnerability remediation actions. This adaptive learning process allows RL-based systems to dynamically adjust their patching strategies based on the current state of the system and the severity of vulnerabilities detected. One of the key advantages of RL in vulnerability management is its ability to prioritise patching activities in a manner that minimises disruptions to critical system operations. RL algorithms can weigh the potential impact of applying patches against the risk posed by unpatched vulnerabilities, thereby optimising the patching process to maximise security while minimising operational downtime. However, RL-based vulnerability management solutions also face several challenges that need to be addressed. One such challenge is ensuring the quality, accuracy and integrity of the data used to train and evaluate RL models. Vulnerability data sources may contain noise, inconsistencies or inaccuracies, which can adversely affect the performance of RL algorithms and lead to suboptimal patching decisions. Therefore, robust data quality assurance processes and validation mechanisms are essential to ensure the reliability of RL-based vulnerability management systems. Addressing these challenges will be essential for unlocking the full potential of RL in vulnerability management. By overcoming data quality and governance issues, organisations can harness the power of RL algorithms to enhance their ability to detect, prioritise and remediate vulnerabilities effectively, thereby strengthening their overall cybersecurity posture. Additionally, effective data governance and management practices are critical for the success of RL in vulnerability management. Proper data governance frameworks help organisations establish policies, procedures and controls for managing vulnerability data throughout its lifecycle, from acquisition and storage to analysis and utilisation. By implementing effective data governance measures, organisations can maintain the confidentiality, integrity and availability of vulnerability data, thus enhancing the trustworthiness and reliability of RL-based vulnerability management solutions.

↣ *Continuous monitoring and analysis* play a crucial role in vulnerability management by enabling organisations to proactively detect and address potential vulnerabilities in their systems and networks. These techniques involve the continuous collection, processing and analysis of data from various sources, such as network traffic, system logs and security alerts, to identify signs of vulnerabilities or suspicious activities. One of the key advantages of continuous monitoring and analysis is its ability to provide real-time visibility into the security posture of an organisation's IT infrastructure. By continuously monitoring network traffic, system logs and other data sources, organisations can promptly identify and respond to emerging threats or vulnerabilities before they can be exploited by attackers. This proactive approach to vulnerability management helps organisations mitigate security risks and minimise the likelihood of successful cyberattacks. However, continuous monitoring and analysis also pose challenges, particularly in handling large volumes of data accurately and efficiently. The sheer volume of data generated by modern IT systems can overwhelm traditional monitoring tools and processes, making it difficult for organisations to effectively identify and prioritise potential vulnerabilities. Moreover, the complexity and diversity of data sources further compound the challenge, as organisations must integrate and correlate data from disparate sources to gain a comprehensive view of their security posture. To address these challenges, organisations must invest in advanced monitoring and analysis tools capable of processing and analysing large volumes of data in real-time. These tools often leverage machine learning and data analytics techniques to automatically identify patterns, anomalies and potential vulnerabilities within the data. By harnessing the power of AI and ML, organisations can streamline the monitoring and analysis process, enabling them to more effectively detect and respond to potential vulnerabilities in a timely manner. Furthermore, organisations must implement robust data management and storage solutions to ensure the accuracy, integrity and availability of the data used for continuous monitoring and analysis. This includes establishing data governance policies, implementing data validation mechanisms and employing secure storage and backup practices to protect sensitive information from unauthorised access or tampering. In conclusion, continuous monitoring and analysis are essential components of effective vulnerability management strategies, enabling organisations to proactively detect, prioritise and address potential vulnerabilities in their IT infrastructure. While challenges such as handling large volumes of data accurately may arise, leveraging advanced monitoring tools and data analytics techniques, along with implementing robust data management practices, can help organisations overcome these obstacles and enhance their cybersecurity resilience.

↣ *Integration with other security measures* is vital for a comprehensive vulnerability management strategy as it allows organisations to leverage existing security infrastructure and tools to enhance their ability to detect, prioritise and remediate vulnerabilities effectively. By integrating vulnerability management solutions with other security measures such as intrusion detection systems (IDS), endpoint protection platforms (EPP) and security information and event management (SIEM) systems, organisations can gain a more holistic view of their security posture and streamline their response to potential threats. One of the key advantages of integrating vulnerability management with other security measures is the ability to correlate vulnerability data with real-time security events and alerts generated by other security tools. For example, integrating vulnerability management with SIEM systems allows organisations to correlate vulnerability scan results with security events detected by IDS or EPP solutions. This correlation enables organisations to prioritise vulnerabilities based on their potential impact on the overall security posture and respond promptly to emerging threats. Additionally, integration with other security measures enables organisations to automate the vulnerability management process and orchestrate response actions across multiple security tools. For example, organisations can automatically trigger vulnerability scans in response to specific security events detected by IDS or EPP solutions, or automatically deploy patches to remediate vulnerabilities identified during scans. This automation helps organisations improve the efficiency of their vulnerability management efforts and reduce the time to detect and remediate vulnerabilities, thereby minimising the risk of exploitation by attackers. However, integration with other security measures may also present challenges, particularly in terms of interoperability and compatibility with existing security infrastructure. Organisations may encounter issues such as data format inconsistencies, communication protocols mismatches or lack of support for standardised integration interfaces. These challenges can hinder the seamless exchange of information between different security tools and impede the effectiveness of the integrated vulnerability management solution. To address these challenges, organisations must carefully evaluate their existing security infrastructure and requirements before embarking on integration efforts. They should prioritise interoperability and compatibility when selecting vulnerability management solutions and seek vendors that offer flexible integration options and support for industry-standard protocols. Additionally, organisations should establish clear integration objectives and requirements, develop comprehensive integration plans and conduct thorough testing to ensure the smooth operation of integrated security solutions. In conclusion, integration with other security measures is essential for a comprehensive vulnerability management strategy, enabling organisations to enhance their ability to detect, prioritise and remediate vulnerabilities effectively. While potential integration issues may arise, organisations can overcome these challenges by prioritising interoperability and compatibility, selecting suitable integration solutions and following best practices for integration planning and implementation. By integrating vulnerability management with other security measures, organisations can strengthen their cybersecurity defences and mitigate the risk of cyber threats effectively.

Vulnerability management is essential for proactively identifying and mitigating security weaknesses in systems and networks. By leveraging AI and machine learning, organisations can streamline and automate the vulnerability management process, thereby improving overall security posture and resilience against cyber threats. However, it does not come without challenges. These challenges underscore the importance of addressing data quality, accuracy and integration concerns to fully leverage the benefits of AI and ML techniques in vulnerability management.

As organisations strive to bolster their cybersecurity defences through comprehensive vulnerability management strategies, it becomes evident that a critical component of success lies in fostering a culture of security awareness and education. In parallel to integrating vulnerability management with other security measures, organisations must invest in equipping their workforce with the knowledge and skills necessary to identify and mitigate cybersecurity risks effectively. This underscores the recognition that cybersecurity is not solely reliant on technological solutions but also on the human factor. AI and machine learning have the potential to be utilised in cybersecurity for enhancing security education and awareness. As cyberattacks become more sophisticated, it is imperative for both individuals and organisations to gain insights into cybersecurity best practices. AI and machine learning technologies can contribute to the development of more effective security education and awareness initiatives.

- ↣ *Natural language processing (NLP)* holds immense potential in revolutionising security awareness and education by enabling the creation of personalised training content. Through NLP techniques, training materials can be dynamically customised to meet the specific needs and knowledge levels of individual learners. For instance, NLP algorithms can analyse the proficiency level of learners based on their interactions with the training platform, previous assessment scores or self-reported information. Subsequently, the training content can be adapted to address areas where learners exhibit weaknesses or gaps in understanding. The personalised nature of NLP-driven training content ensures that learners receive instruction that is relevant and engaging, maximising the effectiveness of the educational experience. By catering to the individual learning styles and preferences of users, NLP-powered training programs can foster deeper comprehension and retention of security concepts. For example, visual learners may receive content with rich graphical representations, while auditory learners may benefit from audio-based explanations. However, despite its transformative potential, ensuring the quality and accuracy of NLP-generated training content presents a significant challenge. NLP algorithms rely on large datasets and sophisticated linguistic models to generate text that is grammatically correct, contextually relevant and semantically accurate. Achieving this level of precision requires ongoing refinement and optimisation of NLP algorithms, as well as rigorous validation processes to verify the accuracy of generated content. Moreover, NLP-driven training content must adhere to industry standards, regulatory requirements and best practices in cybersecurity education. Ensuring compliance with these guidelines while maintaining the personalised nature of the content adds another layer of complexity to the challenge. Additionally, the evolving nature of cybersecurity threats and technologies necessitates continuous updates and revisions to training content to reflect the latest developments and insights. In summary, while NLP holds tremendous promise for enhancing security awareness and education through personalised training content, addressing the challenges associated with ensuring quality and accuracy is essential for realising its full potential. By leveraging advanced NLP techniques alongside robust validation processes and ongoing content refinement, organisations can develop highly effective and engaging security training programs tailored to the unique needs of individual learners.

↣ The *integration of gamification elements* represents a compelling approach to enhancing security awareness and education by infusing training programs with interactive and engaging features. Gamification leverages principles from game design to transform traditional learning experiences into dynamic and immersive activities that motivate and captivate learners. By incorporating elements such as points, badges, leaderboards, challenges and rewards, gamified training platforms can incentivise participation, stimulate competition and foster a sense of achievement among learners. One of the key advantages of gamification is its ability to increase learner engagement and motivation. By presenting security concepts in the context of interactive games and challenges, gamified training programs make learning enjoyable and rewarding, encouraging participants to actively participate and invest effort in their education. Moreover, gamification taps into intrinsic human desires for mastery, autonomy and social interaction, leveraging these motivational drivers to promote sustained engagement with training content. Furthermore, gamification fosters experiential learning by providing learners with opportunities to apply security principles in simulated scenarios. Through interactive simulations and role-playing exercises, participants can practise identifying and responding to security threats in a risk-free environment, thereby enhancing their decision-making skills and situational awareness. Additionally, gamification encourages collaborative learning and knowledge sharing by enabling learners to compete or collaborate with peers in group challenges or team-based activities. However, despite its potential benefits, measuring the impact of gamification in cybersecurity training poses significant challenges. Traditional metrics such as completion rates or assessment scores may not adequately capture the full extent of learning outcomes or behavioural changes resulting from gamified training experiences. Quantifying the effectiveness of gamification requires the development and implementation of comprehensive evaluation frameworks that assess factors such as knowledge retention, skill acquisition, behavioural change and long-term engagement. Moreover, the subjective nature of engagement and motivation makes it challenging to standardise measurement criteria and establish universally applicable benchmarks for evaluating gamified training programs. Additionally, the effectiveness of gamification may vary depending on factors such as learner demographics, cultural backgrounds and individual preferences, further complicating efforts to assess its impact objectively. In summary, while gamification holds considerable promise for enhancing security awareness and education by fostering engagement, motivation and experiential learning, measuring its impact remains a complex and multifaceted endeavour. By employing a combination of qualitative and quantitative assessment methods, organisations can gain insights into the effectiveness of gamified training programs and refine their approaches to maximise learning outcomes and behavioural change.

↣ *Chatbots* represent a valuable tool for enhancing security awareness and education by offering immediate assistance and guidance to individuals seeking information or support on security-related matters. These AI-driven conversational agents leverage natural language processing (NLP) and machine learning algorithms to interpret user queries, provide relevant information and offer personalised recommendations in real time. By serving as virtual assistants, chatbots streamline the process of obtaining help and guidance, making security-related resources more accessible and user-friendly for individuals across diverse contexts and proficiency levels. One of the primary advantages of chatbots in security awareness and education is their ability to deliver timely and contextually relevant information to users whenever they need it. Whether individuals are seeking clarification on security policies, troubleshooting technical issues or requesting guidance on best practices, chatbots can instantly respond to their inquiries and offer tailored solutions or resources to address their concerns. This immediate accessibility to information ensures that users receive timely support and guidance, thereby empowering them to make informed decisions and take appropriate actions to enhance their security posture. Moreover, chatbots facilitate interactive and personalised learning experiences by engaging users in meaningful conversations and providing targeted assistance based on their specific needs and preferences. Through natural language interactions, chatbots can adapt their responses and recommendations to match the user's level of knowledge, learning style and prior interactions, creating a customised learning journey tailored to each individual's requirements. By delivering personalised guidance and support, chatbots can cater to diverse learning preferences and effectively address the unique challenges and concerns faced by users in their security education journey. However, while chatbots offer numerous benefits for security awareness and education, ensuring the quality and accuracy of their responses poses an ongoing challenge. The effectiveness of chatbots hinges on their ability to accurately understand user queries, interpret contextual nuances and provide relevant and accurate information in response. Achieving this level of precision requires continuous improvement and refinement of chatbot algorithms through iterative training, testing and optimisation processes. Additionally, chatbots must be regularly updated with the latest security knowledge, guidelines and best practices to ensure that their responses remain current and relevant in an ever-evolving threat landscape. Furthermore, maintaining user trust and confidence in chatbot interactions necessitates transparent communication about their capabilities, limitations and data handling practices. Users should be informed about the boundaries of chatbot functionality, the types of queries it can address and the steps taken to safeguard their privacy and confidentiality. Establishing clear expectations and providing adequate support channels for escalating complex or sensitive inquiries can help mitigate potential frustrations or misunderstandings arising from chatbot interactions. In summary, chatbots offer valuable opportunities for enhancing security awareness and education by providing real-time assistance, personalised guidance and interactive learning experiences. However, ensuring the quality, accuracy and user trustworthiness of chatbot responses requires ongoing attention and investment in algorithmic refinement, knowledge updates and transparent communication practices. By leveraging chatbots effectively as part of a comprehensive security education strategy, organisations can empower individuals to develop the knowledge, skills and behaviours necessary to protect themselves and their digital assets against emerging cyber threats.

↣ *Machine learning (ML) algorithms* play a pivotal role in enhancing security awareness and education by offering personalised learning experiences and facilitating the assessment of program effectiveness. Through the integration of ML techniques, security education platforms can dynamically adjust the difficulty levels and content of educational materials to align with the abilities and learning preferences of individual users. By analysing user interactions, performance metrics and historical data, ML algorithms can identify patterns and trends indicative of each user's knowledge level, learning pace and areas of strength or weakness. This enables the customisation of learning pathways and the delivery of targeted content that optimally supports each user's learning journey. One of the primary advantages of ML algorithms in security awareness and education is their ability to create adaptive learning environments that cater to the diverse needs and skill levels of users. By leveraging data-driven insights, ML-powered platforms can dynamically modify the difficulty of challenges, quizzes and interactive exercises in real-time, ensuring that users are consistently engaged and appropriately challenged throughout their learning experience. For novice users, ML algorithms may introduce foundational concepts and basic principles in a scaffolded manner, gradually increasing complexity as users demonstrate proficiency and confidence. Conversely, for advanced learners, ML algorithms can present more challenging scenarios and advanced topics to further deepen their understanding and expertise in cybersecurity concepts. Additionally, ML algorithms enable the continuous assessment and optimisation of security education programs by providing insights into learner progress, engagement levels and knowledge retention rates. By analysing user interactions, completion rates and performance metrics, ML algorithms can identify areas of improvement and opportunities for refinement within educational content and delivery methods. This feedback loop allows educators and program administrators to iteratively enhance the effectiveness and relevance of security education initiatives, ensuring that they remain aligned with evolving cybersecurity threats and industry best practices. However, the efficacy of ML algorithms in security awareness and education is contingent upon the availability and quality of data used for training and improvement purposes. ML models rely on large volumes of diverse and representative data to generalise patterns, make accurate predictions and generate actionable insights. Therefore, obtaining high-quality training data that encompasses a wide range of cybersecurity scenarios, user behaviours and learning outcomes is crucial for the successful deployment of ML algorithms in educational settings. Moreover, ensuring data privacy, confidentiality and security throughout the data lifecycle is essential to maintain user trust and compliance with regulatory requirements. In summary, ML algorithms offer significant opportunities for enhancing security awareness and education by providing personalised learning experiences, assessing program effectiveness and driving continuous improvement initiatives. By leveraging data-driven insights and adaptive learning techniques, ML-powered platforms can empower users to develop the knowledge, skills and behaviours necessary to mitigate cyber threats effectively. However, addressing the challenges associated with data quality, privacy and security is paramount to maximising the benefits of ML in security education and fostering a culture of cyber resilience across organisations and communities.

AI and ML hold the potential to improve security education and awareness initiatives by tailoring training content, incorporating gamification elements and offering immediate support and advice. Continuous enhancements to AI/ML algorithms, as well as the refinement of training materials, chatbot interactions and gamification strategies, are essential. Additionally, staying informed about the latest cybersecurity trends and best practices is crucial for both individuals and organisations.

3.4.5 Defence mechanisms and adversarial training

Efforts to counter adversarial attacks include adversarial training, where models are exposed to both standard and adversarial examples during training to enhance their resilience. Researchers and practitioners are also exploring regularisation techniques and architectural enhancements to mitigate vulnerabilities and foster the development of more robust AI models. Adversarial training methods represent a pivotal development in the quest to fortify machine learning models against adversarial attacks. This innovative approach involves training models not only on standard examples but also on adversarial inputs crafted to deceive the model. By exposing the model to these adversarial examples during training, it becomes more adept at recognising and mitigating such threats in real-world scenarios. The concept of adversarial training stems from the realisation that traditional machine learning models, particularly deep neural networks, are susceptible to manipulation by adversaries. These adversaries can subtly alter input data in ways imperceptible to humans, leading the model to produce incorrect outputs with high confidence. Adversarial examples pose a significant challenge to the reliability and security of machine learning systems, especially in security-critical applications such as autonomous driving, facial recognition and malware detection. To counteract this vulnerability, adversarial training techniques introduce adversarial examples into the training data, augmenting the model's learning process. During training iterations, the model is exposed to both benign and adversarial inputs, forcing it to learn robust features that are resilient to manipulation attempts. Through this iterative process, the model gradually adapts to the presence of adversarial perturbations, learning to differentiate between genuine and adversarial inputs more effectively. Adversarial training methods have demonstrated promising results in bolstering the robustness of machine learning models against various types of attacks. By incorporating adversarial examples into the training pipeline, these techniques enhance the model's ability to generalise and defend against adversarial manipulation in diverse environments. Moreover, adversarial training serves as a proactive defence mechanism, equipping models with the capacity to detect and mitigate potential threats before they manifest in real-world scenarios. Despite their effectiveness, adversarial training methods are not without challenges. Generating diverse and representative adversarial examples can be computationally intensive, requiring substantial resources for training and evaluation. Moreover, there is a delicate balance between improving robustness and maintaining model performance on standard inputs, necessitating careful tuning of training parameters and regularisation techniques. Adversarial training represents a crucial advancement in fortifying machine learning models against adversarial attacks. By exposing models to adversarial inputs during training, these methods enhance their resilience and efficacy in security-critical applications. Continued research and innovation in adversarial training techniques hold the potential to further strengthen the security and reliability of machine learning systems in the face of evolving threats. The ethical considerations surrounding adversarial machine learning are significant. As AI becomes increasingly integrated into critical systems such as healthcare diagnostics, autonomous vehicles and financial applications, the potential for adversarial manipulation raises concerns about the reliability and security of these systems.

Recent advancements in computer vision and natural language processing have elevated the role of trained classifiers in critical security systems, such as vision for autonomous vehicles, face recognition and malware detection. As machine learning models become more integral to security, the ability to resist adversarial inputs has emerged as a key objective. Despite the effectiveness of trained models in classifying benign inputs, recent research reveals that adversaries can manipulate inputs to induce incorrect outputs from the model. This issue, particularly prevalent in deep neural networks, has sparked a growing body of research. Notably, in computer vision, even minor alterations to input images can deceive advanced neural networks with high confidence, often without perceptible changes to a human observer. Beyond its security implications, this phenomenon underscores the need for models to learn underlying concepts robustly.

The exploration of adversarial attacks and defence mechanisms has grown substantially in recent years, with researchers proposing various strategies to address the vulnerabilities inherent in machine learning models. Examples of such mechanisms include defensive distillation, feature squeezing and adversarial example detection approaches. These efforts represent crucial initial steps in understanding and mitigating the impact of adversarial attacks on machine learning systems.

- *Defensive distillation* is a technique used to enhance the robustness of machine learning models, particularly against adversarial attacks. It involves training a model in two stages: first, a teacher model is trained on the original dataset using standard training procedures. Then, a student model is trained on the logits (the raw output scores before applying the softmax function) produced by the teacher model instead of the original labels. The rationale behind defensive distillation is to smooth out the decision boundaries learned by the model during training, making it more resilient to small perturbations in the input data. By training the student model on the softened logits generated by the teacher model, which are essentially probability distributions over the classes, the resulting model tends to be less sensitive to small changes in the input that may be introduced by adversarial attacks. In essence, defensive distillation aims to make the model more robust by incorporating knowledge from a more stable and generalised teacher model during the training process. However, it is worth noting that while defensive distillation has shown some effectiveness in improving robustness against certain types of attacks, it is not foolproof and may not provide complete protection against all adversarial threats. As such, it is often used in conjunction with other defence mechanisms as part of a comprehensive strategy to enhance the security of machine learning systems. In this study, researchers introduced defensive distillation as a mechanism to mitigate the vulnerability of deep neural networks (DNNs) to adversarial samples [34]. Through analytical and empirical analysis, they demonstrated that defensive distillation significantly reduced the effectiveness of adversarial sample creation, from 95% to less than 0.5%, on one of the studied DNNs. This improvement was attributed to distillation's role in reducing gradients used in adversarial sample creation. The study also found that distillation increased the average minimum number of features required to modify for creating adversarial samples by approximately 800% for one of the tested DNNs.

↣ *Feature squeezing* is a defence mechanism proposed to enhance the robustness of machine learning models, particularly deep neural networks (DNNs), against adversarial attacks. It works by reducing the precision of input features, which makes it more difficult for attackers to generate effective adversarial samples. This reduction in precision helps in two ways: it limits the range of potential adversarial perturbations that can be applied to input features, and it increases the model's resilience to small changes in input data. By compressing the input feature space, feature squeezing effectively increases the robustness of the model against adversarial attacks. It has been shown to be effective in mitigating various types of attacks, including those targeting image classification and natural language processing tasks. Feature squeezing can be applied alongside other defence mechanisms to provide additional layers of protection against adversarial manipulation. Overall, feature squeezing represents a promising approach to enhancing the security of machine learning models in adversarial settings, offering a practical and effective means of defending against sophisticated attacks. The study referenced by [35] has explored the effectiveness of feature squeezing as a defence mechanism against adversarial attacks. It concludes that despite its simplicity and low cost compared to other defences, feature squeezing demonstrates surprising effectiveness. The approach is believed to limit the search space available to adversaries, thereby reducing the efficacy of adversarial attacks. While feature squeezing may not be impervious to adversarial adaptation, it substantially alters the adversarial challenge. This research suggests promising avenues for defending against adversarial examples and sheds light on the boundaries of deep neural networks in adversarial scenarios.

- *Adversarial example detection* refers to the process of identifying or detecting instances where machine learning models are susceptible to adversarial attacks. In the context of deep learning, adversarial examples are inputs that are intentionally perturbed to cause the model to make incorrect predictions or classifications. These perturbations are often imperceptible to humans but can significantly alter the model's output. Detection methods for adversarial examples typically involve analysing the model's behaviour when presented with input data and identifying patterns or characteristics that indicate susceptibility to adversarial attacks. This can include monitoring changes in the model's decision boundaries, analysing the sensitivity of the model's predictions to small changes in input data or comparing the model's outputs with ground truth labels. Various techniques have been proposed for adversarial example detection, including:
  - Robustness metrics: Quantifying the robustness of a model by measuring its performance under adversarial attacks.
  - Input perturbation: Applying small perturbations to input data and observing changes in the model's output.
  - Adversarial training: Training the model on both clean and adversarial examples to improve its robustness.
  - Confidence analysis: Examining the confidence or uncertainty of the model's predictions to identify instances where it may be making incorrect classifications.

Overall, adversarial example detection plays a crucial role in assessing the security and reliability of machine learning models, especially in applications where robustness is essential, such as autonomous driving, cybersecurity and healthcare. The study has delved into the challenges posed by adversarial examples (AEs) in deep learning applications, particularly in image classification tasks [36]. It has examined various AE detection methods and provided experimental results using state-of-the-art detectors across multiple datasets.

However, despite the progress made, there remains a significant challenge in quantifying the effectiveness and guarantees provided by these defence mechanisms [37]. One key issue is the inability to ascertain whether a given attack has identified the 'most adversarial' example within a given context. Similarly, it is challenging to determine whether a specific defence mechanism can effectively counter all possible adversarial attacks within a well-defined class. This lack of certainty complicates efforts to assess the robustness of machine learning models against adversarial manipulation and evaluate their potential security implications accurately.

As researchers continue to delve into the realm of adversarial attacks and defences, there is a growing recognition of the need for more comprehensive evaluation frameworks and standardised benchmarks. Such frameworks would enable researchers to systematically assess the efficacy of different defence mechanisms and provide clearer insights into their performance under various attack scenarios. By fostering greater transparency and rigour in the evaluation process, these efforts can facilitate the development of more robust and secure machine learning systems capable of withstanding adversarial threats in real-world applications.

Thus, Nicolas et al. [38] try to answer the question on how we can train deep neural networks that are robust to adversarial inputs. The authors investigated the susceptibility of deep neural networks to adversarial examples, which are inputs that closely resemble natural data but are misclassified by the network. They propose a robust optimisation approach to address this vulnerability, providing a comprehensive perspective on prior research in this area. This principled approach enables the development of reliable methods for training and attacking neural networks, offering concrete security guarantees against a wide range of adversaries. The methods outlined in the study significantly enhance the resilience of trained networks to adversarial attacks and introduce the concept of security against a first-order adversary as a fundamental security criterion. The findings suggest that achieving robustness against well-defined classes of adversaries is a crucial step towards the development of fully resistant deep learning models.

Adversarial training stands out as a crucial defence mechanism against adversarial attacks, contributing significantly to the enhancement of model robustness in the face of subtle manipulations. This technique involves training machine learning models not only on conventional, correctly labelled examples but also on intentionally crafted adversarial examples. The objective is to expose the model to various perturbations during training, fostering an improved ability to withstand and accurately classify both standard and adversarial inputs.

The process of adversarial training typically unfolds in several steps. Initially, the model is trained on a standard dataset to learn the underlying patterns and features within the data. Subsequently, adversarial examples are generated by applying specific perturbations to the input data, creating instances designed to mislead the model. These adversarial examples are then incorporated into the training dataset, alongside the standard examples. The model is then retrained on this augmented dataset, iteratively refining its ability to accurately classify both conventional and adversarial inputs.

The effectiveness of adversarial training lies in its capacity to expose the model to a more diverse set of scenarios, enabling it to learn features that contribute to accurate predictions while simultaneously discerning and minimising the impact of adversarial perturbations. By incorporating adversarial examples into the training process, models develop a more robust understanding of the underlying data distribution and are better equipped to handle unexpected variations in input.

This approach has proven successful across various machine learning domains, including computer vision, natural language processing and speech recognition. Adversarial training has been particularly instrumental in fortifying models against attacks that leverage subtle manipulations of input data.

However, it is essential to recognise that adversarial training is not a one-size-fits-all solution. The efficacy of this defence mechanism may vary based on the specific characteristics of the model, the nature of the input data and the intricacies of the adversarial attacks it faces. By training models on both standard and adversarial examples, developers enhance the robustness and resilience of machine learning systems, mitigating the impact of subtle manipulations and bolstering their ability to provide accurate and reliable predictions in the face of evolving security challenges.

3.4.6 Real-world implications and security risks

Adversarial machine learning represents a formidable challenge across a spectrum of security-critical applications, spanning from autonomous vehicles and healthcare diagnostics to financial systems. The real-world implications of adversarial attacks in these domains are profound and multifaceted, posing significant risks to both the integrity of the systems and the safety and well-being of individuals.

In the context of autonomous vehicles, adversarial attacks can manifest in various forms, with potentially catastrophic consequences on road safety. By subtly manipulating input data, such as altering traffic signs or pedestrian signals, malicious actors can deceive the vehicle's perception systems, leading to misinterpretations of the environment and incorrect decision-making by the vehicle's control mechanisms. For instance, an adversary could craft adversarial stop signs that appear normal to human observers but are misclassified by the vehicle's object detection algorithms, resulting in the vehicle failing to stop at intersections or yielding incorrectly.

Similarly, adversarial attacks targeting healthcare diagnostics have the potential to compromise the accuracy and reliability of medical systems, thereby jeopardising patient outcomes and safety. By tampering with medical images, patient records or diagnostic algorithms, adversaries could introduce subtle alterations that go undetected by healthcare professionals but lead to misdiagnosis or inappropriate treatment plans. For instance, an adversarially crafted medical image could contain imperceptible alterations that cause an AI-powered diagnostic system to misclassify benign anomalies as malignant tumours, leading to unnecessary medical procedures or delays in critical treatments.

In the realm of financial systems, adversarial machine learning poses significant risks to the stability and integrity of markets and transactions. Attackers could exploit vulnerabilities in machine learning algorithms employed for fraud detection, risk assessment or stock market predictions to manipulate outcomes for financial gain. For example, adversarial perturbations introduced into transaction data could deceive fraud detection systems, allowing fraudulent transactions to evade detection and resulting in financial losses for individuals and institutions. Moreover, adversaries could launch targeted attacks to manipulate stock prices or trading algorithms, leading to market disruptions and undermining investor confidence.

The pervasiveness of machine learning in these critical applications amplifies the impact of adversarial attacks, necessitating robust defence mechanisms and proactive security measures to mitigate risks effectively. Strategies for addressing adversarial threats may include the development of resilient machine learning models that are resistant to manipulation, the implementation of rigorous testing and validation procedures to detect vulnerabilities, and the deployment of advanced threat detection techniques to identify and respond to adversarial behaviour in real time. Additionally, collaboration across interdisciplinary teams, including cybersecurity experts, machine learning researchers and domain-specific professionals, is essential to comprehensively address the complex challenges posed by adversarial machine learning and safeguard the security and reliability of critical systems.

3.4.7 Regularisation techniques

Mitigating adversarial vulnerabilities and enhancing model robustness are imperative goals in the development of artificial intelligence (AI). Regularisation techniques and architectural enhancements play a pivotal role in achieving these objectives, offering strategies to fortify AI models against subtle manipulations and improve their resilience in real-world scenarios.

Regularisation methods involve adding constraints to the training process to prevent models from becoming overly complex or overfitting to the training data. Regularisation methods serve as indispensable tools in the machine learning practitioner's toolkit, allowing them to strike a delicate balance between model complexity and generalisation performance while mitigating the risk of overfitting. By incorporating appropriate regularisation techniques into the training process, practitioners can build more robust and reliable machine learning models capable of effectively capturing underlying patterns in the data. In addition to regularisation techniques, architectural enhancements such as skip connections in neural networks and ensemble learning strategies further contribute to model robustness by facilitating information flow and diversifying model predictions.

- ↣ L1 and L2 Regularisation – L1 regularisation, also known as Lasso regularisation, is a method used to prevent overfitting in machine learning models by adding a penalty term to the loss function during training.

$$\sum_{i=1}^{n}(Y_i - \sum_{j=1}^{p} X_{ij}\beta_j)^2 + \lambda\sum_{j=1}^{p}|\beta_j|$$

This penalty term is proportional to the sum of the absolute values of the model's weights or coefficients. The objective of L1 regularisation is to encourage sparsity in the model, meaning that many of the coefficients become zero, effectively selecting only the most important features for prediction while disregarding less relevant ones. The term 'L1' refers to the L1 norm, which calculates the magnitude of a vector by summing the absolute values of its components. In the context of regularisation, the L1 norm is applied to the vector of model coefficients. By adding the L1 penalty term to the loss function, the optimisation process during training is incentivised to minimise both the error on the training data and the magnitude of the model's coefficients. One of the key advantages of L1 regularisation is its feature selection capability. Because the penalty term encourages sparsity, features that are less important for prediction tend to have their corresponding coefficients driven to zero. This effectively performs automatic feature selection, allowing the model to focus on the most informative features while ignoring irrelevant or redundant ones. As a result, L1 regularisation can lead to simpler and more interpretable models by eliminating unnecessary complexity. Moreover, the sparsity induced by L1 regularisation can also help reduce the risk of overfitting, especially in high-dimensional datasets where the number of features exceeds the number of samples. By limiting the number of non-zero coefficients, L1 regularisation constrains the model's capacity, making it less prone to memorising noise in the training data and improving its ability to generalise to unseen data. However, it is important to note that L1 regularisation may not be suitable for all types of datasets or models. In cases where there is multicollinearity among features, meaning that some features are highly correlated with each other, L1 regularisation may arbitrarily select one feature over another, leading to potential loss of information. In such scenarios, techniques like Elastic Net regularisation, which combines L1 and L2 penalties, may be more appropriate. Overall, L1 regularisation is a powerful technique for promoting sparsity and preventing overfitting in machine learning models. By incorporating L1 regularisation into the training process, practitioners can build more robust and interpretable models that strike a balance between complexity and generalisation performance.

L2 regularisation, also known as Ridge regularisation, is a widely used technique in machine learning to prevent overfitting by adding a penalty term to the loss function during training.

$$\sum_{i=1}^{n}\left(y_i - \sum_{j=1}^{p} x_{ij}\beta_j\right)^2 + \lambda \sum_{j=1}^{p} |\beta_j|$$

This penalty term is proportional to the sum of the squared values of the model's weights or coefficients. The objective of L2 regularisation is to discourage the model from learning large weights, which can lead to overfitting by fitting too closely to the training data. The term 'L2' refers to the L2 norm, also known as the Euclidean norm, which calculates the magnitude of a vector by summing the squares of its components and taking the square root of the result. In the context of regularisation, the L2 norm is applied to the vector of model coefficients. By adding the L2 penalty term to the loss function, the optimisation process during training is incentivised to minimise both the error on the training data and the magnitude of the model's coefficients. One of the key advantages of L2 regularisation is its ability to control the complexity of the model while still allowing all features to contribute to the prediction. Unlike L1 regularisation, which encourages sparsity by driving some coefficients to zero, L2 regularisation penalises large coefficients without necessarily eliminating any of them. This can lead to smoother and more stable models that are less sensitive to small changes in the input data. Moreover, L2 regularisation has the desirable property of being differentiable everywhere, making it well-suited for optimisation algorithms that rely on gradient-based methods, such as stochastic gradient descent (SGD). The smoothness of the L2 penalty term ensures that the gradient of the loss function remains continuous, facilitating efficient optimisation and convergence to a global minimum. Another important aspect of L2 regularisation is its role in improving the conditioning of the optimisation problem. Large weights in the model can cause the optimisation landscape to become steep and narrow, making it difficult for optimisation algorithms to converge. By penalising the square of the weights, L2 regularisation encourages the weights to be spread out more evenly, resulting in a smoother and more well-conditioned optimisation landscape. However, it is worth noting that L2 regularisation tends to shrink the weights towards zero proportionally, rather than driving them all the way to zero as in L1 regularisation. This means that L2 regularisation may not perform feature selection as effectively as L1 regularisation, especially in scenarios where some features are irrelevant or redundant. In summary, L2 regularisation is a powerful technique for preventing overfitting and improving the generalisation performance of machine learning models. By incorporating L2 regularisation into the training process, practitioners can build more robust and stable models that strike a balance between complexity and generalisation performance.

- *Dropout* is a regularisation technique commonly used in neural network training to prevent overfitting and improve the generalisation performance of the model. It works by randomly dropping out, or omitting, a fraction of neurons in the network during each training iteration. This means that certain neurons are temporarily removed from the network, effectively reducing its capacity and forcing the remaining neurons to learn more robust and diverse representations of the data. The dropout process is typically applied to hidden layers of the neural network, where each neuron has a probability p of being dropped out during training. This probability is a hyperparameter that controls the dropout rate, with typical values ranging from 0.2 to 0.5. During each training iteration, the dropout process randomly selects neurons to be dropped out based on the specified probability p. As a result, different subsets of neurons are dropped out in each iteration, leading to a form of ensemble learning where multiple subnetworks are trained simultaneously. By randomly dropping out neurons, dropout encourages the network to learn more robust and less correlated features, reducing its reliance on specific neurons or features. This prevents the network from memorising the training data and helps it to generalise better to unseen examples. Additionally, dropout acts as a form of model averaging during inference, where the predictions are averaged over multiple subnetworks, further improving the model's generalisation performance. One key advantage of dropout is its simplicity and effectiveness in preventing overfitting without introducing additional complexity to the model architecture. It can be easily implemented by adding dropout layers to the neural network architecture, with minimal computational overhead. Dropout is particularly effective in deep neural networks with a large number of parameters, where overfitting is a common concern. However, it is important to note that dropout should be used judiciously and in conjunction with other regularisation techniques, as excessive dropout rates may hinder the learning process and slow down convergence. Additionally, dropout is typically applied during training and disabled during inference, as it introduces randomness that is not desirable during prediction. Adaptive learning rate algorithms, such as Adam (adaptive moment estimation) and RMSprop (root mean square propagation), are optimisation algorithms commonly used in training neural networks. These algorithms dynamically adjust the learning rate during training based on the gradients of the loss function with respect to the model parameters. The main advantage of adaptive learning rate algorithms is their ability to automatically adapt the learning rate for each parameter based on its past gradients. This allows the algorithm to converge faster and more reliably compared to traditional optimisation algorithms with fixed learning rates. By adapting the learning rate on a per-parameter basis, adaptive learning rate algorithms can overcome challenges such as vanishing or exploding gradients, which can occur in deep neural networks with complex architectures. Adam, in particular, combines the advantages of both momentum-based optimisation and RMSprop by maintaining separate learning rates for each parameter and adjusting them based on the first and second moments of the gradients. This enables Adam to converge quickly and efficiently, even in the presence of noisy or sparse gradients. Similarly, RMSprop adapts the learning rate for each parameter based on the moving average of the squared gradients, effectively normalising the learning rates across different parameters. This prevents the learning rates from becoming too large or too small, leading to more stable and reliable optimisation. Overall, incorporating adaptive learning rate algorithms like Adam or RMSprop can significantly enhance the training process by dynamically adjusting the learning rates to suit the characteristics of the optimisation landscape. This can lead to faster convergence, improved generalisation performance and better overall training efficiency.

↣ *Batch normalisation* is a technique commonly used in neural networks to address the problem of internal covariate shift, which refers to the change in the distribution of input values to the layers of a neural network during training. This phenomenon can hinder the convergence of the network and make training unstable. Batch normalisation aims to mitigate internal covariate shift by normalising the inputs to each layer of the network. The process of batch normalisation involves normalising the activations of each layer by subtracting the mean and dividing by the standard deviation of the activations within a mini-batch of data. This is done independently for each feature dimension, ensuring that the activations have a mean of zero and a standard deviation of one. Additionally, batch normalisation introduces two learnable parameters, usually referred to as scale and shift parameters, which allow the network to learn the optimal scaling and shifting of the normalised activations. By normalising the activations within each mini-batch, batch normalisation helps to stabilise the training process and accelerate convergence. It reduces the likelihood of vanishing or exploding gradients by keeping the activations within a reasonable range, which allows for more stable and efficient optimisation. This enables the network to train faster and more reliably, even when using higher learning rates or deeper architectures. Furthermore, batch normalisation acts as a form of regularisation by adding noise to the network during training. This noise helps to prevent overfitting by introducing randomness into the optimisation process, which encourages the network to learn more robust and generalisable representations of the data. Batch normalisation also has the benefit of making the network less sensitive to the initialisation of the weights and biases, as the normalisation process helps to standardise the input distributions across layers. This can lead to more consistent performance and faster convergence across different training runs. Overall, batch normalisation is a powerful technique for stabilising training, accelerating convergence and enhancing the robustness of neural networks. It has become a standard component of modern neural network architectures and is widely used in practice to improve the performance and efficiency of deep learning models.

↣ *Residual networks (ResNets)* are a type of deep neural network architecture that utilise skip connections to address the challenge of vanishing gradients during training. These skip connections allow information to bypass one or more layers of the network, enabling the direct flow of information from earlier layers to later layers. In the case of ResNets, the use of skip connections introduces a form of implicit regularisation. These skip connections allow for the direct flow of information from earlier layers to later layers, effectively creating shortcuts through the network. This shortcut path helps to mitigate the vanishing gradient problem, where gradients become too small to effectively update the weights of earlier layers during training. By facilitating the flow of information and gradients through the network, skip connections enable more stable and efficient training of deep neural networks. This can be seen as a form of regularisation, as it helps to prevent the degradation of training performance that can occur with very deep networks. The main idea behind ResNets is the concept of residual learning. Instead of directly learning the mapping from input to output, ResNets learn residual functions, which represent the difference between the desired output and the input. This is achieved by adding shortcut connections, also known as skip connections, which bypass one or more layers and directly feed the input of a layer to a later layer. By incorporating skip connections, ResNets alleviate the vanishing gradient problem, which occurs when gradients become too small as they are back-propagated through many layers of the network during training. This problem can hinder the training process, as it makes it difficult for the network to learn meaningful representations of the data. With skip connections, the gradient signal has a shorter path to propagate through the network, allowing it to reach earlier layers more easily. This facilitates the flow of information and gradients through the network, enabling more effective training of deep architectures with many layers. As a result, ResNets are able to learn deeper and more complex representations of the data, leading to improved performance on a wide range of tasks, including image classification, object detection and semantic segmentation. The skip connections in ResNets enable the network to effectively capture both low-level and high-level features in the data, leading to more robust and accurate predictions.

↣ *Adversarial training* is a technique used in machine learning to improve the robustness of models against adversarial attacks. Adversarial examples are inputs that are intentionally crafted to mislead a machine learning model, causing it to make incorrect predictions. These examples are generated by applying small, imperceptible perturbations to legitimate inputs, resulting in outputs that differ significantly from what a human observer would expect. The process of adversarial training involves exposing the model to both standard (legitimate) examples and adversarial examples during the training process. By training on a mixture of both types of examples, the model learns to better understand the underlying distribution of the data and becomes more robust to adversarial perturbations. In essence, adversarial training acts as a form of implicit regularisation by encouraging the model to learn more robust and generalisable representations of the data. This regularisation effect helps to improve the model's resilience to adversarial attacks while also enhancing its overall performance on standard examples. By incorporating adversarial training into the learning process, models can become more robust and reliable in real-world scenarios, where they may encounter adversarial inputs. During adversarial training, the model is typically trained using a modified loss function that incorporates adversarial examples. This loss function encourages the model to make accurate predictions not only on standard examples but also on examples that have been perturbed to be adversarial. By optimising this combined loss function, the model learns to recognise and correctly classify both legitimate and adversarial inputs. Adversarial training can be performed using various techniques, such as projected gradient descent, where adversarial examples are generated by perturbing the input in the direction that maximises the model's loss. Alternatively, adversarial examples can be generated using more sophisticated algorithms, such as the fast gradient sign method (FGSM) or the basic iterative method (BIM). One of the challenges of adversarial training is finding a balance between improving the model's robustness to adversarial examples and maintaining its performance on standard examples. Training on adversarial examples can sometimes lead to a decrease in accuracy on standard examples, as the model learns to focus more on defending against attacks rather than generalising well to the underlying data distribution.

Overall, adversarial training is an important technique for enhancing the security and reliability of machine learning models, particularly in applications where security is critical, such as autonomous driving systems, healthcare diagnostics and financial transactions. By exposing the model to a diverse range of examples, including adversarial ones, adversarial training helps to improve the model's resilience to attacks and enhance its overall performance in real-world scenarios.

↣ *Randomised smoothing* is a sophisticated defence mechanism in the realm of adversarial robustness, designed to fortify machine learning models against subtle perturbations and adversarial attacks. This technique operates by injecting random noise into input data during the inference phase, thereby generating an ensemble of predictions. By incorporating randomness into the prediction process, randomised smoothing serves to obscure the model's decision boundaries and reduce its susceptibility to small perturbations in the input space. Essentially, this approach introduces variability into the model's predictions, making it more challenging for adversaries to craft adversarial examples that reliably manipulate the model's outputs. The underlying principle of randomised smoothing lies in the notion that the aggregation of multiple noisy predictions can lead to more robust and stable decisions, effectively mitigating the impact of adversarial perturbations. Through the strategic utilisation of randomisation, randomised smoothing offers a powerful defence mechanism that enhances the resilience of machine learning models in the face of adversarial attacks.

↣ *Feature space transformation models* represent a sophisticated approach to bolstering the robustness of machine learning models against adversarial attacks by fundamentally altering the representation of input data. Unlike traditional models that operate directly on the raw input features, transformation models manipulate the feature space itself, aiming to reduce the model's sensitivity to subtle perturbations and adversarial manipulations. At their core, these transformation models introduce alterations to the input features, effectively modifying their distribution or structure in a manner that renders the model less susceptible to adversarial attacks. By transforming the feature space, these models seek to reshape the landscape in which the model operates, making it more resilient to the subtle variations and manipulations that adversaries may introduce. From a regularisation standpoint, feature space transformation models align closely with the objective of mitigating overfitting and enhancing the generalisation capabilities of machine learning models. By introducing controlled transformations to the input features, these models impose constraints on the complexity of the learned decision boundaries, thereby preventing the model from relying too heavily on specific features or patterns that may be vulnerable to adversarial manipulation. Moreover, feature space transformation can be viewed as a form of data augmentation, where synthetic examples are generated to enrich the training dataset and expose the model to a diverse range of input variations. By expanding the diversity of the input space through transformations, these models effectively regularise the learning process, encouraging the model to learn more robust and generalisable representations of the underlying data distribution. In essence, feature space transformation models offer a principled approach to enhancing the robustness of machine learning models by reshaping the input space in a way that diminishes the impact of adversarial perturbations. By introducing controlled transformations and augmentations, these models not only mitigate the risks posed by adversarial attacks but also contribute to the overall regularisation and generalisation capabilities of the model, making it more adept at handling the complexities and uncertainties inherent in real-world data.

↣ *Ensemble techniques* in the realm of artificial intelligence (AI) involve combining predictions from multiple models to improve overall performance and robustness. This approach encompasses various methods, i.e., bagging, boosting and stacking, each offering unique benefits in enhancing the resilience of AI systems against adversarial attacks. Bagging, short for bootstrap aggregating, involves training multiple instances of the same model on different subsets of the training data and then combining their predictions through averaging or voting. By leveraging diverse subsets of the data, bagging reduces the variance of the model's predictions and enhances overall stability. In the context of adversarial attacks, the diversity among the models trained via bagging can mitigate the impact of attacks targeting specific vulnerabilities in individual models. Even if one model is compromised by an adversarial example, the ensemble's collective decision-making process can remain robust and resilient. Boosting, on the other hand, focuses on iteratively training a sequence of weak models, each one emphasising the data instances that were misclassified by previous models. By iteratively correcting errors and focusing on challenging data points, boosting gradually constructs a strong predictive model. Similar to bagging, the ensemble nature of boosting can enhance robustness against adversarial attacks by leveraging the collective wisdom of multiple models. Adversarial perturbations that may fool individual models are less likely to affect the entire ensemble, as the diverse set of weak learners can collectively counteract the impact of such attacks. Stacking, also known as stacked generalisation, is another ensemble technique used in machine learning to improve model performance and robustness. Unlike bagging and boosting, which focus on training multiple models independently and combining their predictions, stacking involves training a meta-model on the outputs of multiple base models. In stacking, the base models are trained on the same dataset, and their predictions on the validation set are used as features for training the meta-model. This meta-model learns to combine the predictions of the base models to make the final prediction. By learning from the diverse perspectives of the base models, the meta-model can often achieve better performance than any individual base model alone. One of the key advantages of stacking is its ability to capture complex patterns in the data by leveraging the strengths of different base models. Each base model may excel in capturing certain aspects of the data or be more robust to specific types of noise or uncertainty. By combining their predictions, stacking can produce a more robust and accurate final model. In essence, ensemble techniques serve as a powerful defence mechanism against adversarial attacks in AI systems by leveraging the collective intelligence of multiple models to enhance robustness and resilience. By combining predictions from diverse sources, ensemble methods mitigate the vulnerabilities inherent in individual models and provide a more reliable defence against adversarial manipulation of data.

↣ *Explainable AI (XAI)* represents a pivotal advancement in the field of artificial intelligence, particularly in contexts where transparency and interpretability are paramount. At its core, XAI prioritises the development and utilisation of machine learning models that can be readily understood and explained by humans. This emphasis on interpretability serves multiple critical purposes within AI systems, extending far beyond mere comprehension of model outputs. First and foremost, the use of interpretable models in XAI facilitates a deeper understanding of how these models arrive at their decisions. Traditional black-box models, while often highly accurate, lack transparency in their decision-making processes, making it challenging for stakeholders to comprehend the underlying reasoning behind model predictions. In contrast, interpretable models offer clear insights into the features and factors influencing decision outcomes, empowering users to gain actionable insights from model outputs. Importantly, this transparency inherent in interpretable models also plays a crucial role in the identification of vulnerabilities within AI systems. By providing visibility into the inner workings of the model, XAI techniques enable stakeholders to uncover potential weaknesses, biases or blind spots that may exist within the model architecture or training data. This heightened awareness of vulnerabilities facilitates proactive measures to address and mitigate risks before they manifest into significant issues or adverse outcomes. Moreover, XAI contributes to the crafting of more robust AI models by fostering a collaborative approach to model development and refinement. By enabling stakeholders to interrogate and validate model decisions, interpretable models facilitate iterative improvements and refinements based on real-world feedback and domain expertise. This iterative process of model validation and enhancement helps enhance the robustness and reliability of AI systems, ultimately leading to better performance and trustworthiness in deployment scenarios. In the context of regularisation, XAI techniques intersect with traditional regularisation methods by emphasising the importance of model interpretability as a regularisation constraint. While traditional regularisation methods focus on controlling model complexity to prevent overfitting and improve generalisation performance, XAI techniques extend this notion by incorporating interpretability as an additional regularisation criterion. By prioritising the development of interpretable models, XAI effectively imposes constraints on model complexity, encouraging the creation of more transparent and comprehensible models that align with human intuition and domain knowledge. In summary, XAI represents a paradigm shift in AI research and development, placing a premium on transparency, interpretability and human-centric design principles. By emphasising the use of interpretable models, XAI facilitates a deeper understanding of AI systems, enhances vulnerability detection and mitigation, fosters collaborative model development and aligns with the goals of regularisation by promoting model transparency and simplicity.

Regularisation techniques and architectural enhancements are integral components of robust AI development. As the field advances, continuous research into novel regularisation methods, innovative architectures and the integration of adversarial training will be essential for creating AI systems that can effectively navigate the challenges posed by adversarial manipulation while maintaining high levels of performance and reliability.

3.4.8 Intrusion kill chain

The kill chain concept, originally developed by Lockheed Martin in the context of military operations, has been adapted for cybersecurity to describe the stages of a cyberattack [39]. It provides a structured framework for understanding the lifecycle of an attack, from initial reconnaissance to final exfiltration of data. Here's a detailed breakdown of each stage (Figure 3.5):

- *Reconnaissance*: The attacker gathers information about the target system or organisation, often through publicly available sources, social engineering or scanning tools. This stage involves identifying potential vulnerabilities and entry points for exploitation.
- *Weaponisation*: In this stage, the attacker creates or obtains a malicious payload, such as malware or exploit kits, and prepares it for deployment. This payload is often tailored to exploit specific vulnerabilities identified during reconnaissance.
- *Delivery*: The attacker delivers the malicious payload to the target system or network. This can occur through various vectors, including email attachments, malicious links, drive-by downloads or physical media.
- *Exploitation*: Once the malicious payload reaches the target system, the attacker exploits vulnerabilities to gain unauthorised access. This may involve executing code, escalating privileges or bypassing security controls to establish a foothold within the network.
- *Installation*: With access to the target system, the attacker installs additional tools or malware to maintain persistence and establish control over the compromised system. This stage often involves creating backdoors, installing remote access Trojans (RATs) or modifying system configurations.
- *Command and control (C2)*: The attacker establishes communication channels with the compromised systems to remotely control and manage the attack. This typically involves connecting to command and control servers or utilising covert communication channels to evade detection.
- *Actions on objectives*: In the final stage, the attacker achieves their primary objectives, which may include data exfiltration, data destruction, financial fraud or espionage. The attacker may exploit the compromised systems to steal sensitive information, disrupt operations or further propagate the attack within the network.

Understanding the kill chain model enables security professionals to identify and disrupt attacks at various stages of execution. By analysing each

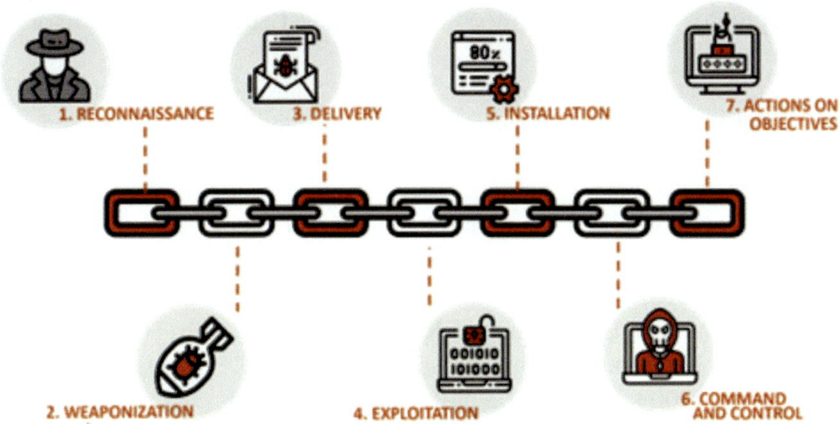

Figure 3.5 Intrusion kill chain.

phase of the kill chain, organisations can implement proactive security measures, such as intrusion detection systems, endpoint protection and network segmentation, to detect, mitigate and prevent cyber threats. Additionally, mapping observed threats to the kill chain framework helps organisations prioritise security controls and allocate resources effectively to mitigate the most significant risks.

References

[1] Rozenman, Georgi & Kundu, Neel Kanth & Liu, Ruiqi & Zhang, Leyi & Maslennikov, Alona & Reches, Yuval & Youm, Heung. (2023). The quantum internet: A synergy of quantum information technologies and 6G networks. IET Quantum Communication. 4 n/a-n/a. 10.1049/qtc2.12069.

[2] C. H. Bennett and G. Brassard. "Quantum cryptography: Public key distribution and coin tossing". In Proceedings of IEEE International Conference on Computers, Systems and Signal Processing, volume 175, page 8. New York, 1984.

[3] Ekert, Artur K. "Quantum cryptography based on Bell's theorem". Physical Review Letters. 67 (6): 661–663. August 1991. doi:10.1103/PhysRevLett.67.661

[4] Charles H. Bennett, Gilles Brassard, and N. David Mermin: Quantum cryptography without Bell's theorem, Phys. Rev. Lett. 68, 557. February 1992.

[5] Mu, Yi; Seberry, Jennifer; Zheng, Yuliang, "Shared cryptographic bits via quantized quadrature phase amplitudes of light". Optics Communications. 123 (1–3): 344–352. 1996. doi:10.1016/0030-4018(95)00688-5.

[6] Bruss, D. "Optimal Eavesdropping in Quantum Cryptography with Six States". Phys. Rev. Lett. 81 (14): 3018–3021. 1998. doi:10.1103/PhysRevLett.81.3018

[7] Hwang, Won-Young. "Quantum Key Distribution with High Loss: Toward Global Secure Communication". Physical Review Letters. 91 (5): 057901. 2003. doi:10.1103/physrevlett.91.057901

[8] Lo, Hoi-Kwong. Quantum key distribution with vacua or dim pulses as decoy states. Proceedings of 2004 IEEE International Symposium on Information Theory. New York: IEEE Press. p. 137. 2004. doi:10.1109/ISIT.2004.1365174

[9] Valerio Scarani; Antonio Acín; Grégoire Ribordy; Nicolas Gisin (2004). "Quantum Cryptography Protocols Robust against Photon Number Splitting Attacks for Weak Laser Pulse Implementations". Physical Review Letters. 92 (5). 2004. doi:10.1103/PhysRevLett.92.057901

[10] Kak, Subhash, "A Three-Stage Quantum Cryptography Protocol". Foundations of Physics Letters. 19 (3): 293–296. 2006. doi:10.1007/s10702-006-0520-9.

[11] Mubashir Khan, Muhammad; Murphy, Michael; Beige, Almut, "High error-rate quantum key distribution for long-distance communication". New Journal of Physics. 11 (6): 2009. doi:10.1088/1367-2630/11/6/063043

[12] Ding, Yunhong; Bacco, Davide, "High-dimensional quantum key distribution based on multicore fiber using silicon photonic integrated circuits". npj Quantum Information. 3: 25. 2017. doi:10.1038/s41534-017-0026-2

[13] A. Shields and I. Abram, Semiconductor sources of single photons and photon pairs, "Quantum Information Processing & Communications in Europe" (9 pages), March 2005

[14] O. Thomas, C. L. Salter, A. J. Bennett, R. M. Stevenson, M. A. Pooley, M. B. Ward, R. B. Patel, A. B. de la Giroday, N. Skold, I. Farrer, C. A. Nicoll, D. A. Ritchie and A. J. Shields, Semiconductor Single Photon Devices for Quantum Information Processing. AIP Conf. Proc.,

vol 1363, pp. 339-344, 17 October 2011 ISBN: 978-0-7354-0921-7 Edited by Timothy Ralph and Ping Koy Lam Quantum Communication, Measurement and Computing (QCMC): The Tenth International Conference

[15] Grünenfelder, F., Boaron, A., Resta, G.V. et al. Fast single-photon detectors and real-time key distillation enable high secret-key-rate quantum key distribution systems. Nat. Photon. 17, 422–426 (2023). doi:10.1038/s41566-023-01168-2

[16] Morton, J., Tyryshkin, A., Brown, R. et al. Solid-state quantum memory using the 31P nuclear spin. Nature 455, 1085–1088 (2008). doi:10.1038/nature07295

[17] Bartolucci, S., Birchall, P., Bombín, H. et al. Fusion-based quantum computation. Nat Commun 14, 912 (2023). doi:10.1038/s41467-023-36493-1

[18] Li, Chi-Kwong & Nakahara, Mikio & Poon, Yiu & Sze, Nung-Sing & Tomita, Hiroyuki. (2011). Efficient Quantum Error Correction for Fully Correlated Noise. Physics Letters A - PHYS LETT A. 375. 10.1016/j.physleta.2011.07.027.

[19] Sebastianus A. Goorden, Marcel Horstmann, Allard P. Mosk, Boris Škorić, and Pepijn W. H. Pinkse, "Quantum-secure authentication of a physical unclonable key," Optica 1, 421-424 (2014)

[20] Philip Sibson, Jake E. Kennard, Stasja Stanisic, Chris Erven, Jeremy L. O'Brien, and Mark G. Thompson, "Integrated silicon photonics for high-speed quantum key distribution," Optica 4, 172-177 (2017)

[21] ITU-T, Y.3800, Overview on networks supporting quantum key distribution, 2019.

[22] ITU-T, Technical Report 2021, Quantum key distribution network protocols: Quantum layer, 2021.

[23] Mannalatha, V., Mishra, S. & Pathak, A. A comprehensive review of quantum random number generators: concepts, classification and the origin of randomness. Quantum Inf Process 22, 439 (2023)

[24] Quantis QRNG (Quantum Random Number Generator) - ID Quantique - https://www.idquantique.com/random-number-generation/products/quantis-random-number-generator/

[25] Quantis QRNG Chip receives NIST Entropy Source Validation (ESV) Certification on IID Track - https://www.idquantique.com/qrng-chip-nist-certification/

[26] The National Institute of Standards and Technology (NIST) - https://www.nist.gov/

[27] The National Institute of Standards and Technology (NIST), NIST IR 8413: Status Report on the Third Round of the NIST Post-Quantum Cryptography Standardization Process

[28] International Organization for Standardization (ISO) - https://www.iso.org/

[29] International Electrotechnical Commission (IEC) - https://www.iec.ch/homepage

[30] Quantum Information Technology Standardization (ISO/IEC JTC 1 Workshop) - https://www.iec.ch/node/275995

[31] ETSI Cyber Quantum Safe Cryptography (QSC) Working Group - https://www.etsi.org/technologies/quantum-safe-cryptography

[32] ETSI Quantum-Safe Cryptography (QSC) working group, Technical Report TR 103 619

[33] Sarker, I. H., Furhad, M. H., & Nowrozy, R. (2021). Ai-driven cybersecurity: An overview, security intelligence modeling and research directions. SN Computer Science, 2(3), 1–18. https://doi.org/10.1007/s42979-021-00557-0

[34] Papernot, Nicolas & McDaniel, Patrick & Wu, Xi & Jha, Somesh & Swami, Ananthram. (2016). Distillation as a Defense to Adversarial Perturbations Against Deep Neural Networks. 582-597. 10.1109/SP.2016.41.

[35] Weilin Xu, David Evans, Yanjun Qi. Feature Squeezing: Detecting Adversarial Examples in Deep Neural Networks. 2018 Network and Distributed System Security Symposium. 18-21 February, San Diego, California.

[36] Aldahdooh, A., Hamidouche, W., Fezza, S.A. et al. Adversarial example detection for DNN models: a review and experimental comparison. Artif Intell Rev 55, 4403–4462 (2022).

[37] Madry, Aleksander & Makelov, Aleksandar & Schmidt, Ludwig & Tsipras, Dimitris & Vladu, Adrian. (2017). Towards Deep Learning Models Resistant to Adversarial Attacks.

[38] Papernot, Nicolas & McDaniel, Patrick & Sinha, Arunesh & Wellman, Michael. (2016). Towards the Science of Security and Privacy in Machine Learning.

[39] Hutchins, Eric & Cloppert, Michael & Amin, Rohan. (2011). Intelligence-Driven Computer Network Defense Informed by Analysis of Adversary Campaigns and Intrusion Kill Chains. Leading Issues in Information Warfare & Security Research. 1.

4

Standardisation, Regulation, Policy and Ethical Considerations

In the era of 6G, where standardisation plays a critical role alongside regulation in ensuring security and privacy, the proliferation of advanced technologies and the interconnectedness of digital ecosystems underscore the importance of regulatory frameworks. These frameworks aim to safeguard individuals' privacy rights, ensure the security of sensitive data and mitigate potential risks associated with emerging technologies. Here are several key aspects of regulation within security and privacy in the 6G era, coupled with the imperative of standardisation:

- *Data protection regulations*: With the exponential growth of data generation and utilisation in 6G networks, robust data protection regulations are essential to safeguard individuals' privacy rights and prevent unauthorised access or misuse of personal data. Regulatory frameworks, such as the General Data Protection Regulation (GDPR) in the European Union, establish guidelines for the collection, processing, storage and sharing of personal data, imposing strict requirements on organisations to ensure transparency, consent and accountability in data handling practices.
- *Cybersecurity standards and compliance*: Regulatory bodies and industry organisations develop cybersecurity standards and compliance frameworks to address evolving cyber threats and vulnerabilities in 6G networks. These standards outline best practices for securing network infrastructure, protecting against cyberattacks and responding to security incidents. Compliance with established cybersecurity standards, such as the ISO/IEC 27001 series, NIST Cybersecurity Framework or industry-specific regulations, is essential for organisations to demonstrate their commitment to maintaining robust security posture and safeguarding critical assets.

- *Privacy by design and default*: In the 6G era, privacy considerations are integrated into the design and development of network architectures, protocols and applications through the concept of privacy by design and default. Regulatory requirements mandate that privacy features and safeguards are embedded into technology solutions from the outset, ensuring that privacy principles, such as data minimisation, encryption and user consent, are prioritised throughout the product lifecycle. By adopting privacy-enhancing technologies and practices, organisations can mitigate privacy risks and build trust among users.
- *Regulatory oversight of emerging technologies*: Regulatory agencies monitor the development and deployment of emerging technologies, such as artificial intelligence (AI), Internet of Things (IoT) and edge computing, to address potential security and privacy concerns. Regulatory oversight ensures that innovations comply with legal and ethical standards, adhere to principles of fairness and non-discrimination and uphold individuals' rights to privacy and data protection. Additionally, regulatory authorities may impose restrictions or guidelines on the use of sensitive technologies in critical sectors, such as healthcare, finance and transportation, to mitigate risks to public safety and national security.
- *International collaboration and harmonisation*: Given the global nature of 6G networks and digital services, international collaboration and harmonisation of regulatory frameworks are essential to facilitate cross-border data flows, promote interoperability and address transnational cyber threats. Regulatory bodies, industry associations and standardisation organisations work together to develop common principles, guidelines and protocols for ensuring security and privacy in the 6G ecosystem. By aligning regulatory approaches and fostering cooperation among stakeholders, countries can effectively address emerging challenges and promote a secure and trusted digital environment worldwide.

Overall, regulation within security and privacy in the 6G era aims to strike a balance between promoting innovation and protecting individuals' rights, ensuring that technological advancements are deployed responsibly and ethically to benefit society while mitigating potential risks and vulnerabilities. By establishing clear legal frameworks, enforcing compliance measures and fostering collaboration among stakeholders, regulatory authorities play a crucial role in shaping the future of cybersecurity and privacy in the 6G landscape.

4.1 6G Standardisation Timeline

The advent of 6G marks its transition into the preliminary phase before formal standardisation (Figure 4.1). By the close of 2023, the 3rd Generation Partnership Project (3GPP) pledged its commitment to crafting the sixth-generation mobile system. This dedication was further reinforced with the establishment of a roadmap for 6G standardisation during the 3GPP meetings held in March 2024 in Maastricht, the Netherlands. Additionally, various industry standardisation bodies, such as the Open Radio Access Network (O-RAN) Alliance, are actively engaged in shaping specific aspects of 6G networks. We will delineate the timeline set forth by 3GPP, its alignment with the International Telecommunication Union (ITU), and underscore pivotal principles guiding the development of 6G.

The International Telecommunication Union (ITU) assumes a pivotal role in the standardisation process by establishing the criteria for classifying a system as an International Mobile Telecommunications (IMT) technology. This IMT classification is particularly significant as it grants access to a broad spectrum of frequency bands globally or regionally recognised as IMT bands. Such classification serves as a crucial milestone in paving the way for the establishment of a comprehensive global commercial ecosystem for 6G. Within the ITU framework, 6G is denoted as IMT-2030, following the categorisation of previous generations, with 5G labelled as IMT-2020, 3G as IMT-2000 and 4G as IMT Advanced. The ITU's efforts towards IMT-2030 entail a series of distinct tasks, some of which have been finalised while others are on the verge of commencement. The following delineation offers a high-level overview of the various steps that the ITU will undertake in defining IMT-2030.

The initial phase involved the finalisation of two key deliverables: 'The Future Technology Trends' [1] and the 'Framework for IMT-2030 and Beyond' [2]. Between 2024 and the conclusion of 2026, the ITU will focus on delineating the technical performance criteria and corresponding evaluation methodologies for IMT-2030. These criteria will encompass functional aspects, such as supporting specific functions, as well as quantitative metrics, including spectral efficiency, latency and positioning accuracy, under specified conditions. Following the completion of the requirements, the process of soliciting technologies for IMT-2030 is set to commence in 2027 and extend until early 2029. For this purpose, the 3GPP will submit self-assessments of 6G to the ITU by the end of 2028 or the beginning of 2029. The final phase, which involves the ITU's decision to designate a technology as IMT-2030, is

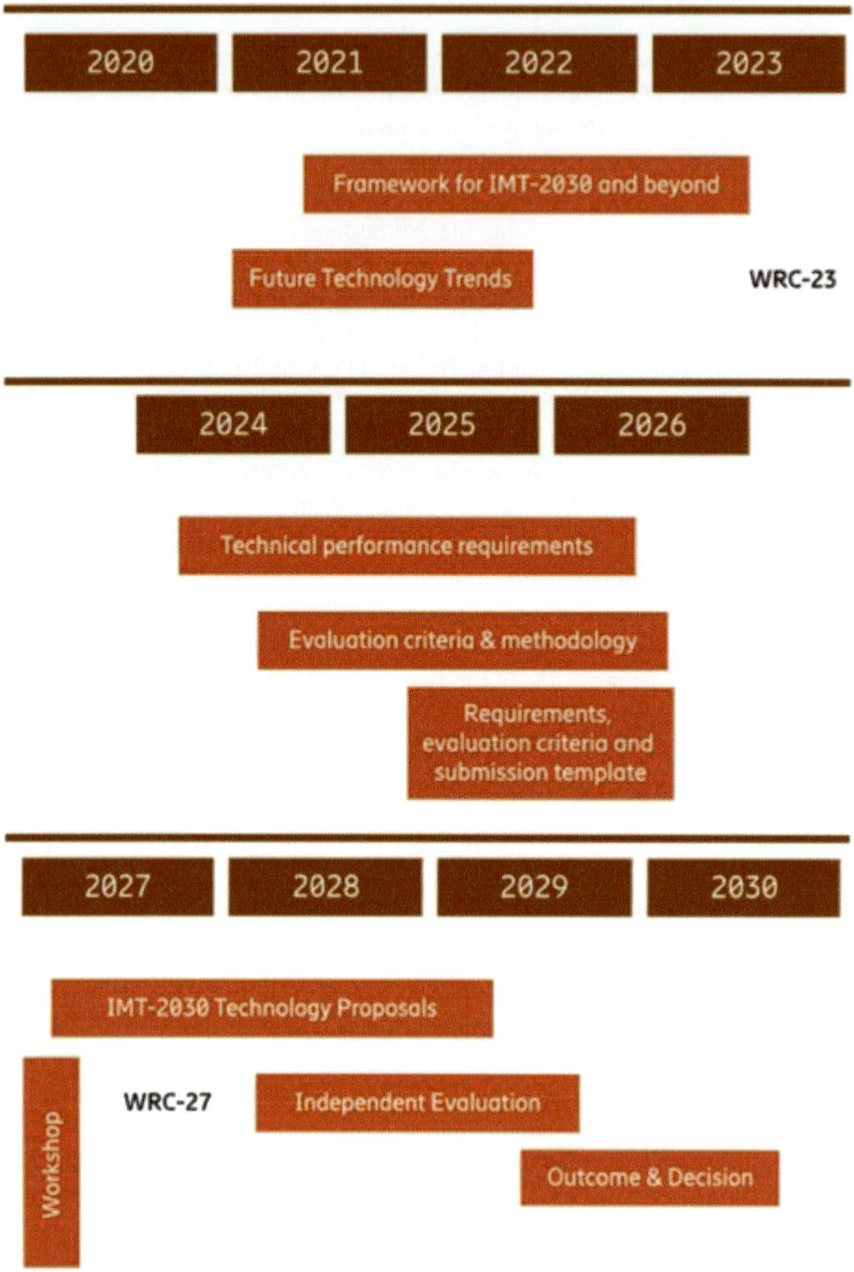

Figure 4.1 6G standardisation timeline.

anticipated to conclude by 2030. Subsequently, there will be opportunities to update submissions with the latest specifications during early 2030, paving the way for potential commercial 6G deployments by 2030. Concerning technology submissions, organisations and companies (referred to as proponents) present proposals to the ITU for classification as IMT technology. These submissions include a detailed description of the technology alongside a declaration of its performance, showcasing how it aligns with the IMT-2030 requirements established by the ITU. To ensure accuracy, the ITU employs independent evaluation groups to assess the declared performance of candidate technologies. Based on feedback from these evaluation groups, the ITU then determines whether to grant the technology the IMT-2030 designation.

By 2023, 3GPP had committed to the development of 6G specifications. To reinforce this commitment, during the March 2024 meetings, 3GPP took a significant step by establishing a timeline for 6G. Here, we will delve into the timeline of this project and provide a broad overview of the various tasks involved. The 3GPP timeline is depicted in Figure 4.2. Typically, 3GPP's work is organised into releases, and the work on Release 19 commenced at the beginning of 2024. At the conclusion of each release, 3GPP updates its specifications to reflect the progress made during that time. Technical specification is a detailed set of instructions or rules describing how a particular 3GPP technology or system should be designed and implemented. The final, agreed-upon version of a set of 3GPP specifications is converted into a standard by 3GPP's organisational partners (e.g., ETSI). Adherence to this standard by all members ensures seamless interoperability among different devices and networks worldwide. Given the extensive nature of developing a new generation of technology, the work spans across multiple releases. For instance, 5G began with Release 14, with the initial specifications finalised

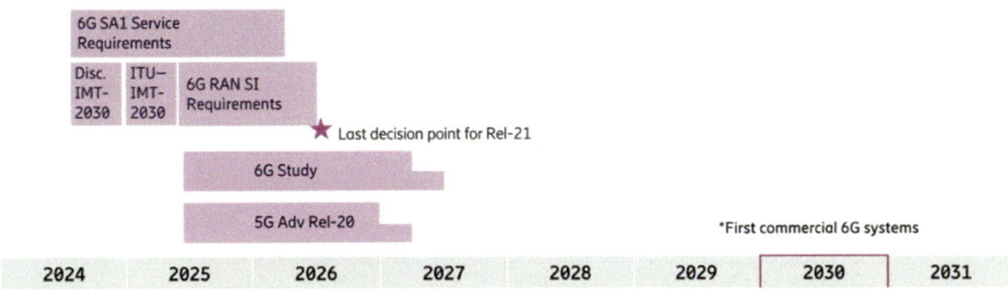

Figure 4.2 3GPP timing.

in Release 15. In the case of 6G, work within 3GPP will commence in 2024 during Release 19, focusing on requirements-related tasks. According to Ericsson's perspective [3], the first specifications are expected to be completed by the end of 2028 in Release 21. This endorsed timeline by 3GPP paves the way for initial commercial systems to enter the market by 2030, aligning with the ITU's timeline. It is important to note that while 3GPP is dedicated to developing 6G, the evolution of 5G Advanced will continue across several releases, introducing new technology that will serve the global market until 2030 and beyond. This ensures not only the ongoing evolution of 5G Advanced in the market but also facilitates a seamless transition to 6G.

Now, let us delve deeper into the various phases of 3GPP's work on 6G, highlighting key milestones and their relation to the earlier described ITU work. The work can be broadly divided into the following phases:

- A use case and requirements study during Release 19 and 20.
- A technical study in Release 20, extending into the beginning of Release 21.
- The initiation of a 6G work item and a self-evaluation study in Release 21.

Commencing in May 2024, the groundwork for defining 6G service requirements within 3GPP will commence. Representatives from the market will provide insights into innovative aspects to be considered for 6G, prompting discussions within 3GPP to outline the scope of the service requirement study.

Approval for the study is anticipated by September 2024. Typically, service-level requirements delineate, at a macro level, the specific demands posed by a particular functionality on the entire communication system. This encompasses user equipment (UE), radio access network (RAN) equipment, core network, security architecture, operational procedures and maintenance, among other factors. Given that 6G is a nascent system, the study will encompass both novel use cases and enhancements of functionalities already present in 5G. Furthermore, dedicated efforts will focus on requirements pertaining to UE and RAN. These demands are somewhat more granular. One facet involves addressing the ITU requirements. Preliminary deliberations will commence in September 2024, with a more concrete scope of work expected by December 2024, culminating in the agreement on a study item. The majority of the work concerning ITU-related requirements is slated for completion by June 2025. The latter segment of the requirement endeavours aims to tackle any overarching requirements stemming from commercial considerations that may not be encompassed by the ITU mandates. An illustration of such a requirement is the seamless migration from 5G to 6G. The study item addressing these demands will kick off in June 2025 and conclude by June 2026. To summarise, this initiates a comprehensive RAN-level requirement study phase, commencing in September 2024 and concluding in June 2026.

3GPP's primary objective will be crafting the 6G system, with technical endeavours commencing in Q3 2025 within the working groups. The system's design will unfold across two phases spanning two releases. The initial phase involves a comprehensive study of various techniques, followed by an in-depth design phase culminating in fully implementable 6G specifications in Release 21. This study initiates in Q3 2025 and extends over 21 months, running parallel to the evolution of 5G Advanced during Release 20, which spans 18 months. Throughout the technical study and requirements development, the 3GPP community will gain clearer insights into the timeline for finalising 6G. Taking these insights and evolving commercial demands into account, 3GPP aims to determine, no later than June 2026, when the Release 21 work item will reach finalisation, thus creating the initial versions of the 6G specifications.

With the timeline established, the discussion will pivot towards delineating the study item's scope and formulating the actual 6G design. While the term '6G' encompasses a broad spectrum beyond connectivity services, several fundamental principles can be outlined. Primarily, 6G should constitute a global standard, not only accommodating new, unforeseen use cases but crucially facilitating the widespread adoption of emerging 5G use cases like extended reality (XR). Key sectors such as low-power wide area (LPWA) IoT, fixed wireless access (FWA), non-terrestrial networks (NTN) and dependable, time-critical communication need to be addressed proactively. Historically, supporting these scenarios came as an afterthought, often leading to overly complex solutions and limited practical adoption. Spectrum-wise, 6G should operate across a broad spectrum range, encompassing FR1, FR2 and the cm-wave range. Efficient multi-RAT spectrum sharing (MRSS) between 5G and 6G is imperative to ensure expansive 6G coverage, and MRSS should be seamlessly integrated into the 6G design from inception. Fortunately, the streamlined design of 5G suggests that 5G–6G sharing can be highly efficient, with minimal overhead (unlike the less efficient 4G–5G sharing due to the inherent complexities of the 4G design). Additionally, transitioning from 5G to 6G must be seamless, following a single migration path. A crucial lesson learned from 5G is to avoid an array of architectural options that fragment the market and impede the adoption of new technology. This implies: The 6G radio access network (RAN) should interface with an evolution of the 5G core network, leveraging its flexible architecture that can readily accommodate new 6G features. Building upon the established foundation of the 5G core network facilitates the smooth and cost-effective introduction of the 6G RAN and other 6G features. 6G should solely support standalone operation, with devices connected to either 5G or 6G at any given time. Despite the initial allure of dual connectivity across generations for aggregating spectrum resources, in reality, it often leads to subpar performance, with traffic predominantly traversing on one leg only. MRSS emerges as the preferred migration path. 6G should incorporate open interfaces to foster a vibrant ecosystem. Hence, standardisation endeavours should prioritise key interfaces where multi-vendor interoperability is both commercially valuable and technically viable. This includes the RAN-CN interface, the air interface, the next-generation lower-layer split and inter-RAN node mobility interfaces. Observability is pivotal for enabling widespread utilisation of artificial intelligence/machine learning (AI/ML) and automation. Therefore, provisions for necessary device-side measurements and reports should be specified from the outset. Lastly, energy efficiency stands out as a paramount consideration. Network-side enhancements, building upon the ultra-lean paradigm of 5G, should extend into spatial and frequency domains by segregating idle and connected mode designs. To ensure prolonged device battery life, baseline design features like wake-up signals should be incorporated.

In summary, the International Telecommunication Union (ITU) has been laying the groundwork for IMT-2030, with a focus on technical performance requirements set to commence in 2024. Meanwhile, 3GPP took its first steps towards 6G in 2023, committing to develop specifications and initiating requirement work in 2024. According to the approved timeline, the actual development of 6G technology within 3GPP is slated to begin in mid-2025, starting with a 21-month study item to assess technology options. By June 2026, 3GPP aims to determine the duration of Release 21 work, paving the way for the first versions of 6G specifications. This timeline targets the introduction of commercial 6G systems to the market by 2030.

4.2 Liability, Accountability and Government Policies

Liability and accountability in 6G networks are pivotal aspects that require thorough examination to ensure the integrity, security and ethical use of emerging technologies. The multifaceted landscape of legal, ethical and regulatory frameworks is shaping the responsibilities of stakeholders in the deployment and operation of 6G networks.

In the rapidly evolving landscape of 6G networks, educating stakeholders is paramount to fostering awareness and understanding of the inherent risks and challenges. Industry stakeholders, including developers, policymakers and end-users, must be equipped with the knowledge to comprehend the imminent threat posed by advanced cryptographic algorithms such as Shor's algorithm. By emphasising the potential vulnerabilities and implications of quantum computing, stakeholders can better grasp the urgency of implementing quantum-resistant cryptographic solutions. Advocating for a strategic shift towards adopting quantum-resistant cryptographic algorithms is imperative to mitigate the risks associated with quantum computing. By raising awareness about the necessity of transitioning to post-quantum cryptographic algorithms, stakeholders can proactively safeguard 6G networks against potential security breaches and vulnerabilities. This strategic shift requires concerted efforts from industry leaders, policymakers and regulatory bodies to prioritise the integration of quantum-resistant cryptographic solutions in the design and deployment of 6G networks.

Global collaboration plays a pivotal role in addressing the quantum threat and standardising post-quantum cryptographic algorithms. International efforts aimed at developing standardised cryptographic solutions underscore the importance of collaborative endeavours in preparing for the quantum era. By fostering global collaboration and knowledge sharing, stakeholders can collectively work towards establishing robust and resilient security measures for 6G networks. Industry standards serve as a cornerstone in ensuring interoperability and the widespread adoption of quantum-resistant cryptographic solutions across diverse communication platforms. The role of industry standards in facilitating the integration of standardised cryptographic algorithms cannot be overstated. By adhering to established standards, stakeholders can streamline the implementation process and enhance the interoperability of cryptographic solutions, thereby fortifying the security posture of 6G networks.

The vision of ubiquitous connectivity, a cornerstone of mobile networks, necessitates extensive wide area coverage, rendering the pursuit of higher spectrum bands, such as terahertz bands, impractical for the next generation of mobile technology. However, these bands align with the 6G vision, offering potential integration with short-range radar for enhanced edge-to-user environments. A supportive 6G spectrum policy should prioritise maximising the effectiveness of bands below 6GHz, fostering advanced spectrum sharing research, long-term spectrum allocation planning and spectrum reframing strategies. This approach aims to eliminate the need for next-generation spectrum auctions, establish common frequency networks and pave the way for AI-powered spectrum sharing, ultimately driving the transition towards a 6G world empowered by artificial intelligence.

Institution of Engineering and Technology (IET) offers key recommendations for policymakers to ensure the success of 6G initiatives [4]:

- *Rethinking mobile generation change*: 6G should adopt a new approach that moves beyond the traditional pursuit of higher data speeds in higher spectrum bands, which is no longer sustainable.
- *Setting ambitious goals*: 6G initiatives should be driven by ambitious goals inspired by societal challenges like sustainable economic growth, pandemics and climate change. A robust pre-standardisation research phase is essential to support these goals.
- *Coordinated modernisation*: 6G should serve as a catalyst for comprehensive modernisation efforts, ensuring the simultaneous upgrade of various infrastructures to sustain interoperability and secure global economies through common standards.
- *Guided research phase*: The research phase of 6G should focus on building consensus on promising research directions, such as the Internet of Senses, while remaining open to breakthrough discoveries. It should be viewed as a competitive arena where the best ideas are pulled into standardisation.
- *Rolling programme of improvements*: Implementing 6G as a rolling programme of improvements over the late 2030s will help smooth out investment profiles and ensure continuous development.
- *Role of governments and regulators*: Governments should use 6G initiatives to establish long-term goals for national infrastructure, embracing digital and communications infrastructures to accommodate a future convergence of fixed and mobile worlds.
- *Engaging with industry*: Governments should engage with industry from the outset to create conducive conditions for sustained research and investment in national infrastructures.
- *Spectrum policy*: A supportive spectrum policy for 6G infrastructure, particularly focusing on effective utilisation of bands below 6 GHz for wide area coverage, is crucial for success.
- *Synchronisation of regulation and innovation*: The regulatory landscape and industry dynamics will evolve significantly in the coming years. To

maximise the benefits of 6G, regulation and technology innovation must develop in sync.

↣ *Modernisation of standards bodies*: The 3GPP standards body needs to modernise to meet the challenges of the next decade. Regional standards bodies, such as the European Telecommunications Standards Institute, should initiate discussions on necessary reforms to global standardisation for 6G to build upon current excellence.

The development of 6G, potentially the largest collaborative technology initiative in the coming decade, is not subject to the influence of any single government or entity. Instead, governments are expected to engage with 6G initiatives in multifaceted ways. They can facilitate consensus building domestically, leveraging their influence to foster dialogue within their research communities. Additionally, governments funding national research have the opportunity to amplify the impact of mobile radio research outcomes by fostering regional and international collaboration. Given the cross-border nature of radio wave propagation, regional cooperation is vital in determining the utilisation of mobile bands, necessitating the involvement of governments and national regulators. Governments also bear the responsibility of ensuring long-term improvement plans for national wireless infrastructures, as exemplified by the collaborative efforts seen under the 5G umbrella. Furthermore, governments play a crucial role in preparing industries and society to embrace and derive benefits from 6G technology upon its eventual arrival. Despite short-term challenges demanding immediate attention, governments are urged to prioritise long-term strategic planning and actively participate in national, regional and global discussions surrounding 6G.

In February 2024, a Joint Statement was published [5] by the Governments of the United States of America, Australia, Canada, the Czech Republic, Finland, France, Japan, the Republic of Korea, Sweden and the United Kingdom on the occasion of endorsing principles for sixth generation (6G) wireless communication. They emphasise the importance of collaboration and unity in supporting open, free, global, interoperable, reliable, resilient and secure connectivity. These principles aim to contribute to building a more inclusive, sustainable, secure and peaceful future for all. The governments call upon other nations, organisations and stakeholders to join them in upholding these principles and working towards their implementation. The shared principles include:

↣ *Trusted technology and protective of national security*: Ensuring that 6G technologies are supported by secure and resilient technology, facilitating the protection of national security.

↣ *Secure, resilient and protective of privacy*: Developing 6G technologies with systematic approaches to cybersecurity, ensuring reliability, resilience, safety and privacy protection.

↣ *Global industry-led and inclusive standard setting & international collaborations*: Building 6G technologies on global standards developed through open, transparent and consensus-based decision-making processes.

↣ *Cooperation to enable open and interoperable innovation*: Promoting international cooperation to facilitate open, secure, resilient and interoperable networks.

↣ *Affordability, sustainability and global connectivity*: Ensuring that 6G technologies are energy-efficient, accessible and contribute to reducing environmental impacts, with a focus on bridging digital divides and empowering developing nations.

↣ *Spectrum and manufacturing*: Supporting secure and resilient supply chains, promoting global competitiveness and efficiently utilising spectrum resources for coexistence with incumbent service providers.

Additionally, the European Union (EU) is actively supporting research and innovation in the field of 6G to secure a leadership position in this sector [6]. Established in 2021, the European Smart Networks and Services Joint Undertaking (SNS JU) receives funding from both the EU budget and industry. Collaborating closely with the European Commission, the 6G Smart Networks and Services Industry Association (6G-IA) represents the interests of European industry and research stakeholders, including operators, manufacturers, academics and small- to medium-sized enterprises. With a budget of at least âĆň1.8 billion for 2021–2027, the SNS JU provides financial support through research and innovation grants to advance 6G technology sovereignty and accelerate 5G deployment. Recently, it allocated âĆň129 million for collaborative projects to advance 6G systems and prepare for standardisation activities. Member States within the EU are also driving initiatives towards 6G development, such as Finland's 6G Flagship and 6G Finland. Furthermore, under the EU Recovery and Resilience Facility, Member States are mandated to allocate a portion of funds to support digital transitions, including 5G and 6G projects. In October 2022, the European Commission announced Hexa-X-II, a research initiative funded under the SNS JU, aimed at laying the foundation for 6G technology. With 44 participating organisations, Hexa-X-II will develop a pre-standardised platform for future 6G standardisation efforts. International collaboration is emphasised, with the EU fostering partnerships with countries like the US and Japan. Initiatives such as the EU-US Trade Technology Council and the EU-Japan Digital Partnership aim to facilitate joint research and cooperation on emerging technologies, including 6G. These efforts are guided by principles such as security-by-design and energy efficiency standards, outlined in a joint 6G outlook issued by the EU and its international partners.

The mobile industry's most prosperous phases coincided with regulatory adjustments aligning with technological advancements, a model to emulate for 6G. Even in the preliminary stages, key long-term regulatory considerations emerge, including addressing disparities between entrenched domestic enterprises and dominant foreign players operating under distinct regulatory frameworks. A recalibrated regulatory environment could optimise investments from various stakeholders, including mobile network operators, property owners and public subsidies, ensuring future wireless infrastructure development. The efficacy of net neutrality, pivotal in catalysing video streaming growth, prompts exploration into regulated neutrality's potential role in equitably distributing cost benefits in the 6G era. Engaging governments and regulators alongside industry stakeholders early on is essential to crafting regulatory frameworks conducive to desired 6G technological outcomes, aligning with global challenges.

4.3 Ethical Considerations and Data Privacy

The ethical dimensions surrounding artificial intelligence (AI) encompass a broad spectrum of considerations, ranging from issues of fairness and accountability to transparency and privacy. As AI technologies continue to advance and permeate various aspects of society, including sensitive domains such as security, healthcare and criminal justice, it becomes increasingly imperative to address these ethical concerns to ensure responsible development and deployment of AI systems.

In the context of AI-driven security measures, ethical considerations take on heightened significance due to the potential impact of these technologies on individuals, organisations and society at large.

- ↣ One of the primary ethical considerations revolves around *fairness and bias mitigation* in AI algorithms used for security purposes. Biases inherent in training data or algorithmic decision-making processes can lead to discriminatory outcomes, disproportionately affecting certain groups or individuals. To address this concern, developers and practitioners must implement measures to detect, mitigate and prevent biases in AI systems, thereby ensuring fairness and equity in security-related decision-making processes.

- *Transparency and accountability* are also critical ethical considerations in the development and deployment of AI-driven security measures. As AI algorithms become increasingly complex and opaque, it becomes challenging for stakeholders to understand how these systems arrive at their decisions. Lack of transparency can erode trust in AI systems and hinder stakeholders' ability to hold developers and deployers accountable for their actions. Therefore, efforts to enhance transparency and accountability in AI systems, such as explainable AI (XAI) techniques and algorithmic auditing, are essential for fostering trust and accountability in security applications.
- Moreover, *privacy and data protection* emerge as significant ethical considerations in the context of AI-driven security measures. AI algorithms often rely on vast amounts of data, including sensitive personal information, to make predictions or detect anomalies. Safeguarding individuals' privacy rights and ensuring compliance with data protection regulations are paramount to ethical AI deployment. Developers must implement robust data anonymisation, encryption and access control mechanisms to protect individuals' privacy and mitigate the risk of unauthorised access or misuse of sensitive data.
- Another ethical consideration pertains to the potential *societal impact* of AI-driven security measures, particularly in terms of power dynamics and human autonomy. AI technologies have the potential to augment human capabilities and enhance security outcomes, but they also raise concerns about surveillance, control and the erosion of civil liberties. Responsible deployment of AI systems requires careful consideration of these societal implications, with a focus on preserving individual freedoms, autonomy and human rights.

4.3.1 General Data Protection Regulation (GDPR)

The General Data Protection Regulation (GDPR) stands as the most stringent privacy and security law globally. Originating from the European Union (EU), it extends its obligations to organisations worldwide, as long as they interact with or collect data from individuals within the EU [7]. Enforced on May 25, 2018, the GDPR imposes substantial fines on violators of its privacy and security standards, with penalties that could amount to tens of millions of euros. The GDPR signifies Europe's unwavering commitment to data privacy and security, particularly crucial in an era where reliance on cloud services grows, and data breaches become commonplace. However, the regulation, though comprehensive, lacks specificity, posing a significant challenge for small- and medium-sized enterprises (SMEs) striving for compliance. In response to these challenges, we have developed this website as a resource hub for SME owners and managers, offering insights into navigating GDPR compliance hurdles. While it does not replace legal counsel, it aims to assist in identifying key areas of focus for GDPR compliance efforts. Additionally, we provide recommendations on privacy tools and risk mitigation strategies. As interpretations of the GDPR evolve, we strive to keep readers informed of emerging best practices.

The GDPR's jurisdiction extends to organisations processing the personal data of EU citizens or residents, irrespective of their location. Violations of the GDPR entail severe penalties, including fines of up to âĆň20 million or 4% of global revenue, whichever is higher. Moreover, individuals affected by data breaches retain the right to seek compensation for damages. Key definitions under the GDPR include:

- *Personal data*: Any information related to an identifiable individual, encompassing various data types such as names, email addresses, location information and biometric data.
- *Data processing*: Any action performed on data, including collection, recording, storage and usage.
- *Data controller*: Entity determining the purpose and means of data processing.
- *Data processor*: Third party processing data on behalf of a data controller.

Furthermore, data processing under the GDPR must adhere to seven fundamental principles outlined in Article 5.1-2, emphasising lawfulness, fairness, transparency and accountability. These principles encompass:

- *Lawfulness, fairness and transparency*: Processing must be lawful, fair and transparent to data subjects.
- *Purpose limitation*: Data should be processed for specified, legitimate purposes.
- *Data minimisation*: Only necessary data should be collected and processed.
- *Accuracy*: Personal data must be accurate and up-to-date.
- *Storage limitation*: Data should be retained for the necessary duration.

- *Integrity and confidentiality*: Processing should ensure data security and confidentiality.
- *Accountability*: Data controllers must demonstrate compliance with GDPR principles.
- *Achieving accountability and data security*: Compliance with the GDPR necessitates organisations to demonstrate accountability through various measures, including:
    - *Designating data protection responsibilities*: The GDPR mandates organisations to integrate data protection principles into the design of products and activities, promoting a proactive approach to privacy. By considering data protection from the outset, organisations can minimise risks and enhance compliance with GDPR requirements.
- *Maintaining detailed documentation of data processing activities*: Data processing must be justified under one of the lawful bases outlined in Article 6 of the GDPR, including consent, contract performance, legal obligation, vital interests, public task and legitimate interests. Organisations must document their legal basis for processing and ensure transparency with data subjects.
- *Implementing technical and organisational security measures*: The GDPR imposes stringent requirements for obtaining consent from data subjects, emphasising clarity, specificity and the right to withdraw consent. Organisations must maintain records of consent and respect individuals' privacy rights, including the right to access, rectification, erasure and objection to data processing.
- *Establishing data processing agreement (DPA) contracts with third-party processors*: A DPA contract delineates the responsibilities and obligations of both the data controller (the organisation collecting and managing the data) and the data processor (the entity processing the data on behalf of the controller).
- *Appointing data protection officers (DPOs) when required*: Certain organisations are mandated to appoint data protection officers (DPOs) under the GDPR, responsible for overseeing GDPR compliance and serving as a point of contact for data subjects and regulators. While not obligatory for all, appointing a DPO can facilitate adherence to GDPR requirements.

Furthermore, organisations must prioritise data security by adopting appropriate technical and organisational measures to safeguard personal data.

These measures encompass encryption, staff training and incident response protocols to mitigate the impact of data breaches. Data subjects are endowed with various privacy rights under the GDPR, enabling them to exert control over their personal data. These rights encompass the right to information, access, rectification, erasure, restriction of processing, data portability, objection and protection against automated decision-making.

The GDPR heralds a new era of data protection and privacy rights, demanding heightened accountability and transparency from organisations worldwide. By embracing privacy-by-design principles, implementing robust security measures and upholding individuals' privacy rights, organisations can navigate the complexities of GDPR compliance while fostering trust and confidence among data subjects. As the GDPR landscape evolves, continuous adaptation and adherence to best practices are essential for ensuring sustained compliance and effective data protection.

In terms of 6G, the 6G Smart Networks and Services Infrastructure Association (6G-IA) places a high priority on data protection, as detailed in their data protection declaration [8]. The 6G-IA and its member organisations, represented by the Chair of the Board of the 6G-IA, are fully committed to adhering to the EU General Data Protection Regulation (GDPR) and the German Federal Data Protection Act (Bundesdatenschutzgesetz – BDSG), as well as any other relevant legislation. The 6G-IA ensures that its website and related internet pages, which are controlled by the 6G-IA Association, can be accessed without requiring personal data. However, if a user opts to use special services via the website, the processing of personal data may become necessary. In such cases, where there is no statutory basis for data processing, consent from the data subject will be sought. This commitment to data protection and GDPR compliance is reflected in the numerous technical and organisational measures implemented by the 6G-IA to ensure the protection of personal data processed through its website. Establishing DPAs with third-party processors is a critical part of this compliance framework, ensuring that all external entities handling personal data on behalf of the 6G-IA adhere to the same stringent data protection standards. These DPAs clearly outline the specific responsibilities and duties of the third-party processors, ensuring that they process personal data only under the instructions of the data controller and in compliance with GDPR requirements. The agreements also stipulate the necessity for processors to implement appropriate technical and organisational measures to protect the data, mirroring the measures taken by the 6G-IA itself.

Achieving a delicate equilibrium between security and privacy stands as a formidable challenge in the development and deployment of 6G networks. While security measures are essential for safeguarding against cyber threats and malicious actors, they must not come at the expense of individual privacy rights. One approach to balancing security and privacy involves adopting a privacy-by-design approach, wherein security measures are integrated into the architecture of 6G systems from the outset. This entails embedding privacy-enhancing features into network protocols, ensuring end-to-end encryption and implementing robust authentication mechanisms. Moreover, regulatory frameworks must strike a careful balance between enabling security measures and upholding privacy rights. This requires ongoing dialogue between policymakers, industry stakeholders and privacy advocates to develop nuanced regulations that mitigate security risks without compromising individuals' privacy. Addressing the ethical considerations surrounding AI-driven security measures necessitates a multifaceted approach that prioritises fairness, transparency, accountability, privacy and societal impact. By integrating ethical principles into the design, development and deployment of AI systems, stakeholders can harness the potential of 6G while mitigating risks and safeguarding fundamental rights and values.

References

[1] ITU-R M.2516 Future technology trends of terrestrial International Mobile Telecommunications systems towards 2030 and beyond
[2] ITU-R M.2160 IMT-2030 Framework (2160 : Framework and overall objectives of the future development of IMT for 2030 and beyond (itu.int))
[3] Ericsson, 6G standardisation – an overview of timeline and high-level technology principles, March 2024.
[4] Institution of Engineering and Technology (IET) - 6G for policy makers
[5] U.S. Department of State, Joint Statement Endorsing Principles for 6G: Secure, Open, and Resilient by Design, February 2024.
[6] European Parliamentary Research Service (EPRS), The path to 6G, January 2024.
[7] Complete guide to GDPR compliance, gdpr.eu
[8] 6G-IA, Data protection declaration, https://6g-ia.eu/data-protection-declaration/

5

Practical Applications: Real-world 6G Security Concrete Scenarios and Implementations

As the world transitions to 6G technology, the security landscape must evolve to address the unique challenges and opportunities presented by this next generation of wireless communication. This chapter explores concrete scenarios and implementations where 6G technology would be applied to enhance security across various sectors. By examining real-world use cases, we can understand the practical applications of advanced security mechanisms and their implications for the future.

When implementing 6G security solutions, performance considerations are paramount.

- *Computational overhead*: A significant concern in adopting quantum-resistant cryptographic algorithms is the potential computational overhead. These advanced algorithms, while essential for securing communication against quantum threats, can impose substantial processing demands on systems. It is crucial to address these concerns by optimising algorithms and leveraging hardware acceleration to ensure that the performance of communication systems is not unduly compromised. Solutions such as specialised cryptographic processors and efficient software implementations can help mitigate the impact on system performance.
- *Quantifying security gains*: Developing robust methodologies to quantify the security gains achieved through the adoption of quantum-resistant cryptography is essential. This involves creating benchmarks and metrics that can evaluate the effectiveness of these security measures in real-world scenarios. By balancing security enhancements with practical implementation considerations, such as computational efficiency and latency, organisations can make informed decisions about deploying

quantum-resistant solutions. Quantitative assessments help in demonstrating the tangible benefits of enhanced security, facilitating broader acceptance and implementation.

Seamless integration with existing systems and communication infrastructures is a critical aspect of implementing quantum-resistant cryptographic solutions. Ensuring interoperability and backward compatibility is vital for a smooth transition without compromising system compatibility.

- ↣ *Interoperability*: Ensuring seamless integration of quantum-resistant cryptographic solutions with existing communication infrastructures is critical for a smooth transition. This requires the development of standard protocols and interfaces that support interoperability between new and legacy systems. Strategies such as modular integration, where quantum-resistant components can be gradually introduced without disrupting existing operations, play a vital role. Interoperability ensures that organisations can enhance security while maintaining the continuity and reliability of their current systems.
- ↣ *Backward compatibility*: Maintaining backward compatibility with legacy systems while progressively implementing quantum-resistant cryptographic measures is a complex but necessary challenge. Approaches to achieving this include designing hybrid cryptographic systems that support both traditional and quantum-resistant algorithms. This allows for a phased transition, where older systems can continue to operate securely alongside newer, more secure solutions. Techniques such as dual-layer encryption, where data is encrypted with both conventional and quantum-resistant algorithms, ensure that communication remains secure throughout the transition period.

By addressing these performance considerations and integration challenges, 6G technology can be effectively deployed to secure various critical sectors. The following case studies highlight specific real-world applications of 6G security.

5.1 Secure Healthcare IoT

In the healthcare sector, the Internet of Things (IoT) is revolutionising patient care by enabling remote monitoring, real-time data collection and advanced diagnostics. However, the integration of 6G technology into healthcare IoT devices necessitates robust security measures to protect sensitive patient data and ensure the integrity of medical devices. The global rise in population and the ageing demographic are pushing current healthcare systems to their limits, making them unsustainable for the future. To address this, wireless health solutions need to be implemented, enabling continuous and cost-effective monitoring and management of health for all citizens. 6G technology is expected to play a pivotal role in realising wireless healthcare, integrating the Internet of Bio-Nano-Things (IoBNT) into our daily lives [1]. This technology will facilitate the embedding of low-complexity wearable and implantable devices into our routines, allowing the collection of health and lifestyle data from everyday interactions, such as using a smart drug dispenser or drinking from a connected water bottle.

The Internet of Medical Things (IoMT) will require a robust and intelligent network that offers extensive connectivity, high data rates, low latency and enhanced healthcare experiences. Unlike 5G, the 6G communication system is anticipated to support Smart IoMT (SIoMT) solutions ubiquitously, significantly improving the quality of life [2]. The conceptual framework of 6G includes the integration of various advanced networking technologies, such as wireless optical networks, cell-free communication systems and quantum telecommunications, along with a decentralised security framework within the SIoMT context. This will enable new models of healthcare delivery, connecting homes to hospitals, healthcare personnel, medical supplies and facilities through ultra-reliable, low-latency networks.

Germany's 6G Health project, funded by the Federal Ministry of Education and Research, is a prime example of these advancements [3]. VDE, in collaboration with 18 partners, aims to make 6G technology suitable for medical devices and systems [4]. This initiative includes the establishment of four research hubs across Germany, coordinated by the Fraunhofer Heinrich Hertz Institute (HHI), focusing on integrating communication and sensing to enhance healthcare environments. These efforts aim to improve patient monitoring, streamline hospital workflows and reduce the workload on healthcare staff through networked robotics and augmented reality (AR) applications.

From a clinical perspective, several primary use cases are being addressed (Figure 5.1):

↣ *Patient monitoring*: Real-time remote monitoring of biosignals, such as blood pressure, body temperature and respiratory rate, ensures continuous clinical collaboration even after hospital discharge. This involves innovative, non-invasive sensor technology combined with advanced 6G-mediated network intelligence for extended clinical applications in perioperative and telemedical settings.

- *Collaborative medical teamwork*: Enhanced network functionalities will enable better collaboration among doctors and nurses. For instance, AR and telemedicine can allow medical professionals to view 3D representations of organs and tissues for preoperative planning or consult specialists for complex interventions remotely.
- *Smart hospital*: 6G will facilitate the networking of medical devices and communication infrastructures, enabling efficient and safer treatment and logistics processes. High-speed, low-latency connections will ensure quick and accurate transmission of medical images and data, which is crucial in emergencies and routine care for homebound or elderly patients. Real-time remote monitoring of chronic illnesses and connected implants, such as pacemakers, will provide healthcare professionals with up-to-date patient data, allowing for timely interventions.
- *Telemedicine*: High-speed, low-latency connections will be crucial for transmitting medical images and data quickly and accurately, which is especially important in emergency situations. Even in routine care, such as monitoring homebound or elderly patients, low-latency video calls can enhance trust and care quality.
- *Remote monitoring*: Patients with chronic illnesses or those requiring constant follow-up will benefit from real-time monitoring through connected implants and wearables. These devices will transmit health data to healthcare professionals in real time, enabling quick responses to any issues.
- *Augmented reality (AR) and virtual reality (VR)*: AR and VR can be valuable tools for training healthcare professionals and treating patients. High-speed, low-latency connections will enable real-time image transmission and collaboration among professionals in different locations, enhancing precision in virtual procedures.
- *Automation and robotics*: Automating healthcare processes can minimise errors and improve efficiency. Remotely controlled surgical robots, utilising low-latency 6G connections, will perform surgical procedures with higher precision, reducing the likelihood of errors.
- *Networked robotics*: Networked robotics, whether for logistics or exoskeleton control systems, will help manage heavy workloads, reducing the physical strain on healthcare workers and improving patient care.

The potential applications of 6G in healthcare are vast and promising. For example, AR and VR can enhance the training and education of healthcare

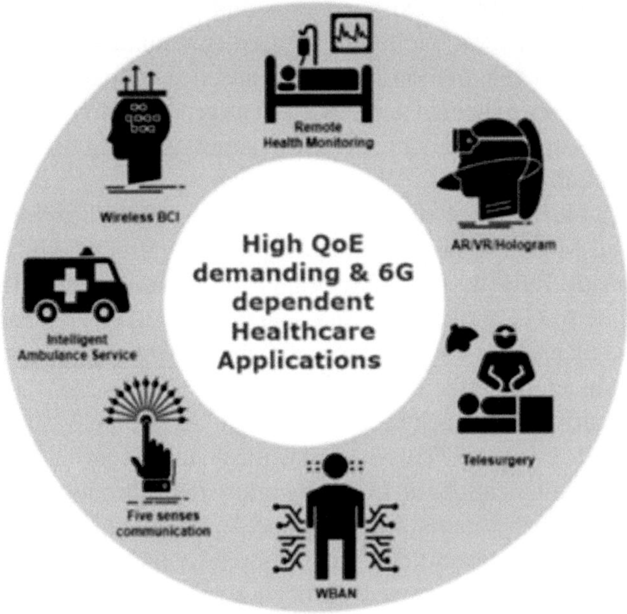

Figure 5.1 6G-reliant healthcare applications.

professionals, as well as enable precise virtual procedures through real-time image transmission and collaboration. Automation and robotics, facilitated by low-latency 6G connections, will improve the precision and efficiency of surgical procedures, reducing the likelihood of errors.

6G will also revolutionise telemedicine, providing high-speed, reliable connections for real-time consultations, enhancing trust and care quality. The ongoing development of 6G-based medical applications, such as the 6G-Health project led by Fraunhofer HHI, aims to lay the foundation for integrating sensing, mobile communications and computing power into healthcare. This integration will optimise clinical processes, improve patient outcomes and support healthcare professionals in their daily activities by leveraging AI and other advanced technologies.

In addition to robust security measures like multi-factor authentication (MFA), several innovative approaches have emerged to bolster security in 6G healthcare systems. For instance, in a study titled ‘A Novel Three-factor Authentication Protocol for Multiple Service Providers in 6G-Aided Intelligent Healthcare Systems’ [5], researchers integrated a three-factor mechanism combining smart cards, passwords and biometrics. This protocol ensures fast authentication, facilitating secure communications between patients and providers while demonstrating enhanced functionality and cost efficiency compared to existing solutions. Security validation was rigorously conducted using RoR model, AVISPA simulation and BAN logic, underscoring its reliability.

Furthermore, blockchain-based MFA techniques, as explored in 'Blockchain-based Multi Factor Authentication for Future 6G Cellular Networks: A Systematic Review' [7], offer promising avenues to address vulnerabilities specific to 6G applications and cellular networks. By leveraging blockchain, these techniques enhance security and authentication protocols, mitigating potential attacks effectively.

Moreover, AI-driven approaches, as detailed in 'AI-Driven Multi-Factor Authentication and Dynamic Trust Management for Securing Massive Machine Type Communication in 6G Networks' [8], introduce dynamic trust management and behavioural profiling models. These AI-based systems accommodate the diverse capabilities and resource limitations of machine-type devices in 6G networks, thereby fortifying security in machine-type communications (MTC).

In addition to robust security measures like multi-factor authentication (MFA), innovative approaches such as differential privacy are crucial in enhancing data collection practices within 6G healthcare systems. Differential privacy techniques enable healthcare providers to anonymise patient data effectively, preserving individual privacy while allowing for comprehensive data collection and analysis. This is particularly significant in research and public health monitoring, where aggregated data plays a vital role in understanding health trends without compromising the confidentiality of individual patient information.

For instance, in studies focusing on 6G applications, differential privacy ensures that data can be utilised for research purposes while adhering to strict privacy standards. By applying differential privacy mechanisms, healthcare providers can confidently collect and analyse data, knowing that individual identities remain protected against unauthorised access or disclosure.

Together, these advancements underscore the critical role of multifaceted security measures in safeguarding sensitive healthcare information within evolving 6G environments. Such innovations not only enhance authentication protocols but also contribute to the overall resilience and integrity of healthcare data management systems.

5.2 Secure Autonomous Vehicles Network

Autonomous vehicles (AVs) rely on a network of sensors, communication devices and control systems to operate safely and efficiently. The deployment of 6G technology in AV networks enhances connectivity and data transmission but also introduces new security challenges [9]. 6G networks represent a significant leap forward from 5G, particularly in the realm of autonomous vehicles (AVs) and drones. These technologies, which rely on sophisticated sensors and AI algorithms for navigation and decision-making, stand to benefit immensely from the capabilities of 6G.

Current 5G networks have paved the way for Beyond 5G (B5G) systems, specifically designed to support autonomous services such as swarms of unmanned aerial vehicles (UAVs). These advancements promise enhanced capacity expansion strategies to tackle issues like massive connectivity and ensure ultra-high throughput with minimal latency. In emergency scenarios where network density and traffic patterns fluctuate, these capabilities become crucial.

6G technology integrates artificial intelligence (AI), machine learning (ML), Internet of Things (IoT) and blockchain to establish secure, intelligent and ubiquitous UAV networks. For example, blockchain and other distributed ledger technologies (DLTs) can secure transactions and communications between AVs and infrastructure. A blockchain-based system can manage the secure exchange of data between vehicles and traffic management systems, ensuring that data is tamper-proof and transparent. However, these innovations also bring new challenges, particularly concerning security, privacy, intelligence and energy efficiency in UAV swarms operating within 6G mobile networks.

Security measures are pivotal, especially when considering distributed ledger technology (DLT) like blockchain for secure transactions and communications between AVs and infrastructure. By employing blockchain, data exchange between vehicles and traffic management systems becomes tamper-proof and transparent, ensuring integrity across the network. Furthermore, privacy solutions tailored to user-centric needs protect personal data within AV networks. These techniques prevent unauthorised tracking of vehicle movements and safeguard individual identities, bolstering public trust and compliance with stringent privacy regulations.

The integration of 6G networking with AVs offers transformative potential for traffic management systems. The ultra-low latency of 6G – potentially 50 times faster than 5G – will enable real-time communication between autonomous vehicles, paving the way for intelligent traffic flow management. Imagine a scenario where self-driving cars communicate seamlessly, adjusting speeds to avoid congestion and optimising routes without the need for traditional traffic lights.

Moreover, edge computing capabilities in 6G facilitate real-time decision-making for AVs, reducing latency by processing data closer to its source. This enables critical functions such as autonomous vehicle control and real-time object detection for drones, enhancing safety and efficiency in urban and remote environments alike.

Despite these advancements, challenges remain, including interoperability between different AV platforms, cybersecurity risks and regulatory frameworks. Addressing these issues is crucial to ensuring the safe and responsible integration of autonomous vehicles and drones into 6G networks, ultimately realising their full potential to revolutionise transportation and logistics sectors worldwide.

In conclusion, the evolution towards 6G Autonomous Intelligent Transportation Systems (6G-AITS) promises a future where AVs and drones operate autonomously, intelligently and efficiently. By leveraging advanced technologies and overcoming existing challenges, we can harness the transformative power of 6G to create safer, more sustainable transportation solutions for the future.

5.3 Secure Smart Grid Infrastructure

6G wireless networks hold tremendous promise for transforming smart energy grids, offering enhanced capabilities in monitoring, data transmission, cybersecurity and operational efficiency. This section explores the potential of 6G technology within smart grid management (SEGM), focusing on several key technological advancements that could revolutionise energy grid operations [10].

Smart grids utilise advanced communication networks to optimise electricity generation, distribution and consumption [11]. The integration of 6G technology holds promise for improving efficiency and reliability in smart grid operations, contingent upon robust cybersecurity measures to safeguard critical infrastructure. For instance, multi-factor authentication (MFA) enhances security by restricting access to authorised personnel, thereby mitigating the risk of cyberattacks that could disrupt power distribution or compromise grid integrity. Additionally, blockchain technology offers a decentralised and secure method for managing transactions within smart grids, ensuring transparency and preventing fraud in energy trades between producers and consumers. Furthermore, the application of differential privacy techniques protects consumers' energy usage data while enabling utilities to analyse consumption patterns and optimise grid performance efficiently. These advancements underscore the potential of 6G to transform smart grid management while addressing critical security and privacy concerns.

Real-time monitoring is foundational to efficient smart energy grids, necessitating capabilities enabled by technologies like terahertz (THz) spectrum, massive multiple input multiple output (MIMO), optical wireless communication (OWC), and visible light communication (VLC). These technologies facilitate instantaneous data transfer and monitoring across grid components, ensuring timely responses to dynamic energy demands and grid conditions.

Fast data transmission is critical for managing the vast amounts of data generated within smart grids. Technologies such as network slicing, dynamic spectrum access (DSA) and edge computing play pivotal roles in ensuring swift and efficient data transmission. Network slicing allows for the creation of virtual networks tailored to specific applications within the grid, optimising bandwidth allocation and latency management. Combined with DSA, which enables flexible spectrum utilisation, and edge computing, which processes data closer to its source, these technologies enhance the overall responsiveness and scalability of smart grid operations.

Cybersecurity remains a paramount concern in smart grids, where the integrity and privacy of data must be safeguarded against cyber threats. 6G technologies such as network slicing, DSA, edge computing, blockchain and cyber-twinning contribute significantly to bolstering cybersecurity measures. Network slicing isolates and secures critical grid communications, while DSA adapts to changing threat landscapes by dynamically reallocating spectrum resources. Edge computing enhances data processing efficiency and security by reducing the exposure of sensitive information to external networks. Meanwhile, blockchain and cyber-twinning technologies provide robust mechanisms for data integrity verification and real-time threat detection within smart grid infrastructures.

Scalability and flexibility are essential for adapting smart grids to evolving energy demands and technological advancements. Technologies including network slicing, DSA, edge computing, artificial intelligence (AI) and machine learning (ML), intelligent sensing and Internet of Things (IoT), virtual reality (VR) and augmented reality (AR), and blockchain (BC) are pivotal in enabling agile and responsive grid management. These technologies empower grids to dynamically adjust operations, optimise resource allocation and integrate renewable energy sources efficiently.

The integration of 6G networks promises to address critical challenges faced by conventional energy grids, including the variability of renewable sources, scalability limitations and cybersecurity vulnerabilities. By harnessing the capabilities of 6G technology, energy grids can achieve greater resilience, reliability and sustainability. However, successful deployment necessitates addressing infrastructure development, regulatory frameworks and standardisation challenges to ensure interoperability and seamless integration across smart grid components.

In conclusion, 6G technology represents a transformative leap forward for smart grid management, offering unprecedented opportunities to enhance operational efficiency, cybersecurity and sustainability. By leveraging advanced wireless communication technologies within smart energy grids, stakeholders can pave the way for a more resilient and intelligent energy infrastructure capable of meeting future energy demands effectively.

This discussion underscores the crucial role of interdisciplinary research, collaboration and innovation in realising the full potential of 6G technology for smart grid applications. Addressing technological challenges and regulatory considerations will be key to unlocking the benefits of 6G and advancing towards sustainable energy solutions for smart cities and beyond.

5.4 Ensuring Secure 6G-enabled Smart Cities

Smart cities utilise interconnected systems to enhance urban living, from traffic management to public safety. Smart cities leverage advanced technologies like IoT, AI, data analytics and connectivity to create interconnected urban ecosystems, enhancing transportation, energy management, public safety, healthcare, waste management and urban planning. Crucially, 5G and upcoming 6G networks provide high bandwidth, minimal latency and extensive device connectivity essential for deploying IoT devices and real-time data analytics in smart cities. Supporting this infrastructure requires comprehensive network coverage, dense small cell deployment, edge computing capabilities, robust data centres and stringent security measures. These advancements promise improved efficiency, enhanced public safety, sustainable development and enhanced quality of life. Yet, challenges such as infrastructure costs, regulatory frameworks and bridging the digital divide must be addressed to ensure equitable and sustainable smart city development.

SC innovation hinges on advancements like enhanced computing power, 5G and emerging 6G networks, and technologies such as blockchain, quantum computing, extended reality and digital twins. Artificial intelligence (AI) is pivotal for improving SC efficiency, sustainability and citizen quality of life, optimising energy use, traffic flow and public safety through data-driven decisions. Data management and analytics are critical, handling vast IoT-generated data for informed urban planning and service enhancements. Connectivity via 5G, 6G, Wi-Fi 6 and IoT is foundational, facilitating robust SC systems for seamless operations. Emerging digital services like digital twins, metaverse, virtual reality, robotics and blockchain promise transformative potential, offering new avenues for SC development and innovation. Cloud platforms (e.g., city platforms, cloud computing) and IoT further support SC evolution, enabling scalable, efficient and interconnected urban environments.

To achieve the essential components of a smart city (SC), handling substantial amounts of data is imperative. The integration of heterogeneous technologies, including various radio access technologies (RATs), has intensified the demand for multimedia content and adaptive network management. Effective network selection is crucial for ensuring high quality of service (QoS) amidst limited operator resources and varying traffic loads across cells. Techniques like load balancing dynamically allocate traffic, optimising resource use across congested and underutilised areas. Recent research proposes adaptive algorithms such as ARMANS and E-ARMANS to enhance multimedia streaming efficiency and conserve energy. Additionally, innovations like TYDER and M-IoT ReMIoT leverage network reputation and traffic differentiation to improve service delivery across diverse applications and IoT domains [12]. Emerging technologies like 5G and machine learning (ML) further enhance network performance by refining access strategies and resource allocation based on user behaviours and content demands. These advancements underscore the evolving complexity and opportunities in managing SCs for optimal urban service delivery and resource efficiency.

The ongoing digital transformation impacting society and economies is a dynamic evolution driven by rapid technological advancements, particularly in AI, and the widespread availability of digital data. AI is instrumental in automating processes and improving service delivery across various sectors, including public services where AI-driven chatbots enhance customer interaction and fraud detection. In smart city (SC) contexts, AI optimises traffic flows, enhances public safety through sensor data analysis and monitors environmental conditions. Challenges persist in SC deployments due to diverse city requirements and interpretation discrepancies. Key SC applications include:

↣ *Public transport*: Cities with extensive transportation systems leverage numerous applications to enhance user experience. Mobile apps enable real-time management, offering alternative routes during delays due to breakdowns, accidents or unforeseen events within smart cities (SCs). IoT sensors on physical infrastructure facilitate smart maintenance scheduling, optimising efficiency through continuous feedback. Intelligent transportation systems (ITSs) and digital signage provide real-time updates on delays, empowering travellers to adjust routes dynamically. Enhanced IoT sensor utilisation benefits both users and facilitates maintenance of monitoring facilities.

↣ *Traffic management*: Traffic mitigation is crucial in SCs, aiming to reduce congestion and enhance safety through technological interventions. SCs employ technology to improve traffic flow efficiency and minimise environmental impact. Applications reducing road congestion are pivotal, especially in cities heavily reliant on public and private transport. Real-time car navigators update drivers on traffic conditions, estimate arrival times and facilitate route adjustments. Smart parking apps minimise emissions and search times by directing drivers to available spaces, addressing contemporary urban challenges effectively.

↣ *Air quality monitoring*: SCs utilise air quality sensors to detect harmful pollutants like CO2, SO2, ozone, and particulate matter, alerting authorities to potential health risks. Air quality modelling tools forecast pollution levels, enabling preemptive measures. With escalating air pollution concerns, SCs monitor air quality index (AQI) in urban zones. For instance, innovative solutions like smart bus stops integrate sensors (temperature, humidity, barometer, PM10) and crowd detectors to inform waiting passengers, exemplifying SCs' commitment to environmental stewardship.

↣ *Solid waste reduction*: Modern waste management systems integrate IoT technologies for efficient waste reduction, tracking and payment management. Real-time waste monitoring ensures proper disposal and reduces waste generation. Payment systems incentivise waste reduction behaviours while IoT facilitates real-time system monitoring. Technologies like GPS tracking and RFID tags monitor waste disposal, ensuring compliance and efficiency. Such innovations improve waste management efficacy, supporting SCs' sustainability goals and enhancing urban cleanliness.

These advancements underscore the transformative potential of SCs in enhancing urban living through technology-driven solutions and efficient resource management.

As the demand for advanced technological solutions in smart cities (SCs) continues to rise, there is increasing discourse on the potential role of 6G networks in providing the necessary infrastructure for these futuristic cities. While 5G networks have significantly enhanced connectivity and supported the Internet of Things (IoT), 6G networks are anticipated to offer even faster speeds, lower latency and higher capacity, making them well-suited for the complex systems and devices integral to SCs.

6G networks could enable new SCs to harness a variety of advanced technologies, including autonomous vehicles, smart grids and remote healthcare. Moreover, these networks could facilitate innovative applications such as augmented reality, virtual reality and immersive gaming experiences, opening up new opportunities for businesses and residents in these urban environments.

However, the development of 6G networks is still in its nascent stages, and it may take several years before they become widely accessible. In the interim, researchers and industry experts are actively exploring the potential benefits and use cases of 6G networks in new SC developments. Representative use cases in the context of SCs include:

- *Intelligent transport and logistics*: Autonomous vehicles and drones are expected to enhance safe, efficient and environmentally friendly transportation by 2030 and beyond.
- Connected robotics and autonomous systems: Self-driving vehicles equipped with sensors like LiDAR, radar, GPS and sonar will perceive their surroundings autonomously.
- *Global ubiquitous connectivity*: Network coverage across maritime and river environments will monitor and manage ecosystems, particularly in cities with rivers or ports.
- *Pervasive intelligence*: Increasing deployment of connected devices such as robots, smart cars and drones will drive new applications requiring advanced AI technologies like computer vision, SLAM, face and speech recognition, natural language processing and motion control.

Enabling technologies that are useful for developing these new applications are shown in Figure 5.2.

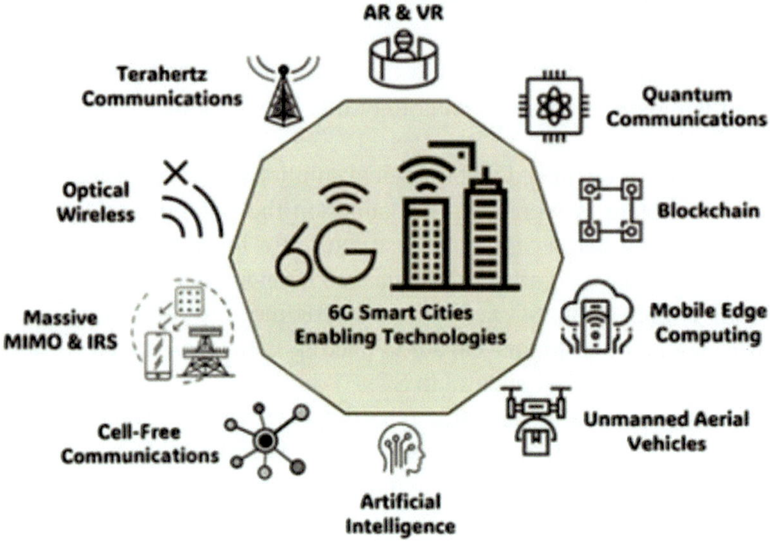

Figure 5.2 6G-reliant enabling technologies for SC.

Smart cities (SCs) and 6G technologies are poised to revolutionise our future lifestyles and work environments. However, their integration presents significant challenges that must be carefully navigated. SCs encounter obstacles such as interoperability issues among diverse devices and systems, the critical need for secure data handling to protect sensitive information and the digital divide stemming from unequal access to expensive SC technologies. Moreover, implementing SC infrastructure requires substantial investments in resources and infrastructure, posing financial challenges for many cities.

Similarly, 6G faces multifaceted challenges including technical complexities, spectrum availability limitations in certain regions, high deployment costs and concerns about security and regulatory compliance. The development of 6G networks necessitates new infrastructure and technologies, substantial spectrum allocation and global coordination to establish standardised network protocols. Overcoming these challenges is crucial to achieving widespread 6G coverage and ensuring its effectiveness in supporting advanced SC applications.

Despite these challenges, the synergy between SCs and 6G promises transformative benefits. 6G networks are expected to enhance SC capabilities with faster data speeds, lower latency and robust connectivity, enabling innovations in mobility, healthcare, energy management and public safety.

These networks will support real-time data transfers for autonomous systems and advanced healthcare services, facilitate smart energy grids and strengthen public safety measures through efficient communication channels. Overall, the evolution towards 6G networks represents a pivotal advancement in urban development, offering cities unprecedented opportunities to enhance efficiency, sustainability and quality of life through advanced technological integration.

5.5 Enhancing Supply Chain Security with 6G

The global supply chain is becoming increasingly complex and interconnected. 6G technology can enhance supply chain management by improving real-time tracking, data analytics and communication. However, it also requires advanced security measures to protect sensitive information and ensure the integrity of the supply chain. Regardless of the industry, an efficient supply chain is crucial for achieving success. Central to this efficiency are data utilisation, financial planning and logistical expertise encompassing manufacturing and distribution. 6G technology promises advancements in these areas and beyond.

Enhancing supply chain security through the integration of 6G networks represents a strategic leap forward in optimising supply chain management across its core stages: design, planning and operation [13]. Supply chain design involves the formulation of long-term strategies that dictate internal operational frameworks and external collaborations. These decisions are pivotal in establishing a robust supply chain network that aligns with the company's overarching goals and market dynamics, ensuring long-term competitiveness and sustainability.

In the planning phase, short-term operational tasks are meticulously integrated into the designed supply chain framework. This includes demand forecasting, inventory management, pricing strategies and marketing targets. The goal here is to translate strategic decisions into actionable plans that optimise resource allocation, minimise operational costs and maximise supply chain efficiency. Effective planning ensures that the supply chain network is agile and responsive to market fluctuations, thereby enhancing customer satisfaction and maintaining competitive edge.

During supply chain operation, the focus shifts to real-time execution and coordination across network nodes. This stage involves the seamless flow of goods and information through various supply chain nodes, from suppliers to end customers. Rapid decision-making becomes crucial to respond swiftly to demand changes, supply disruptions and logistical challenges. It requires robust communication channels and sophisticated monitoring systems to ensure operational continuity and mitigate risks effectively.

The integration of 6G IoT networks introduces transformative capabilities that revolutionise supply chain management. Technologies such as airborne anchor nodes (AN) and UAVs equipped with received signal strength indicator (RSSI) sensors enable precise tracking and monitoring of mobile IoT devices within the supply chain. These advancements enhance operational visibility, optimise asset management and improve overall supply chain resilience.

Despite technological advancements, modern supply chain management faces persistent challenges that necessitate innovative solutions. These challenges include the need for adaptable network models that cater to diverse industries, robust security measures against cyber threats and the integration of advanced technologies like big data analytics and machine learning for predictive insights.

Blockchain technology emerges as a promising solution to these challenges by providing decentralised transactional security, ensuring data integrity and enhancing transparency throughout supply chain processes. By establishing a tamper-proof digital ledger, blockchain simplifies transaction processes, reduces costs associated with intermediaries and accelerates operational workflows. It fosters trust and collaboration among supply chain partners while enabling seamless tracking of goods from production to delivery.

Moreover, machine learning algorithms empower supply chain networks by leveraging extensive datasets to forecast demand patterns, optimise production schedules and mitigate supply chain risks. These algorithms enhance decision-making capabilities by providing actionable insights into consumer behaviour, market trends and operational performance. By automating repetitive tasks and predictive analytics, machine learning enables proactive risk management and operational excellence.

Effective communication is pivotal within supply chain logistics, where numerous components such as manufacturers, warehouses and suppliers must coordinate seamlessly to prevent delays and loss of inventory. Building on the achievements of its predecessor, 6G technology is projected to elevate global communication standards significantly. With an anticipated release around 2030, 6G aims to deliver unparalleled download speeds, eliminate latency and alleviate congestion on mobile and Wi-Fi networks. Moreover, it will facilitate advancements like virtual reality and the metaverse, enhancing communication capabilities across supply chain nodes through multiple networks and devices. In addition to bolstering communication, the advancements brought by 6G will optimise automated processes integral to supply chain operations, such as those employed by manufacturers and distributors. Automation is increasingly crucial in mitigating labour shortages and enhancing operational efficiency while minimising workplace hazards. By integrating seamlessly with the Internet of Things (IoT), a wireless network technology, 6G is set to revolutionise both wired and wireless computer networks, providing a more stable foundation for automated systems. Furthermore, the enhanced security features of 6G networks will fortify defences against cyber threats, safeguarding critical supply chain operations from potential disruptions. Cloud-based artificial intelligence systems excel in efficiently managing vast datasets critical for supply chain operations, ranging from inventory management to safeguarding client confidentiality. 6G networks promise to significantly boost the efficiency of these AI systems by expanding storage capacities, enhancing security measures and accelerating communication with cloud-based platforms. As a result, supply chains relying on sophisticated computer systems will operate more efficiently and securely.

In conclusion, the convergence of blockchain, machine learning and 6G-enabled IoT technologies represents a paradigm shift in enhancing supply chain security, resilience and sustainability. This integrated approach not only strengthens real-time monitoring and transaction security but also positions supply chains to anticipate and adapt to future technological advancements and market dynamics. By embracing innovation and leveraging cutting-edge technologies, supply chains can achieve sustained operational success, enhance customer satisfaction and drive business growth in the era of 6G connectivity.

5.6 Securing Industry 4.0 with 6G

Industry 4.0 represents the fourth industrial revolution, characterised by the integration of digital technologies into manufacturing and production. 6G technology can enhance Industry 4.0 by improving connectivity, automation and data analytics, but it also requires robust security measures to protect industrial systems. In the fast-evolving landscape of technology, rapid transformation is the norm. The emergence of 6G, Industrial IoT, and Industry 4.0 signifies a new era of connectivity that is reshaping our digital interactions; the convergence of these cutting-edge technologies, emphasises the role of cloud computing, the importance of hardware encryption, and their profound impact on the energy and utilities sector.

The Industrial Internet of Things (IIoT) serves as the foundation of Industry 4.0, creating an interconnected ecosystem where machines, devices and humans collaborate in real time [14, 15]. This network of sensors and actuators enables data-driven decision-making, predictive maintenance, and enhances operational efficiency across industrial infrastructures. Industry 4.0, as the fourth industrial revolution, integrates smart technologies into manufacturing and operational processes, paving the way for highly automated and efficient industrial environments.

Cloud computing stands at the forefront of these transformative technologies, providing essential infrastructure for data storage, processing and analysis. It facilitates seamless scalability, collaboration and accessibility, playing a pivotal role in the era of 6G, Industrial IoT and Industry 4.0.

Furthermore, digital twin (DT) technology has been a focal point in communication networks for several years, garnering significant attention. The telecommunications community widely acknowledges its potential to revolutionise 6G communication systems. The survey [16] has underscored the immense capability of DT technology in supporting Industry 4.0 connectivity over future 6G mobile networks. On one hand, digital twins facilitate monitoring, simulation and control, complemented by the pervasive, high-capacity and dependable radio access provided by 6G. This synergy outlines a blueprint for an emerging ecosystem of industrial digital twins, interconnecting all facets of industrial operations and maximising their potential impact (Figure 5.3).

Ensuring the security of interconnected devices and sensitive data becomes paramount in this digital landscape. Hardware encryption emerges as a crucial solution, securing data at the device level and mitigating cyber threats. By encrypting data at the hardware level, the integrity and confidentiality of information exchanged within vast networks of connected devices are safeguarded, contributing to a resilient security framework.

In the energy and utilities sector, the digital transformation driven by 6G, Industrial IoT and Industry 4.0 brings significant advancements. Smart grids, predictive maintenance, real-time monitoring and improved consumption and production predictions enhance efficiency and sustainability. These technologies optimise resource utilisation, reduce downtime and support sustainable practices, thereby shaping a greener future.

In conclusion, the convergence of 6G, Industrial IoT and Industry 4.0 represents a paradigm shift in connectivity and industrial operations. Cloud

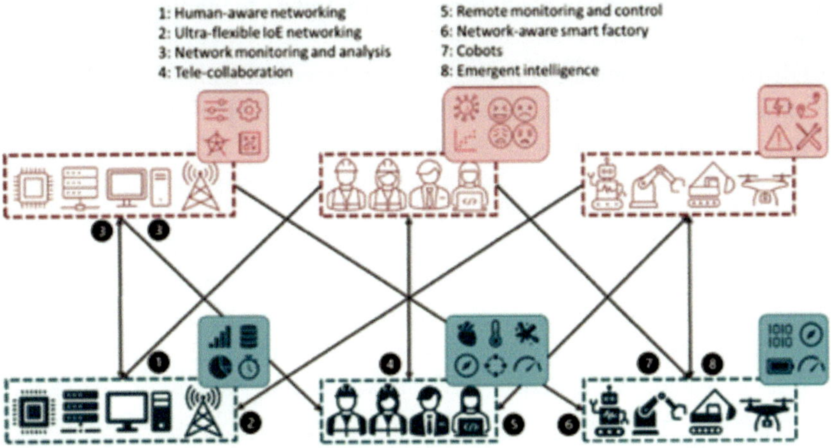

Figure 5.3 Industry 4.0 and 6G DT.

computing, hardware encryption and advancements in energy and utilities underscore this transformative journey. As we navigate this era of unprecedented connectivity, the potential for innovation is limitless, marking a profound shift towards smarter, more efficient industrial systems. Welcome to the future, where connectivity knows no bounds.

By exploring these real-world scenarios and implementations, it becomes evident that 6G technology holds significant potential to enhance security across various sectors. However, achieving this requires a comprehensive approach to security, incorporating advanced technologies and strategies to protect sensitive information and ensure the integrity of interconnected systems.

References

[1] L. Mucchi et al., "How 6G Technology Can Change the Future Wireless Healthcare," 2020 2nd 6G Wireless Summit (6G SUMMIT), Levi, Finland, 2020, pp. 1-6, doi:10.1109/6GSUMMIT49458.2020.9083916.

[2] P. V. Matre, A. Kumbhare, R. Gedam, A. Sharma, N. K. Vaishnav and D. Naidu, "6G Enabled Smart IoT in Healthcare System: Prospect, Issues and Study Areas," 2023 International Conference on Artificial Intelligence for Innovations in Healthcare Industries (ICAIIHI), Raipur, India, 2023, pp. 1-6, doi:10.1109/ICAIIHI57871.2023.10489451.

[3] Medica Tradefair, 6G in healthcare: better wireless technology for better care, 2023

[4] VDE Health, 6G networks in medicine and medical technology, 2023

[5] Nasralla, M.M.; Khattak, S.B.A.; Ur Rehman, I.; Iqbal, M. Exploring the Role of 6G Technology in Enhancing Quality of Experience for m-Health Multimedia Applications: A Comprehensive Survey. Sensors 2023, 23, 5882. DOI:10.3390/s23135882

[6] T. -V. Le, C. -F. Lu, C. -L. Hsu, T. K. Do, Y. -F. Chou and W. -C. Wei, “A Novel Three-Factor Authentication Protocol for Multiple Service Providers in 6G-Aided Intelligent Healthcare Systems,” in IEEE Access, vol. 10, pp. 28975-28990, 2022, doi:10.1109/ACCESS.2022.3158756.

[7] Asim, J.; Khan, A.S.; Saqib, R.M.; Abdullah, J.; Ahmad, Z.; Honey, S.; Afzal, S.; Alqahtani, M.S.; Abbas, M. Blockchain-based Multifactor Authentication for Future 6G Cellular Networks: A Systematic Review. Appl. Sci. 2022, 12, 3551. doi:10.3390/app12073551

[8] Nasralla, M.M.; Khattak, S.B.A.; Ur Rehman, I.; Iqbal, M. Exploring the Role of 6G Technology in Enhancing Quality of Experience for m-Health Multimedia Applications: A Comprehensive Survey. Sensors 2023, 23, 5882. doi:10.3390/s23135882

[9] Xiaoheng Deng, Leilei Wang, Jinsong Gui, Ping Jiang, Xuechen Chen, Feng Zeng, Shaohua Wan, A review of 6G autonomous intelligent transportation systems: Mechanisms, applications and challenges, Journal of Systems Architecture, Volume 142, 2023, 102929, ISSN 1383-7621, doi: 10.1016/j.sysarc.2023.102929.

[10] Mohammed H. Alsharif, Abu Jahid, Raju Kannadasan, Mun-Kyeom Kim, Unleashing the potential of sixth generation (6G) wireless networks in smart energy grid management: A comprehensive review, Energy Reports, Volume 11, 2024, Pages 1376-1398, ISSN 2352-4847, doi:10.1016/j.egyr.2024.01.011.

[11] Al Amin, A.; Hong, J.; Bui, V.-H.; Su, W. Emerging 6G/B6G Wireless Communication for the Power Infrastructure in Smart Cities: Innovations, Challenges, and Future Perspectives. Algorithms 2023, 16, 474. doi:10.3390/a16100474

[12] Murroni, M.; Anedda, M.; Fadda, M.; Ruiu, P.; Popescu, V.; Zaharia, C.; Giusto, D. 6G—Enabling the New Smart City: A Survey. Sensors 2023, 23, 7528. doi> 10.3390/s23177528

[13] Liang, W.; Zhang, L.; Kadoch, M. 6G IoT Tracking- and Machine Learning-Enhanced Blockchained Supply Chain Management. Electronics 2023, 12, 40. doi:10.3390/electronics12010040

[14] Rojek, I.; Kotlarz, P.; Dorożyński, J.; Mikołajewski, D. Sixth-Generation (6G) Networks for Improved Machine-to-Machine (M2M) Communication in Industry 4.0. Electronics 2024, 13, 1832. doi:10.3390/electronics13101832

[15] Waidner, Michael & Kasper, Michael. (2016). Security In Industrie 4.0 — Challenges and Solutions for the Fourth Industrial Revolution. 1303-1308. 10.3850/9783981537079_1005.

[16] B. Han et al., "Digital Twins for Industry 4.0 in the 6G Era," in IEEE Open Journal of Vehicular Technology, vol. 4, pp. 820-835, 2023, doi: 10.1109/OJVT.2023.3325382.

6

The Road Ahead for Shaping a Secure 6G Future

As we advance toward the era of 6G networks, it is crucial to prioritise proactive security measures to mitigate emerging threats and safeguard the integrity, confidentiality and availability of communication systems. The importance of these measures becomes evident when considering the key challenges in 6G security: quantum computing, AI and machine learning, decentralised edge computing and IoT and connected devices.

Quantum computing poses a significant threat to current cryptographic protocols due to its potential to solve complex mathematical problems much faster than classical computers. Traditional encryption methods, which are the cornerstone of data security, could be rendered obsolete, making sensitive information vulnerable to exposure. Proactive security measures must include the development and implementation of quantum-resistant cryptographic algorithms to ensure that data remains secure against the computational power of quantum computers.

AI and machine learning are double-edged swords in the context of 6G security. On one hand, they offer powerful tools for detecting and mitigating threats through advanced anomaly detection and predictive analytics. On the other hand, they can be exploited by adversaries to develop sophisticated attacks that can bypass traditional security mechanisms. It is imperative to incorporate robust AI-driven security solutions while simultaneously advancing research in adversarial AI to defend against AI-powered attacks. Continuous monitoring and adaptive learning mechanisms will be essential to stay ahead of evolving threats.

Decentralised edge computing, a key feature of 6G networks, enhances latency and bandwidth efficiency by processing data closer to its source. However, this decentralisation also introduces new security challenges, such as increased attack surfaces and the difficulty of maintaining a unified security policy across distributed nodes. Proactive measures must include secure edge computing frameworks that ensure data integrity, secure communication channels and robust access controls. Additionally, decentralised trust mechanisms and secure orchestration of edge devices will be crucial to maintaining a resilient security posture.

The proliferation of IoT and connected devices in 6G networks exponentially increases the number of potential entry points for attackers. These devices often have limited computational resources, making it challenging to implement traditional security measures. Proactive security strategies should focus on lightweight cryptographic protocols, secure firmware updates and strong authentication mechanisms tailored for IoT devices. Network segmentation and anomaly detection systems specifically designed for IoT environments can help in isolating and mitigating potential threats.

Proactive security measures in 6G networks are not merely optional but essential to address the sophisticated challenges posed by quantum computing, AI and machine learning, decentralised edge computing and IoT and connected devices. By anticipating these threats and implementing forward-looking security strategies, we can pave the way for a secure 6G future that ensures the trust and reliability of next-generation communication systems.

6.1 Future Prospects for Cryptographic Advancements

As we move toward the 6G era, cryptographic advancements will play a pivotal role in ensuring the security and privacy of communications and data. Three key areas – AI-driven cybersecurity solutions, blockchain and distributed ledger technologies (DLT) and privacy-preserving technologies – offer promising prospects for enhancing cryptographic security in future networks.

6.1.1 AI-driven cybersecurity solutions

Adaptive security measures represent a transformative approach in the realm of cybersecurity, particularly in the context of AI-driven solutions [1]. As the threat landscape becomes increasingly complex and dynamic, traditional security measures often fall short in providing comprehensive protection. AI-driven adaptive security measures, however, offer a proactive and robust defence mechanism that evolves in real time to counteract emerging threats. AI-driven cybersecurity systems are designed to continuously monitor network activities and learn from them. Unlike static security systems that rely on predefined rules and signatures, AI systems employ machine learning algorithms to understand and analyse traffic patterns, user behaviours and system anomalies. This continuous learning process enables the system to adapt to new threats that have not been previously encountered.

By leveraging machine learning, adaptive security measures can perform in-depth behavioural analysis of both network traffic and user activities. These analyses help in identifying deviations from normal behaviour that might indicate a potential security breach. For instance, an AI system can detect unusual login times, abnormal data access patterns or atypical file modifications, which might suggest compromised accounts or insider threats. Traditional anomaly detection methods often produce a high number of false positives, leading to alert fatigue among security professionals. AI-driven systems, however, refine anomaly detection by learning from the vast amount of data they process. Advanced algorithms, such as deep learning and neural networks, can distinguish between benign anomalies and actual threats with high accuracy, thereby reducing false positives and enabling more effective threat detection.

One of the key advantages of AI-driven adaptive security measures is the ability to automatically identify and classify threats in real time [2]. When a potential threat is detected, the system can quickly determine the nature and severity of the threat, allowing for immediate action. This rapid identification is crucial in minimising the window of opportunity for attackers. Once a threat is identified, AI systems can autonomously deploy mitigation strategies. These strategies might include isolating affected systems, blocking malicious IP addresses or terminating suspicious processes. The ability to respond swiftly without human intervention ensures that threats are neutralised before they can cause significant damage. AI-driven systems can also contribute to the broader cybersecurity ecosystem by sharing threat intelligence. By analysing patterns and correlating data from various sources, AI systems can generate insights that are shared with other security systems and organisations. This collective intelligence helps in pre emptively identifying and defending against widespread threats.

The algorithms used in AI-driven security systems are designed to evolve based on the feedback they receive. For example, reinforcement learning algorithms can optimise their performance by learning from past incidents and adapting their strategies accordingly. This evolutionary approach ensures that the security measures remain effective against new and sophisticated attack vectors. AI enhances the capability for proactive threat hunting by automating the search for potential vulnerabilities and threats within the network. Automated threat hunting tools can simulate attack scenarios, identify weak points and recommend remediation actions. This proactive stance significantly reduces the risk of undetected threats. Future advancements in AI-driven adaptive security measures might include self-healing capabilities. Such systems could autonomously repair and fortify themselves after detecting an attack, ensuring continuous protection and resilience. This self-healing property is especially valuable in maintaining the integrity of critical infrastructure and minimising downtime.

Adaptive security measures powered by AI represent a significant advancement in cybersecurity. By continuously analysing network patterns and behaviours, these systems can dynamically adapt to evolving threats, providing a robust defence mechanism. The ability to detect anomalies in real-time, automatically identify and mitigate threats and evolve based on feedback ensures that AI-driven cybersecurity solutions remain a step ahead of cyber adversaries. As we move towards more interconnected and complex digital environments, the role of adaptive security measures will become increasingly crucial in safeguarding our networks and data.

Predictive analytics, empowered by artificial intelligence, stands as a pivotal advancement in cybersecurity, offering the ability to foresee and counteract potential cyber threats before they fully emerge. This proactive approach is critical in the modern threat landscape, where cyberattacks are becoming increasingly sophisticated and frequent. By harnessing the power of AI, predictive analytics can analyse vast amounts of historical data to identify patterns, trends and anomalies that may indicate future security breaches.

The foundation of predictive analytics in cybersecurity lies in its ability to process and interpret historical data. AI algorithms are adept at sifting through extensive datasets, uncovering correlations and patterns that might be imperceptible to human analysts. This analysis enables the identification of trends that precede security incidents, such as the frequency of certain types of network traffic, the occurrence of specific user behaviours or the emergence of new types of malware. By recognising these trends, AI can forecast potential vulnerabilities and anticipate the tactics, techniques and procedures that attackers might use.

One of the significant benefits of predictive analytics is its capacity to provide early warnings of potential threats. For instance, if an AI system detects a gradual increase in suspicious login attempts or unusual data access patterns, it can alert security teams to the possibility of an impending attack. This early warning system allows organisations to bolster their defences and take pre-emptive measures, such as enhancing authentication protocols, tightening access controls or patching vulnerable systems, thereby reducing the risk of a successful breach.

In addition to identifying potential threats, predictive analytics can also assess the likelihood and potential impact of these threats. By evaluating historical incidents and their outcomes, AI can estimate the probability of similar events occurring in the future and their possible repercussions. This risk assessment helps organisations prioritise their security efforts and allocate resources more effectively [3]. For example, if a particular type of attack is deemed highly probable and could result in significant data loss or operational disruption, security teams can focus on fortifying defences against that specific threat.

Another crucial aspect of predictive analytics is its role in vulnerability management. AI can analyse past vulnerabilities and their exploitation patterns to predict which current vulnerabilities are most likely to be targeted by attackers. This foresight enables organisations to prioritise their patching and remediation efforts, addressing the most critical vulnerabilities before they can be exploited. Consequently, predictive analytics enhances the overall security posture by ensuring that the most significant risks are mitigated promptly.

AI-driven predictive analytics also plays a vital role in enhancing incident response strategies. By anticipating potential threats, security teams can develop and refine their response plans in advance. This preparation includes conducting simulated attack scenarios, improving communication protocols and ensuring that all necessary tools and resources are readily available. When a predicted threat materialises, the organisation is better equipped to respond swiftly and effectively, minimising the impact of the attack.

Furthermore, predictive analytics facilitates continuous improvement in cybersecurity. By continuously monitoring and analysing data, AI systems can learn from each security incident, refining their predictive models and enhancing their accuracy over time. This iterative process ensures that the organisation's security measures evolve in response to new threats and changing attack patterns. As a result, predictive analytics fosters a dynamic and adaptive security environment, capable of staying ahead of emerging threats.

The integration of predictive analytics into cybersecurity also promotes a culture of proactive security. Instead of merely reacting to incidents as they occur, organisations can adopt a forward-thinking approach, continuously seeking to anticipate and mitigate potential threats. This proactive stance not only strengthens the organisation's defences but also fosters a sense of vigilance and preparedness among security teams, reducing the likelihood of successful attacks.

Predictive analytics, driven by AI, offers a powerful tool for enhancing cybersecurity by anticipating potential threats before they materialise. Through the analysis of historical data and the identification of trends, AI can predict vulnerabilities and pre-emptively address them, significantly strengthening the overall security posture. By providing early warnings, assessing risks, managing vulnerabilities, enhancing incident response and promoting continuous improvement and proactive security, predictive analytics plays a crucial role in safeguarding organisations against the ever-evolving landscape of cyber threats.

Automated threat hunting represents a significant advancement in cybersecurity, leveraging the capabilities of artificial intelligence to streamline and enhance the process of identifying and neutralising threats [4, 5]. This approach reduces reliance on human intervention, providing a faster and more efficient means of dealing with sophisticated and persistent threats that often evade traditional security measures. The integration of AI into threat hunting not only improves detection rates but also frees up human analysts to focus on more complex and strategic aspects of cybersecurity.

At the core of automated threat hunting is the ability of AI to process and analyse vast amounts of data at speeds far beyond human capabilities. Traditional threat hunting relies heavily on skilled analysts manually sifting through logs, network traffic and other data sources to identify anomalies and indicators of compromise. This process is time-consuming and prone to errors due to the sheer volume of data and the complexity of modern cyber threats. AI-driven systems, however, can automate this data analysis, continuously monitoring and evaluating data from various sources in real time.

AI algorithms excel at recognising patterns and anomalies within the data. Machine learning models can be trained on historical data to understand what constitutes normal behaviour within a network and, conversely, what deviations might indicate a potential threat. These models can detect subtle and complex indicators of compromise that might be missed by human analysts, such as unusual patterns of data access, unexpected changes in network traffic or atypical user behaviour. By identifying these anomalies, AI can flag potential threats for further investigation or even initiate automated response measures.

One of the key advantages of automated threat hunting is its ability to deal with sophisticated and persistent threats, often referred to as advanced persistent threats (APTs). These threats are typically well-funded, highly skilled and employ stealthy techniques to avoid detection by traditional security measures. APTs can remain undetected within a network for extended periods, gathering intelligence and slowly expanding their foothold. AI-driven threat hunting systems are particularly effective against such threats because they can continuously analyse network activity and detect the subtle signs of an ongoing attack, such as lateral movement within the network or the exfiltration of data.

In addition to detecting threats, AI can also play a crucial role in neutralising them. Automated threat hunting systems can be programmed to initiate predefined response actions when certain criteria are met. For example, if the AI detects a potential threat, it can automatically isolate the affected system, block suspicious network traffic or alert the security team. This rapid response capability is essential in minimising the impact of a threat and preventing it from spreading further within the network.

Another significant benefit of automated threat hunting is the reduction in the workload for human analysts. Cybersecurity professionals are often overwhelmed by the volume of alerts and potential threats they must investigate. By automating the initial stages of threat hunting, AI can filter out false positives and prioritise genuine threats, allowing human analysts to focus their efforts on the most critical and complex cases. This not only improves the efficiency of the security team but also reduces the risk of burnout and human error.

The continuous nature of AI-driven threat hunting also ensures that threats are detected and responded to in real time. Traditional security measures, such as scheduled scans or periodic audits, may leave windows of vulnerability that sophisticated attackers can exploit. In contrast, AI systems operate 24/7, providing constant vigilance and immediate detection of any anomalies. This proactive approach is crucial in today's fast-paced threat landscape, where new vulnerabilities and attack vectors can emerge rapidly.

Moreover, automated threat hunting systems can adapt and improve over time. Machine learning models can be updated with new data, including information about newly discovered threats and attack techniques. This continuous learning process ensures that the AI remains effective against evolving threats, maintaining its relevance and efficacy in a constantly changing cybersecurity environment.

Automated threat hunting, powered by AI, offers a transformative approach to cybersecurity by automating the detection and neutralisation of threats. This capability enhances the efficiency and effectiveness of threat-hunting processes, particularly against sophisticated and persistent threats that evade traditional security measures. By leveraging AI's ability to analyse vast amounts of data, recognise patterns and respond in real time, automated threat hunting reduces reliance on human intervention and enables security teams to focus on more strategic tasks. This proactive and adaptive approach significantly strengthens an organisation's security posture, ensuring continuous protection against emerging cyber threats.

Enhanced encryption techniques, driven by the capabilities of artificial intelligence, represent a crucial frontier in the ongoing effort to secure digital communications and data. As the threat landscape evolves, particularly with the advent of quantum computing, traditional encryption methods face increasing challenges [6]. AI's ability to process vast amounts of data and identify weaknesses in existing cryptographic methods offers significant potential for developing new, more resilient encryption algorithms. This proactive approach is essential in safeguarding sensitive information against both current and future threats.

AI's role in optimising and developing new encryption algorithms starts with its capacity for advanced data analysis. Traditional methods of creating encryption standards often rely on human expertise and trial-and-error processes, which, while effective, can be time-consuming and limited by the scope of human analysis. AI, on the other hand, can analyse extensive datasets rapidly, identifying patterns, anomalies and potential vulnerabilities that might be overlooked by human researchers. This capability allows for a more comprehensive evaluation of existing encryption methods and the identification of areas that require strengthening.

One of the significant contributions of AI to encryption is its ability to simulate and predict the effectiveness of cryptographic algorithms under various attack scenarios. Machine learning models can be trained on historical data of cryptographic attacks, learning the techniques and strategies employed by attackers. This knowledge enables AI systems to anticipate potential weaknesses in new and existing encryption algorithms, providing insights into how these algorithms can be fortified. By understanding the tactics of adversaries, AI can help design encryption methods that are inherently more resistant to a broader range of attacks.

In the context of quantum computing, the role of AI in developing enhanced encryption techniques becomes even more critical. Quantum computers have the potential to break many of the cryptographic algorithms currently in use, such as RSA and ECC, by leveraging their immense computational power to solve complex mathematical problems that are infeasible for classical computers. AI can aid in the development of quantum-resistant cryptographic algorithms by simulating quantum attacks and testing the resilience of proposed encryption methods. This proactive approach ensures that encryption standards can evolve in parallel with advancements in quantum computing, maintaining the security of sensitive data.

Furthermore, AI can contribute to the optimisation of encryption algorithms by improving their efficiency and performance. Encryption and decryption processes can be computationally intensive, particularly for large datasets or real-time communications. AI-driven optimisation techniques can streamline these processes, reducing the computational overhead while maintaining or even enhancing the security of the encryption. This balance is crucial for applications that require both high security and high performance, such as financial transactions, secure communications and data storage.

AI's ability to process and analyse data in real time also enables dynamic encryption strategies. Traditional encryption methods typically involve static keys and algorithms, which can be vulnerable to prolonged attacks. AI can facilitate the development of adaptive encryption techniques that change dynamically based on the threat environment. For example, an AI system could monitor network traffic for signs of an ongoing attack and automatically switch to a more secure encryption method or increase the complexity of the encryption key. This adaptability enhances the overall security posture by making it more difficult for attackers to exploit static vulnerabilities.

In addition to developing new encryption algorithms, AI can play a significant role in improving key management practices. Effective key management is essential for maintaining the security of encrypted data, but it can be challenging to implement at scale. AI can automate key generation, distribution and rotation processes, ensuring that encryption keys are managed securely and efficiently. This automation reduces the risk of human error, which can be a significant source of vulnerabilities in cryptographic systems [7].

Moreover, AI driven techniques can enhance the resilience of encryption methods against side-channel attacks, which exploit physical or implementation-specific characteristics of cryptographic systems to gain access to sensitive information. By continuously monitoring and analysing the physical parameters of cryptographic devices, such as power consumption, electromagnetic emissions or execution time, AI can detect and mitigate potential side-channel attack vectors. This proactive approach ensures that encryption methods remain secure even in the face of sophisticated attack techniques that target their physical implementation.

Enhanced encryption techniques, powered by AI, are crucial for the future of cybersecurity. AI's advanced data analysis capabilities, predictive modelling and optimisation techniques enable the development of more robust and resilient encryption algorithms. These advancements are essential for protecting sensitive information against evolving threats, including those posed by quantum computing. By leveraging AI to simulate attacks, optimise performance and implement dynamic encryption strategies, the security of encrypted data can be significantly strengthened, ensuring its confidentiality and integrity in an increasingly complex threat landscape.

6.1.2 Blockchain and distributed ledger technologies (DLT)

Decentralised trust models offered by blockchain and distributed ledger technologies (DLT) represent a significant paradigm shift in how security and trust are managed in digital networks [8]. Unlike traditional systems that rely on centralised authorities to validate and secure transactions or data, decentralised trust models distribute these responsibilities across a network of nodes, reducing the risk associated with single points of failure and enhancing the overall security and resilience of the network.

One of the key advantages of decentralised trust models is their ability to eliminate the need for central authorities. In traditional centralised systems, trust is placed in a single entity or a small group of entities that are responsible for maintaining the security and integrity of the data or transactions. This centralisation creates vulnerabilities, as these authorities become attractive targets for cyberattacks. If compromised, they can lead to widespread disruption or data breaches. Decentralised trust models mitigate this risk by distributing the validation process across multiple independent nodes. Each node maintains a copy of the ledger and participates in a consensus mechanism to agree on the state of the ledger. This distribution makes it significantly more challenging for an attacker to compromise the entire network, as they would need to gain control of a majority of the nodes, a feat that is often prohibitively difficult and resource-intensive.

Blockchain and DLT use consensus mechanisms to ensure the integrity and authenticity of data. Consensus mechanisms are protocols that allow distributed networks to agree on a single version of the truth without the need for a central authority. There are various types of consensus mechanisms, each with its own strengths and trade-offs. For example, proof of work (PoW) requires nodes to solve complex cryptographic puzzles to validate transactions and add them to the ledger, making it highly secure but energy-intensive. Proof of stake (PoS) and delegated proof of stake (DPoS) offer more energy-efficient alternatives by relying on the stake or reputation of nodes to validate transactions. These mechanisms not only secure the network but also make it resistant to various attacks, including double-spending and Sybil attacks.

Cryptographic hashing plays a crucial role in securing decentralised trust models. Hash functions transform input data into a fixed-size string of characters, which appears random but is deterministic for a given input. In blockchain and DLT, cryptographic hashes are used to link blocks of data together in a chain, where each block contains the hash of the previous block. This chaining ensures that any alteration to a block's data would change its hash, breaking the chain and signalling tampering. This property makes blockchain and DLT highly tamper-evident, as any unauthorised changes to the data are immediately detectable.

The decentralised nature of blockchain and DLT also enhances transparency and auditability. Since all transactions are recorded on a public ledger that is accessible to all participating nodes, any changes or additions to the data can be independently verified. This transparency is particularly valuable in applications where trust and accountability are paramount, such as supply chain management, financial transactions and voting systems. By providing a verifiable and immutable record of transactions, blockchain and DLT reduce the potential for fraud and corruption.

Moreover, decentralised trust models facilitate improved data privacy and security. In traditional centralised systems, sensitive data is often stored in large, centralised databases that are vulnerable to breaches. Decentralised systems can employ techniques such as data sharding and encryption to distribute and secure data across multiple nodes. Each node only has access to a portion of the data, and cryptographic techniques ensure that even if a node is compromised, the data remains protected. Additionally, decentralised identity management systems leverage blockchain to provide users with greater control over their personal information, allowing them to selectively disclose information without relying on centralised identity providers.

The adoption of decentralised trust models is also driving innovation in smart contracts, which are self-executing contracts with the terms of the agreement directly written into code. Smart contracts automatically enforce and execute the terms of a contract when predefined conditions are met, without the need for intermediaries. This automation not only reduces the risk of human error and fraud but also enhances the efficiency and speed of contractual processes. Blockchain-based smart contracts are being used in a wide range of applications, from financial services and insurance to real estate and supply chain management.

Decentralised trust models enabled by blockchain and DLT offer a robust and secure alternative to traditional centralised systems. By distributing trust and validation responsibilities across a network of nodes, these technologies mitigate the risks associated with central points of failure, enhance data integrity and authenticity through consensus mechanisms and cryptographic hashing and provide greater transparency, auditability and privacy. As these technologies continue to evolve, they hold the potential to transform various industries by enabling more secure, efficient and trustworthy digital interactions.

Secure transactions and smart contracts are among the most transformative applications of blockchain technology, offering significant advancements in security, transparency and efficiency across various sectors [9, 10]. Blockchain's decentralised and immutable ledger enables secure and transparent transactions, which can be leveraged in financial services, supply chain management and IoT ecosystems to address longstanding challenges and create new opportunities.

In the financial services sector, blockchain technology facilitates secure and transparent transactions by eliminating the need for intermediaries such as banks and payment processors [11]. This reduction in intermediaries not only decreases transaction costs but also speeds up the processing time. Each transaction recorded on the blockchain is cryptographically secured and linked to previous transactions, ensuring data integrity and making it tamper-evident. This feature is particularly beneficial in cross-border payments, where traditional systems can be slow and costly. Blockchain enables near-instantaneous settlement of international transactions, enhancing the efficiency and reliability of global financial networks. Moreover, the transparency of blockchain transactions helps in regulatory compliance and reduces the risk of fraud and money laundering.

In supply chain management, blockchain's ability to provide a transparent and immutable record of transactions can significantly enhance the traceability and accountability of goods as they move through the supply chain. Each participant in the supply chain can record transactions on the blockchain, creating a permanent and verifiable history of the product's journey from origin to destination. This transparency helps in detecting and preventing fraud, counterfeiting and unethical practices such as forced labour. For instance, in the food industry, blockchain can be used to trace the origin of food products, ensuring their authenticity and safety. In the event of a contamination outbreak, blockchain enables swift and precise identification of the affected products, reducing the scope of recalls and protecting consumer health. Additionally, blockchain enhances the efficiency of supply chain operations by automating processes such as inventory management, order fulfilment and payments.

In IoT ecosystems, blockchain technology can secure and streamline the interactions between connected devices. The proliferation of IoT devices has led to an exponential increase in data generation and the need for secure, efficient and scalable methods to manage device communications and transactions. Blockchain addresses these challenges by providing a decentralised framework that ensures data integrity, security and privacy. Each IoT device can act as a node in the blockchain network, recording transactions and interactions in a secure and verifiable manner. This decentralised approach eliminates the single point of failure inherent in centralised systems, enhancing the resilience of IoT networks. Moreover, blockchain's consensus mechanisms ensure that all devices in the network agree on the state of transactions, preventing unauthorised access and tampering. For example, in smart cities, blockchain can be used to manage IoT-enabled infrastructure such as traffic lights, energy grids and public transportation systems, ensuring secure and efficient operations.

Smart contracts further extend the capabilities of blockchain by automating and securing complex transactions without human intervention. Smart contracts are self-executing agreements with the terms and conditions of the agreement directly written into code. Once the predefined conditions are met, the smart contract automatically enforces the terms, reducing the need for intermediaries and minimising the risk of human error and fraud. In financial services, smart contracts can automate processes such as loan approvals, insurance claims and trade settlements, streamlining operations and reducing administrative costs. For instance, a smart contract for a loan could automatically disburse funds when the borrower's credit score and income meet the lender's criteria, and subsequently, deduct monthly repayments from the borrower's account.

In supply chain management, smart contracts can automate various tasks, such as tracking shipments, verifying the authenticity of products and releasing payments. For example, a smart contract can be programmed to release payment to a supplier once the shipment is verified to have reached its destination and passed quality checks. This automation reduces delays and disputes, ensuring timely and accurate transactions. Additionally, smart contracts enhance transparency and trust among supply chain participants, as the terms of the agreement are visible and immutable.

In IoT ecosystems, smart contracts can manage and automate interactions between devices, ensuring secure and efficient operations. For instance, in a smart home, a smart contract can control the interactions between IoT devices, such as adjusting the thermostat based on weather conditions or turning off lights when no motion is detected. In industrial IoT, smart contracts can automate maintenance schedules, ordering replacement parts when sensors detect wear and tear. This automation reduces downtime and maintenance costs, enhancing operational efficiency.

In conclusion, the integration of secure transactions and smart contracts within blockchain technology presents significant advancements in various sectors. By providing secure, transparent and efficient transaction mechanisms, blockchain enhances the reliability and integrity of financial services, supply chain management and IoT ecosystems. Smart contracts further extend these benefits by automating and securing complex transactions, reducing the need for intermediaries and minimising the risk of human error and fraud. As blockchain technology continues to evolve, its applications in secure transactions and smart contracts will likely expand, driving innovation and transforming industries.

Tamper-proof records are a fundamental feature of blockchain technology, deriving from its immutable nature, which ensures that once data is recorded, it cannot be altered or deleted. This characteristic is crucial for maintaining the integrity and trustworthiness of records in various sensitive applications such as healthcare, legal documentation and identity verification. In these fields, the ability to ensure that records remain unaltered is paramount to safeguarding against fraud, errors and unauthorised modifications [12].

In healthcare, the immutability of blockchain can revolutionise the way medical records are managed. Patient data, including medical histories, treatment records and test results, can be securely stored on a blockchain. Each entry into a patient's medical record is time-stamped and cryptographically linked to previous entries, creating a chronological and tamper-proof log of the patient's health information. This ensures that healthcare providers have access to accurate and unaltered records, which is critical for delivering appropriate care and making informed medical decisions. Additionally, the use of blockchain can enhance patient privacy and data security, as patients can control who has access to their medical information. This decentralised approach reduces the risk of data breaches and unauthorised access, which are significant concerns in the healthcare industry.

In the realm of legal documentation, blockchain's tamper-proof records can provide a robust solution for maintaining the integrity of legal documents such as contracts, deeds and wills. Legal documents recorded on a blockchain are immutable, ensuring that the terms and conditions agreed upon by the parties cannot be altered post-execution. This feature is particularly valuable in scenarios where the authenticity and integrity of documents are critical, such as in property transactions, intellectual property rights and contractual agreements. For example, a smart contract stored on a blockchain can automatically enforce the terms of an agreement once predefined conditions are met, eliminating the need for intermediaries and reducing the potential for disputes. In the event of a legal dispute, the blockchain provides a verifiable and tamper-proof record of the document's original terms, which can serve as evidence in court. This enhances the overall trust and reliability of legal processes.

Identity verification is another area where blockchain's immutable records can provide significant benefits. Traditional identity verification systems often rely on centralised databases, which are vulnerable to hacking, data breaches and unauthorised alterations. Blockchain technology, with its decentralised and tamper-proof nature, offers a more secure alternative for identity management. By recording identity attributes on a blockchain, individuals can have a secure and immutable digital identity that can be verified by multiple parties without the need for a central authority. For instance, a digital identity stored on a blockchain can include various verified credentials, such as government-issued IDs, educational qualifications and professional certifications. Each credential is cryptographically secured and linked to the individual's identity, ensuring that it cannot be altered or tampered with. This provides a higher level of assurance in identity verification processes, reducing the risk of identity theft and fraud.

Moreover, the use of blockchain for maintaining tamper-proof records extends to supply chain management, financial services and government operations. In supply chain management, blockchain can provide a transparent and immutable record of the journey of goods from origin to destination. This ensures the authenticity and traceability of products, which is essential for preventing fraud, counterfeiting and ensuring compliance with regulations. For example, in the food industry, blockchain can track the provenance of food items, ensuring that they meet safety standards and enabling swift action in the event of a contamination outbreak.

In financial services, blockchain's immutable records can enhance the security and transparency of transactions, reducing the risk of fraud and improving regulatory compliance. Each transaction recorded on a blockchain is permanent and verifiable, providing a clear audit trail for financial activities. This is particularly valuable for regulatory reporting, where accurate and unaltered records are required.

In government operations, blockchain can provide secure and tamper-proof records for various public services, such as land registries, voting systems and public records. For instance, recording land ownership and property transactions on a blockchain can prevent fraud and disputes over land titles. Similarly, blockchain-based voting systems can ensure the integrity of the electoral process by providing a transparent and immutable record of votes cast.

The tamper-proof nature of blockchain records is a game-changer for maintaining the integrity and trustworthiness of data in sensitive applications. By ensuring that once data is recorded, it cannot be altered or deleted, blockchain technology provides a robust solution for various fields, including healthcare, legal documentation, identity verification, supply chain management, financial services and government operations. This enhances security, reduces the risk of fraud and unauthorised modifications and builds trust in digital systems and processes. As blockchain technology continues to evolve, its applications in creating and maintaining tamper-proof records are likely to expand, driving innovation and improving security across multiple sectors.

Interoperability and scalability are two critical areas where future advancements in blockchain technology will significantly impact its integration and effectiveness across diverse sectors, particularly as we move toward the era of 6G and beyond. The development of interoperable blockchain systems will be essential for enabling seamless communication and data exchange between different blockchain networks. Currently, many blockchain platforms operate in isolation, with limited ability to interact with other systems. Future improvements will aim to bridge these gaps, allowing different blockchain networks to work together harmoniously, thereby creating a more cohesive and interconnected ecosystem.

Enhanced interoperability will facilitate the integration of blockchain technology into a broader range of applications, from financial services to supply chain management and beyond. By enabling different blockchain systems to communicate and share information, organisations can leverage the strengths of various platforms, leading to more efficient and effective solutions. For instance, in a multi-chain environment where different blockchains serve different purposes – such as one for financial transactions and another for supply chain tracking – interoperability will allow these systems to exchange data and execute transactions seamlessly. This capability will not only streamline operations but also expand the potential use cases for blockchain technology.

On the scalability front, future advancements will focus on increasing the capacity of blockchain networks to handle large volumes of transactions and data without compromising performance. Scalability is a significant challenge for blockchain technology, as many existing systems struggle with limitations in transaction throughput and processing speed. As blockchain becomes more widely adopted, particularly in the context of 6G networks and the burgeoning Internet of Things (IoT), the ability to scale efficiently will be crucial. Enhancements in scalability will ensure that blockchain networks can support high transaction volumes and accommodate the growing demands of large-scale applications.

For example, in the realm of financial services, scalability improvements will be essential for supporting high-frequency trading and global transactions. Similarly, in supply chain management, scalable blockchain solutions will enable real-time tracking and verification of goods across complex global supply chains. As 6G networks drive the proliferation of connected devices and data-intensive applications, scalable blockchain technology will be vital for managing and securing the vast amounts of data generated.

Moreover, advancements in blockchain scalability will also contribute to the overall efficiency and cost-effectiveness of blockchain systems. By optimising transaction processing and reducing latency, scalable blockchain networks can lower operational costs and enhance user experience. This will encourage more widespread adoption and integration of blockchain technology across various industries. The future of blockchain technology will be shaped by its ability to achieve interoperability and scalability. These advancements will enable blockchain networks to work together seamlessly and handle the demands of large-scale applications, paving the way for broader adoption and integration across different sectors. As we move into the 6G era and beyond, the evolution of blockchain technology will play a crucial role in creating a more connected, efficient and secure digital ecosystem.

6.1.3 Privacy-preserving technologies

Homomorphic encryption represents a transformative advancement in the field of data security by enabling computations to be performed directly on encrypted data without the need to decrypt it first [13]. This capability ensures that sensitive information remains confidential throughout the entire processing lifecycle, offering substantial benefits in various applications such as secure data analysis, cloud computing and outsourced computations.

The core principle of homomorphic encryption lies in its ability to perform operations on encrypted data in such a way that when the results are decrypted, they match the outcomes of the operations performed on the plaintext data. This means that data can be encrypted and sent to a third-party service or cloud provider for processing, while the actual data remains inaccessible and protected from unauthorised access. This has profound implications for scenarios where data confidentiality is crucial, such as in healthcare, finance and personal data management.

In the realm of secure data analysis, homomorphic encryption allows organisations to perform complex analytical queries and data processing tasks on encrypted datasets without exposing the underlying sensitive information. For example, a healthcare provider can outsource the analysis of patient data to a cloud-based analytics service without revealing the patients' private medical information. The encrypted data is processed in the cloud, and the results are returned in an encrypted form. Once decrypted, the results provide valuable insights while ensuring that the patient data remains secure and private throughout the analysis process. This capability is particularly valuable in industries where data privacy regulations are stringent and where maintaining confidentiality is paramount.

In cloud computing, homomorphic encryption offers a solution to the challenge of securing data while leveraging the computational power and scalability of cloud services. Traditionally, encrypting data before sending it to the cloud for processing meant that the cloud provider could not perform meaningful operations on the encrypted data, thus limiting the utility of the cloud services. Homomorphic encryption overcomes this limitation by enabling the cloud provider to execute computations on the encrypted data without having access to the plaintext. This not only enhances data security but also allows users to fully utilise cloud computing resources without compromising the confidentiality of their data. As a result, organisations can benefit from cloud-based services while maintaining control over their sensitive information.

In the context of outsourced computations, homomorphic encryption provides a means for performing computations on data without revealing the data itself to the party conducting the computation. This is particularly useful in scenarios where data needs to be shared with external entities for processing, such as in collaborative research or multi-party computations. For instance, in a collaborative research project involving multiple institutions, homomorphic encryption enables each participant to contribute encrypted data for joint analysis without disclosing their individual datasets. The computations are performed on the encrypted data, and the results are returned in an encrypted form. This approach ensures that the privacy of each participant's data is preserved while still allowing for collaborative insights and outcomes.

However, despite its promising advantages, homomorphic encryption also presents challenges related to computational efficiency and performance. The encryption and decryption processes, as well as the computations performed on encrypted data, can be computationally intensive and require significant processing power. As a result, practical implementations of homomorphic encryption must balance the trade-off between security and performance. Ongoing research and advancements in homomorphic encryption aim to improve its efficiency and reduce its computational overhead, making it more feasible for widespread adoption [14]. Homomorphic encryption represents a significant leap forward in ensuring data confidentiality and security throughout the processing lifecycle. By allowing computations to be performed on encrypted data without decryption, this technology addresses critical challenges related to secure data analysis, cloud computing and outsourced computations. As homomorphic encryption continues to evolve and overcome its performance limitations, it has the potential to enhance data security and privacy across various domains, enabling secure and privacy-preserving data management in an increasingly data-driven world.

Differential privacy is a cutting-edge approach to protecting individual privacy in large-scale data collection and analysis, and it holds significant promise for the future of 6G networks [15]. By incorporating statistical noise into data, differential privacy ensures that individual information remains obscured even when analysing aggregate data sets. This method is designed to provide strong privacy guarantees, allowing organisations to gain valuable insights from data while preventing the re-identification of individuals.

In the context of 6G networks, where vast amounts of data will be collected from various sources such as IoT devices, smart sensors and user interactions, differential privacy offers a crucial mechanism for safeguarding sensitive information. With the proliferation of connected devices and the increasing volume of data generated, ensuring privacy becomes a paramount concern. Differential privacy addresses this by adding noise to the data, making it challenging for adversaries to extract specific details about any individual from the aggregate results. This approach ensures that the privacy of users is preserved while still allowing for meaningful analysis and insights to be derived from the data.

For instance, in healthcare applications, differential privacy can be employed to protect patient data while enabling researchers to perform large-scale studies and analyses. Medical data, which often contains sensitive personal information, can be analysed to identify trends and patterns without revealing individual patient details. By applying differential privacy techniques, healthcare providers and researchers can maintain the confidentiality of patient data while still benefiting from the insights gained through data analysis.

Similarly, in social sciences, differential privacy can be used to protect the privacy of individuals participating in surveys or studies. When collecting and analysing social data, it's essential to ensure that the privacy of participants is not compromised, particularly in sensitive research areas. Differential privacy allows researchers to publish statistical results and share aggregate data without disclosing individual responses, thus safeguarding participant privacy.

Moreover, as 6G networks facilitate new applications and services that rely on large-scale data collection and analysis, such as personalised services, smart city infrastructure and advanced machine learning models, differential privacy can play a pivotal role in maintaining user trust and compliance with privacy regulations. With the ability to add controlled noise to data, differential privacy allows organisations to leverage data for innovation while mitigating the risks associated with data breaches and misuse.

However, implementing differential privacy in real-world applications involves balancing privacy with data utility. The process of adding noise to data can introduce trade-offs between privacy and the accuracy of the insights derived from the data. Therefore, ongoing research and advancements in differential privacy aim to refine these techniques to maximise privacy protection while minimising the impact on data quality and usefulness. In the broader context of 6G and the future of connectivity, differential privacy represents a forward-looking approach to data security that aligns with the growing emphasis on user privacy and data protection. As 6G networks become more integral to daily life and enable new technological advancements, incorporating differential privacy techniques will be essential for addressing privacy challenges and ensuring that individuals' personal information remains secure. By embracing differential privacy, 6G networks can enhance their security framework and build a foundation of trust with users, paving the way for secure and privacy-preserving data management in an increasingly connected world.

Zero-knowledge proofs (ZKPs) are poised to play a transformative role in the future of secure communications, particularly within the context of 6G networks and other advanced digital environments. This cryptographic technology enables one party to prove to another that they possess certain information or that a statement is true without revealing the actual information itself. This capability is especially valuable in scenarios where privacy and confidentiality are paramount, allowing for secure verification without exposing sensitive data.

The fundamental advantage of zero-knowledge proofs lies in their ability to preserve privacy while ensuring authenticity. In authentication processes, for example, ZKPs allow users to prove their identity without disclosing any personal details. This means that a user can authenticate themselves to a system or service without revealing passwords or other sensitive information, thereby reducing the risk of identity theft and enhancing overall security. Similarly, in voting systems, ZKPs can be employed to verify that a vote has been cast correctly without disclosing the voter's choice. This ensures the integrity of the voting process while protecting voter privacy.

In the realm of confidential transactions, zero-knowledge proofs enable transactions to be validated without revealing the transaction details. This is particularly useful in financial systems where transaction privacy is critical. For instance, ZKPs can be used to confirm that a transaction meets certain criteria, such as having sufficient funds or adhering to regulatory requirements, without exposing the specifics of the transaction to outside parties. This enhances privacy while maintaining the integrity of the financial system.

The deployment of zero-knowledge proofs in 6G networks could revolutionise how data and transactions are secured and verified. As 6G promises to bring unprecedented levels of connectivity and data exchange, the need for robust privacy-preserving mechanisms will become even more critical. ZKPs will help address these needs by providing a method for secure and private verification that scales with the increased complexity and volume of data in a 6G environment.

The integration of ZKPs into blockchain and distributed ledger technologies will further enhance their security and privacy features. By incorporating zero-knowledge proofs, these technologies can offer enhanced privacy for transactions and data, while still ensuring transparency and immutability. This is particularly relevant for decentralised applications and smart contracts, where privacy and confidentiality are often at odds with the need for transparency. Zero-knowledge proofs represent a significant advancement in cryptographic technology, with wide-ranging applications in authentication, voting systems and confidential transactions. As we advance towards the 6G era, the ability of ZKPs to provide privacy-preserving verification while maintaining data integrity will be crucial. Their integration into future digital systems will enhance security and privacy, addressing the evolving challenges of the digital age.

Secure multi-party computation (SMPC) represents a groundbreaking advancement in privacy-preserving technology, crucial for the future of collaborative data analysis and processing in contexts like federated learning and collaborative research [16]. SMPC enables multiple parties to jointly compute a function using their private inputs without revealing the inputs themselves. This capability ensures that each participant's data remains confidential throughout the computation process, fostering collaboration while upholding stringent privacy standards.

In practical terms, SMPC allows organisations or individuals to work together on data-driven projects without compromising the confidentiality of their respective datasets. For example, in federated learning, where multiple institutions or entities collaborate to build a shared machine learning model, SMPC can be employed to aggregate model updates from various participants without exposing their individual training data. This is particularly valuable in scenarios where sensitive data – such as medical records, financial information or proprietary business data – is involved. By enabling joint computation while keeping data private, SMPC facilitates the development of robust models and insights without risking data breaches or unauthorised access.

Collaborative research projects also benefit from SMPC, as it allows researchers to analyse data collectively without sharing raw data. For instance, in medical research, different hospitals or research institutions can use SMPC to pool data for large-scale studies or clinical trials, ensuring that patient confidentiality is maintained while deriving valuable insights from combined datasets. This capability accelerates research and innovation by overcoming the barriers of data silos and privacy concerns.

The importance of SMPC extends to various applications in the future of digital security and privacy. As data collection and analysis become more interconnected and complex, the need for technologies that enable secure and private collaboration will only grow. SMPC offers a practical solution to these challenges by ensuring that data remains secure, even when multiple parties are involved in computations.

In the context of emerging technologies like 6G networks, SMPC can play a pivotal role in enabling secure data sharing and processing across diverse and distributed systems. With the proliferation of connected devices and the increasing volume of data exchanged across networks, SMPC will help safeguard privacy while supporting collaborative efforts. This is especially critical as 6G networks aim to integrate various sectors and applications, from smart cities to autonomous vehicles, all of which require secure and private handling of data. Secure multi-party computation stands as a vital technology for the future of privacy-preserving collaborative data analysis. Its ability to allow multiple parties to compute functions over their private inputs without compromising data confidentiality is essential for federated learning, collaborative research and a wide range of other applications. As digital landscapes evolve and data privacy challenges become more pronounced, SMPC will be instrumental in enabling secure and efficient collaboration across diverse domains.

The future of cryptographic advancements is bright, with AI-driven cybersecurity solutions, blockchain and DLT and privacy-preserving technologies poised to revolutionise the security landscape. These advancements will provide robust, scalable and adaptive security measures that can meet the complex demands of the 6G era. By embracing these innovations, we can ensure the secure and private transmission of information, fostering trust and resilience in next-generation communication networks.

6.2 Research and Development Directions for 6G Security

As we rapidly advance toward the implementation of 6G networks, it becomes increasingly imperative to tackle the intricate security challenges associated with this next-generation technology. This task demands a comprehensive and multifaceted strategy that incorporates extensive global collaboration, a broad spectrum of interdisciplinary research and the creation of robust and sophisticated testing environments. Addressing these security concerns effectively requires not only the combined efforts of international stakeholders working together but also the integration of diverse fields of study and expertise. Furthermore, developing advanced testing frameworks is crucial for thoroughly evaluating and ensuring the security measures deployed in 6G networks. This holistic approach will help to anticipate, understand and mitigate potential risks, thereby ensuring a secure and resilient future for 6G technology.

6.2.1 Collaboration and standardisation

The importance of global cooperation in 6G security research cannot be overstated. As 6G networks are envisioned to provide ubiquitous connectivity and integrate various technologies across borders, ensuring their security necessitates a unified global effort. Researchers, industry leaders and policymakers from around the world must collaborate to address shared security challenges and develop coherent strategies. This international collaboration helps in pooling expertise, resources and perspectives, facilitating the creation of comprehensive security frameworks that address diverse threats and vulnerabilities. Successful case studies of such cooperation, like the joint research initiatives led by international consortia or global tech companies, highlight the effectiveness of collaborative approaches in advancing 6G security research.

International standards organisations play a pivotal role in shaping security protocols for 6G networks. These organisations, such as the International Telecommunication Union (ITU), the Institute of Electrical and Electronics Engineers (IEEE) and the 3rd Generation Partnership Project (3GPP), are instrumental in defining the technical standards and security guidelines that ensure interoperability, reliability and security of 6G systems. Their work involves creating standardised protocols and frameworks that address security concerns specific to 6G, such as quantum-resistant encryption and advanced threat detection mechanisms. The involvement of these organisations in setting global standards ensures that security practices are consistent, comprehensive and adaptable to evolving threats.

6.2.2 Interdisciplinary research initiatives

Encouraging interdisciplinary research is crucial for addressing the complex security needs of 6G networks. The convergence of fields like cryptography, artificial intelligence (AI) and network engineering offers innovative solutions to emerging security challenges. Research that integrates these disciplines can lead to the development of advanced cryptographic algorithms resistant to quantum attacks, AI-driven cybersecurity solutions for real-time threat detection and network engineering practices that enhance the resilience and robustness of 6G infrastructure. Interdisciplinary research efforts demonstrate the benefits of combining expertise from various fields. For instance, research projects that integrate cryptographic methods with AI techniques have led to the creation of adaptive security measures capable of responding to dynamic threats. Similarly, collaborative research between cryptographers and network engineers has resulted in the development of secure communication protocols that address vulnerabilities in complex network architectures. These efforts highlight the potential for interdisciplinary approaches to drive innovation and advance security in 6G networks.

6.2.3 Development of testbeds and simulation environments

The development of testbeds and simulation environments is critical for validating security measures in 6G networks [17]. Testbeds provide controlled environments where researchers can evaluate the performance and effectiveness of security protocols and technologies under realistic conditions. These environments facilitate real-world validation of theoretical concepts, enabling researchers to identify and address potential issues before deployment.

Simulation environments play a complementary role by allowing for the modelling of various attack scenarios and network configurations. These simulations help in understanding the behaviour of security mechanisms in different conditions and assessing their resilience against potential threats. Real-world validation through testbeds and simulations contributes to the refinement of security measures, ensuring that they are robust and effective in protecting 6G networks.

In summary, the future of 6G security research and development hinges on global collaboration, interdisciplinary innovation and rigorous testing. By working together on an international scale, leveraging the expertise of various fields and developing advanced testbeds and simulation environments, stakeholders can address the evolving security challenges of 6G networks. These efforts will pave the way for secure, resilient and reliable 6G systems, ensuring their successful deployment and operation in a rapidly advancing technological landscape.

6.3 Policy and Regulatory Frameworks for 6G

The *development of robust policy frameworks* is crucial for ensuring the security and resilience of 6G networks. Proactive policy development involves anticipating potential security threats and addressing them through comprehensive regulations and guidelines. As 6G networks are expected to handle unprecedented volumes of data and connect a vast array of devices, it is essential to establish policies that pre-emptively address security concerns, rather than reactively responding to breaches and vulnerabilities. This approach helps create a secure environment from the outset, reducing the likelihood of successful attacks and ensuring that security measures evolve alongside technological advancements.

Case studies from previous generations of networks, such as 4G and 5G, offer valuable insights into effective policy frameworks. For instance, the implementation of the European Union's General Data Protection Regulation (GDPR) and the United States' Communications Assistance for Law Enforcement Act (CALEA) provided frameworks that addressed privacy and security concerns while balancing the need for technological advancement. These examples highlight the importance of crafting policies that not only protect users but also facilitate innovation by setting clear guidelines and standards.

The *ethical implications* of advanced security measures in 6G networks are a significant concern. As security technologies become more sophisticated, they may involve invasive practices or extensive data collection that could impact individual privacy and civil liberties. For example, the deployment of advanced surveillance technologies and biometric identification systems raises questions about consent, data ownership and the potential for misuse.

Developing governance frameworks to address these ethical concerns is essential for ensuring that security measures are implemented responsibly. Governance frameworks should include ethical guidelines that address the potential impact of security technologies on privacy and human rights. They should also involve stakeholder consultations and public discussions to ensure that diverse perspectives are considered in policy development.

Case studies on ethical governance in technology deployment provide insights into how ethical considerations can be effectively integrated into policy frameworks. For instance, the ethical guidelines developed by the IEEE Global Initiative on Ethics of Autonomous and Intelligent Systems emphasise transparency, accountability and the protection of human rights. Similarly, the establishment of ethical review boards and regulatory bodies for emerging technologies, such as the UK's Centre for Data Ethics and Innovation, demonstrates how governance structures can address ethical concerns while fostering technological innovation.

The development of effective policy and regulatory frameworks for 6G networks is essential for ensuring robust security and addressing ethical considerations. Proactive policy development, informed by case studies from previous generations, helps create a secure and resilient 6G infrastructure. Simultaneously, governance frameworks that address ethical concerns ensure that advanced security measures are implemented responsibly, balancing technological progress with the protection of individual rights and societal values. These efforts will contribute to the successful and ethical deployment of 6G technologies, paving the way for their positive impact on society.

As we move into the 6G era, addressing the multifaceted security challenges of next-generation networks is crucial. The future of network security is being shaped by significant advancements in cryptography, such as AI-driven cybersecurity solutions, blockchain and distributed ledger technologies and privacy-preserving methods. These innovations promise to enhance the security landscape by providing robust, scalable and adaptive defences that meet the complex demands of 6G networks.

AI-driven solutions will enable real-time threat detection and adaptation, enhancing network resilience. Blockchain and DLT will offer decentralised trust models, secure transactions and tamper-proof records, which are essential for maintaining data integrity and transparency. Privacy-preserving technologies like homomorphic encryption and differential privacy will protect sensitive information and ensure confidentiality.

To effectively navigate the security challenges of 6G, continuous research and development are imperative. Stakeholders must work together to develop and implement comprehensive policies and regulatory frameworks that address both technical and ethical issues. By embracing these advancements and fostering collaborative efforts, we can ensure secure and private communication in the 6G era, building trust and resilience in next-generation networks.

References

[1] M. A. AĞCA, S. Faye and D. Khadraoui, "A Survey on Trusted Distributed Artificial Intelligence," in IEEE Access, vol. 10, pp. 55308-55337, 2022, doi:10.1109/ACCESS.2022.3176385.

[2] J. Ferdous, R. Islam, A. Mahboubi and M. Z. Islam, "A Review of State-of-the-Art Malware Attack Trends and Defense Mechanisms," in IEEE Access, vol. 11, pp. 121118-121141, 2023, doi:10.1109/ACCESS.202 3.3328351.

[3] M. M. Rathore, S. A. Shah, D. Shukla, E. Bentafat and S. Bakiras, "The Role of AI, Machine Learning, and Big Data in Digital Twinning: A Systematic Literature Review, Challenges, and Opportunities," in IEEE Access, vol. 9, pp. 32030-32052, 2021, doi:10.1109/ACCESS.2021.30 60863.

[4] A. Adedoyin and H. Teymourlouei, "Methods for Automating Threat Hunting and Response," 2021 International Conference on Electrical, Computer and Energy Technologies (ICECET), Cape Town, South Africa, 2021, pp. 1-6, doi:10.1109/ICECET52533.2021.9698447.

[5] B. Nour, M. Pourzandi and M. Debbabi, "A Survey on Threat Hunting in Enterprise Networks," in IEEE Communications Surveys & Tutorials, vol. 25, no. 4, pp. 2299-2324, Fourthquarter 2023, doi:10.1109/COMST.2023.3299519.

[6] Alexei Khlebnikov; Jarle Adolfsen, Demystifying Cryptography with OpenSSL 3.0: Discover the best techniques to enhance your network security with OpenSSL 3.0 , Packt Publishing, 2022.

[7] Mike Wills, "Cryptography," in The Official (ISC)2 SSCP CBK Reference, Wiley, 2020, pp.335-465, doi:10.1002/9781119601951.ch5.

[8] Ahmed Banafa, "5 Decentralized Applications – DApps," in Introduction to Blockchain Technology , River Publishers, 2023, pp.35-38.

[9] Rishabh Garg, "Distributed Ledger Technology," in Blockchain for Real World Applications , Wiley, 2023, pp.11-22, doi:10.1002/9781119903765.ch2.

[10] Aman Kumar Dhiman; Ajay Kumar, "Integration of Blockchain Technology and Internet of Things," in Machine Learning Applications: From Computer Vision to Robotics , IEEE, 2024, pp.145-159, doi: 10.1002/9781394173358.ch9.

[11] "A Smart Payment Transaction Procedure by Smart Edge Computing," in Smart Edge Computing: An Operation Research Perspective , Wiley, 2024, pp.113-131, doi:10.1002/9781394277599.ch6.

[12] S. Tyagi and M. Kathuria, "Role of Zero-Knowledge Proof in Blockchain Security," 2022 International Conference on Machine Learning, Big Data, Cloud and Parallel Computing (COM-IT-CON), Faridabad, India, 2022, pp. 738-743, doi:10.1109/COM-IT-CON54601.2022.9850714.

[13] Massimo Bertaccini, Cryptography Algorithms: A guide to algorithms in blockchain, quantum cryptography, zero-knowledge protocols, and homomorphic encryption , Packt Publishing, 2022.

[14] "IEEE Standard for Requirements of Privacy-Preserving Computation Integrated Platforms," in IEEE Std 3156-2023 , vol., no., pp.1-30, 23 Feb. 2024, doi:10.1109/IEEESTD.2024.10443763.

[15] Nii O. Attoh-Okine, "Differential Privacy," in Big Data and Differential Privacy: Analysis Strategies for Railway Track Engineering , Wiley, 2017, pp.241-247, doi:10.1002/9781119229070.ch12.

[16] "IEEE Recommended Practice for Secure Multi-Party Computation," in IEEE Std 2842-2021, vol., no., pp.1-30, 5 Nov. 2021, doi:10.1109/IEEE STD.2021.9604029.

[17] E. J. Khatib, C. S. Álvarez-Merino, H. Q. Luo-Chen and R. B. Moreno, "Designing a 6G Testbed for Location: Use Cases, Challenges, Enablers and Requirements," in IEEE Access, vol. 11, pp. 10053-10091, 2023, doi:10.1109/ACCESS.2023.3240775.

7

Conclusions

In envisioning a secure future amidst the rapid advancement of 6G technology, this comprehensive exploration into 6G security and privacy was meant to serve as a resource. The evolution from 1G to 6G over the past five decades has not only revolutionised wireless communication but also introduced unprecedented challenges in cybersecurity. The advent of 6G brings with it transformative technologies such as quantum computing, AI integration and decentralised edge computing, each presenting unique security risks that demand proactive mitigation strategies.

This book addresses the pressing need for robust security measures in 6G networks, recognising quantum computing vulnerabilities, AI-driven attacks and risks to IoT and connected devices as central concerns. Chapters devoted to security-preserving techniques delve into quantum key distribution (QKD), post-quantum cryptography and AI-driven threat detection systems, offering practical insights and real-world applications to fortify network resilience. In envisioning a secure future amidst the advent of 6G technology, it is imperative to anticipate and address emerging trends and challenges that will shape the security landscape of tomorrow's hyperconnected world. As 6G networks evolve, the emergence of quantum computing presents a dual role – both as a potential threat and a solution. Quantum computers have the potential to break traditional encryption algorithms that currently secure data transmissions. To counter this, the development of quantum-resistant encryption techniques and quantum key distribution (QKD) protocols becomes crucial. Quantum-resistant encryption algorithms rely on mathematical principles that are believed to withstand attacks from quantum computers, ensuring data integrity and confidentiality in a post-quantum era. Similarly, QKD enables the secure exchange of cryptographic keys based on the principles of quantum mechanics, providing a robust foundation for secure communications over 6G networks. Moreover, the proliferation of Internet of Things (IoT) devices, integration of artificial intelligence (AI) and the pervasive hyperconnectivity characteristic of 6G networks introduce a multitude of novel attack surfaces. The sheer volume and diversity of interconnected devices increase the attack vectors available to malicious actors, requiring a paradigm shift in cybersecurity strategies. AI integration, while offering transformative benefits such as autonomous threat detection and adaptive security responses, also introduces new risks. AI-driven cyberattacks, leveraging machine learning algorithms to exploit vulnerabilities and launch sophisticated attacks, pose a significant challenge. Predicting and mitigating these emerging threats necessitate proactive security measures, including continuous monitoring, real-time threat intelligence and adaptive security frameworks capable of evolving alongside evolving threats. Furthermore, IoT devices within 6G networks are particularly vulnerable due to their inherent limitations in terms of computing power and security capabilities. Securing IoT devices requires implementing secure-by-design principles, ensuring robust authentication mechanisms and employing encryption protocols to protect data both at rest and in transit. Sophisticated malware designed to target IoT ecosystems further underscores the importance of comprehensive security measures that encompass device integrity verification, anomaly detection and incident response protocols tailored to IoT environments. Securing IoT devices within the 6G ecosystem requires a proactive approach based on secure-by-design principles. IoT devices are often constrained in terms of computational power and may lack robust security features, making them attractive targets for cyber attackers. Implementing stringent security measures from the outset, such as strong authentication mechanisms, encryption of data both at rest and in transit and regular security updates, will be essential to mitigate vulnerabilities and prevent unauthorised access to IoT networks.

An in-depth examination of several cutting-edge technologies and methodologies was conducted to address the security and privacy challenges anticipated with the advent of 6G networks. The discussion began with quantum key distribution (QKD), a revolutionary technique leveraging quantum physics to achieve unparalleled data encryption security. QKD facilitates secure key exchanges through quantum principles, making interception or tampering nearly impossible without detection. This technology is particularly significant in safeguarding against potential threats posed by quantum computing, which could otherwise compromise current encryption standards. Next, quantum random number generators (QRNGs) were covered, which utilise the inherent unpredictability of quantum phenomena to produce truly random numbers. Unlike traditional methods, QRNGs offer a higher level of randomness, crucial for enhancing cryptographic systems and securing communications. This increased randomness supports the generation of robust encryption keys and other essential cryptographic parameters. The same chapter also explored post-quantum cryptography, which focuses on developing cryptographic algorithms capable of resisting attacks from quantum computers. As quantum technology advances, it is anticipated that some current encryption methods may become vulnerable. Post-quantum cryptography aims to counteract this threat by creating algorithms that remain secure even against quantum-powered attacks, thereby ensuring long-term data protection. Finally, the role of AI-driven threat detection was examined. This technology employs artificial intelligence to enhance network security by analysing data patterns and behaviours to detect and respond to threats in real time. AI's ability to adapt and respond to new and evolving threats significantly boosts the resilience and security of 6G networks.

As 6G technology approaches, navigating its complex security and governance landscape requires a multifaceted approach that balances technological innovation with robust regulation and ethical considerations. The development of standardised security protocols is critical to ensure that 6G networks operate securely and consistently across various sectors and regions. This standardisation process involves creating a timeline for implementing security measures that evolve alongside technological advancements, providing a structured path for ensuring global security practices. Liability and accountability are also key concerns, as they define the roles and responsibilities of various stakeholders involved in the deployment and management of 6G networks. Clear government policies are essential to outline these responsibilities and establish compliance requirements. This regulatory framework helps in managing risks and ensuring that all parties adhere to established security protocols. Ethical considerations, particularly around data privacy, play a significant role as 6G networks handle increasingly sensitive and personal information. Striking a balance between advancing technology and protecting individual privacy is crucial. Developing ethical guidelines for data handling ensures that privacy is maintained while supporting the security needs of the network. In addition to these aspects, fostering collaboration among industry leaders, academic researchers and policymakers is vital. Such collaboration helps in creating best practices, guidelines and compliance standards that enhance cybersecurity across different sectors and geographical areas. It also promotes the sharing of information and collective defence strategies to address emerging cyber threats effectively. A coordinated effort to establish robust standards, clear regulations and ethical guidelines is essential for building a secure and trustworthy 6G infrastructure. This approach will ensure that the next generation of communication technologies can meet its security challenges while fostering innovation and protecting privacy.

In the realm of 6G, applying security measures to practical scenarios is essential for ensuring the robust protection of critical infrastructures and everyday technologies. Secure healthcare IoT represents one of the most impactful areas, where advanced communication networks enable the seamless integration of various medical devices and systems. Ensuring these IoT devices remain secure is crucial for protecting sensitive patient data and maintaining the integrity of healthcare operations. Implementing strong security protocols in this sector helps safeguard against potential breaches that could compromise patient privacy and system reliability. Similarly, autonomous vehicles, which rely heavily on network connectivity for safe and efficient operation, must be protected from potential cyber threats. A secure network for these vehicles ensures that communications between vehicles and infrastructure remain reliable and free from malicious interference. This is vital for preventing accidents and maintaining public safety as autonomous driving technology continues to advance. The smart grid infrastructure also benefits greatly from 6G technology, which supports advanced grid management and monitoring systems. Securing these networks is essential for protecting against cyberattacks that could disrupt power distribution and affect critical services. By implementing comprehensive security measures, the stability and reliability of smart grids can be preserved, ensuring that energy resources are managed effectively. In the context of 6G-enabled smart cities, security is paramount for protecting the vast array of connected devices and systems that manage urban environments. From traffic management to environmental monitoring, a secure 6G network ensures that city operations run smoothly and that sensitive data remains protected from unauthorised access. This contributes to creating safer and more efficient urban spaces. Enhancing supply chain security with 6G involves securing the complex web of logistics and inventory systems that span across global markets. The implementation of robust security measures helps protect against threats that could disrupt supply chains and affect the availability of essential goods. By ensuring the integrity of these systems, businesses can maintain operational continuity and resilience. Securing Industry 4.0 with 6G technology is crucial for protecting the next generation of industrial processes and automation. As industries increasingly adopt connected systems and smart manufacturing technologies, safeguarding these networks against cyber threats becomes essential for maintaining operational efficiency and preventing potential disruptions. In each of these real-world scenarios, the application of advanced security techniques tailored to the specific needs of each sector ensures that 6G technology can be leveraged safely and effectively. Addressing these security challenges through concrete implementations not only enhances the reliability of critical systems but also fosters confidence in the capabilities of next-generation communication networks.

Finally, the book offers a forward-looking perspective on the evolving landscape of network security as we transition into the 6G era. It highlights the critical need for advanced security measures to address the complex challenges posed by emerging technologies and provides a roadmap for navigating these issues. Central to this roadmap is the exploration of cutting-edge cryptographic advancements, including AI-driven cybersecurity solutions, blockchain and distributed ledger technologies (DLT) and privacy-preserving techniques. These innovations are set to revolutionise the security landscape by offering robust, scalable and adaptive defences tailored to the intricate demands of 6G networks. AI-driven cybersecurity solutions will enable real-time adaptation to evolving threats through dynamic anomaly detection and predictive analytics. Blockchain and DLT will introduce decentralised trust models, secure transactions and immutable records, which are crucial for maintaining data integrity and transparency. Privacy-preserving technologies, such as homomorphic encryption and differential privacy, will safeguard sensitive information and ensure confidentiality across diverse applications. The necessity for continuous research and development to keep pace with the rapid advancements in technology is underscored. It calls on stakeholders – including researchers, industry leaders, policymakers and regulatory bodies – to collaborate effectively in shaping a secure 6G future. This collaboration will involve developing comprehensive policy and regulatory frameworks that address both the technical and ethical dimensions of security. By fostering a cooperative approach and staying ahead of emerging threats, we can build resilient and trustworthy 6G networks that support secure and private communication for years to come.

As we stand on the brink of the 6G era, it is clear that our approach to network security must evolve in tandem with technological advancements. The future of secure communication hinges on our ability to integrate cutting-edge technologies and foster collaborative efforts across disciplines. Protecting critical infrastructure within a hyperconnected 6G environment requires tailored strategies that address specific vulnerabilities and risks. Industries such as energy grids, healthcare systems and financial services are prime targets for cyberattacks due to their reliance on interconnected systems and sensitive data. Implementing stringent access controls, deploying AI-driven threat detection systems capable of identifying and neutralising sophisticated threats and building redundancy into network architecture to maintain operational continuity during cyber incidents are critical steps toward safeguarding these vital sectors. By embracing innovative cryptographic methods, leveraging AI for real-time threat detection and ensuring privacy through advanced techniques, we can navigate the complexities of this new era with confidence. Safeguarding the integrity, confidentiality and resilience of 6G networks demands a holistic approach that integrates advanced encryption technologies, AI-driven security solutions and rigorous cybersecurity practices. By anticipating the evolving landscape of threats and challenges – ranging from quantum computing vulnerabilities to AI-driven cyber threats – and adopting proactive security strategies, stakeholders can pave the way for a secure and trustworthy 6G future. Collaborative efforts across industry, academia and regulatory bodies will be essential in developing robust security frameworks and standards that uphold privacy, protect critical infrastructure and mitigate emerging cyber risks in a hyperconnected era. Navigating the complexities of 6G security necessitates foresight, innovation and collaboration across disciplines. By proactively addressing quantum threats, anticipating evolving risks and fortifying critical systems, we can shape a resilient and secure 6G future that harnesses the transformative potential of next-generation wireless technology while safeguarding privacy and integrity. The key takeaway is that proactive and adaptive security strategies will be essential in shaping a resilient and trustworthy 6G infrastructure. Staying ahead of emerging threats and continuously refining our security practices will be crucial in safeguarding the digital landscape of tomorrow.

Index

About the Authors

Ramjee Prasad, President of CTIF Global Capsule (CGC) and Professor Emeritus in the Department of Business Development and Technology at Aarhus University, Herning, Denmark, is a renowned expert in future technologies for business ecosystems. A Fellow of IEEE, IET, IETE, and WWRF, he has been a pioneering figure in wireless communication and ICT standardization. He founded the Global ICT Standardization Forum for India in 2009 and has received numerous accolades, including the Ridderkorset of Dannebrogordenen (Knight of the Dannebrog) in 2010 from the Danish Queen for his contributions to telecommunications research and education. Prof. Prasad holds honorary positions at several prestigious institutions, including the University of Cape Town and the University of KwaZulu-Natal in South Africa. He was honored as a Distinguished Professor by the University of Rome "Tor Vergata" and received the Pravasi Bhartiya Samman Puraskaar in 2023. His achievements include over 50 books, more than 1000 journal and conference publications, 15+ patents, and the mentorship of over 150 Ph.D. graduates. Prof. Prasad has also led major European Commission projects such as MAGNET, MAGNET Beyond, and eWALL.

Ana Koren completed her doctoral thesis "System Model for Integration of Wearable Smart Device Data into a Central Health Information System" in October 2023 at the Faculty of Electrical Engineering and Computing, University of Zagreb, Croatia. Throughout her Ph.D. journey, she broadened her research by engaging as a visiting researcher at renowned institutions like TU Graz in Austria, Universidad de Zaragoza in Spain, and Universidad Nacional de Colombia in Bogotá. Her primary research interests lie in e-Health and wireless personal communications. Ana also played a pivotal role in the practical application of her research, contributing to the development of Croatia's Central Health Information System, including the implementation of the country's Electronic Health Record (EHR).

For Product Safety Concerns and Information please contact our EU representative GPSR@taylorandfrancis.com Taylor & Francis Verlag GmbH, Kaufingerstraße 24, 80331 München, Germany